8/23

DAYTRIPS IN FRANCE

DAYTRIPS

IN

FRANCE

*40 One Day Adventures
by Rail, Bus, or Car*

by
Earl Steinbicker

Photos and Maps by the Author

HASTINGS HOUSE / PUBLISHERS
New York

The author would like to thank the following people, whose generous help and encouragement made this book possible:

George L. Hern, of the French Government Tourist Office.

Christian Escudié and Bruce Haxthausen, both of Air France.

Dagobert M. Scher, of the French National Railroads.

Copyright © 1986 by Earl Steinbicker

Library of Congress Cataloging-in-Publication Data

Steinbicker, Earl, 1934–
   Daytrips in France.

   Includes index.
   1. France — Description and travel—1975- —Guide-books. I. Title.
DC16.S73   1985   914.4'04838   85–14030
ISBN   0–8038–1586–7
10 9 8 7 6 5 4 3 2

Printed in the United States of America

Contents

Introduction

Visitors to France can choose from an enormous range of experiences. There are magnificent cities and medieval towns to explore, splendid châteaux and quaint fishing villages to visit, history to be relived and wines to be tasted. Few nations can match its scope of art, architecture, cuisine, or natural splendor. The possibilities for adventures are endless, but the premise of this book is that many of the very best attractions can easily be enjoyed on a daytrip basis. The pages which follow describe forty of the country's most intriguing destinations and tell you, in step-by-step detail, exactly how to go about probing them on your own.

Daytrips in France is not intended to be a comprehensive guide to the entire nation. It focuses, instead, on three broad areas of maximum tourist interest — daytrips from Paris, daytrips in Provence, and daytrips along the Riviera. Each of these has one major city which, for reasons of transportation and accommodation, makes it the most logical base for one-day adventures in its region. These are Paris, Marseille and Nice. Other towns, of course, could be substituted as bases; and these possibilities are suggested in the text whenever practical.

Daytrips have several advantages over the usual point-to-point touring, especially for short-term visitors. You can sample a far greater range in the same time by seeing only those places which really interest you instead of "doing" the region town by town. It also leads to a more varied diet of sights, such as spending one day on a Normandy beach, the next back in Paris, and the third in medieval Beaune.

The benefits of staying in one hotel for several days are obvious. Weekly rates are often more economical than overnight stays, especially in conjunction with airline package plans. Then, too, you won't waste time searching for a room every night. Your luggage remains in one place while you go out on a carefree daytrip. There is no need to pre-plan every moment of your vacation since you are always free to go wherever you please. Feel like seeing Antibes today? Ah, but this is Tuesday, when its sights are closed, so maybe it would be better to head for Monaco instead, or take a glorious rail excursion through the Var Valley. Is rain predicted for the entire day? You certainly don't want to be in Deauville in a shower, so why not try the wonderful museums in Dijon? The operative word here is flexibility; the freedom of not being tied to a schedule or route. You may run up more mileage this way, but that is easily offset by using one of the prepaid unlimited transportation plans described in the next section.

All of the daytrips in this book may be taken by public transportation or by car. Full information for doing this is given in the "Getting There" section of each trip. A suggested do-it-yourself walking tour is outlined in both the text and on the street map provided. Time and weather considerations are included, along with price-keyed restaurant recommendations, background data and sources of additional information.

The trips have been arranged in a geographic sequence following convenient transportation routes. In several cases it is possible to combine two trips in the same day. These opportunities are noted whenever they are practical.

Destinations were chosen to appeal to a wide variety of interests. In addition to the usual cathedrals, castles and museums there are wine centers, boat cruises, Roman ruins, elegant resorts and major cities, great seaports and quaint fishing villages, preserved medieval towns, caves, exquisite gardens, splendid châteaux, places where history was made, homes of famous artists, natural beauty spots and even an exciting railfan excursion. You should really read through all of them before deciding which appeal to you the most.

Many of the attractions have a nominal entrance fee of some sort — those which are free will come as a pleasant surprise. Cathedrals and churches will appreciate a small donation in the collection box.

Finally, a gentle disclaimer. Places have a way of changing without warning, and errors do creep into print. If your heart is absolutely set on seeing a particular attraction, you should always check first to make sure it isn't closed for renovations, or that the opening times are still valid. Phone numbers for the local tourist information offices are included for this purpose.

One last thought — it isn't really necessary to see everything at any given destination. Be selective. Your one-day adventures in France should be fun, not an endurance test. If it starts becoming that, just stroll over to the nearest outdoor café, sit down, and enjoy yourself. There will always be another day.

Happy Daytripping!

Getting Around

Nearly all of the daytrips in this book can be made by rail, all by car, and some by bus. Which of these you choose depends on purely personal factors, but you may want to consider some of the following information before deciding:

BY RAIL:

The French love to travel by rail, which comes as no surprise as they are blessed with the fastest and some of the most modern trains in the world. Trains are the quickest way to travel for the medium distances described in this book. The **French National Railroads** (*Société Nationale des Chemins de Fer Français,* or **SNCF**) operates an average of 1,500 passenger trains a day over a dense network of more than 20,000 miles of track, serving some 4,000 stations. Many of its lines radiate in all directions from Paris, making daytrips from the capital exceptionally fast and easy. In an energy-conscious age it has been the policy of the French government to encourage rail travel by constantly improving the service with expanded schedules and state-of-the-art technology; and by making it readily affordable for both citizens and visitors.

A new era of rail transportation dawned in 1981 when the first TGV trains began service between Paris and Lyon. Presently operating at speeds of 169 mph on their own dedicated line, one of these speed demons has actually been clocked during trials at a phenomenal 238 mph, a new world record! The expanded TGV fleet now serves other destinations as well, sometimes running on regular tracks at reduced speed. A second TGV service, operating from Montparnasse station in Paris, will bring even faster trains to Brittany and the Atlantic coast as far as the Spanish border, probably beginning around 1989, thus greatly expanding the number of destinations within daytrip range. Meanwhile, the running times of other express trains have been improved, with some routinely hitting 125 mph.

Seasoned travelers often consider riding trains to be one of the best ways of meeting the local people, and making new

friends. It is not at all unusual to strike up an engaging conver-
sation which makes your trip all the more memorable. You can
also get a marvelous view of the passing countryside from the
large windows, and have time to catch up on your reading.

All trains operated by the SNCF belong to one of the following
equipment categories, as indicated on schedules and departure
platforms.

TGV — *Train à Grande Vitesse*. The world's fastest trains
offer a smooth, quiet air-conditioned ride between Paris and
Lyon in just two hours flat. Frequent daily departures also serve
Dijon, Avignon, Marseille, Nîmes, Geneva, Lausanne and other
places. Both first- and second-class accommodations are available.
Reservations are an **absolute requirement**, and these may be
made for a small fee up until five minutes before departure,
either at the reservation window or from special machines in the
stations. There is a surcharge during peak travel times, which is
waived for railpass users. Meal service at your seat is available
for first-class passengers. Be sure to arrange for this when you
reserve your seat. A bar car for both classes provides light meals,
sandwiches, snacks and beverages.

TEE — *Trans Europ Express*. These luxurious, first-class-only
trains connect several major cities in France and provide fast
service to neighboring countries. There is a premium surcharge
on all departures, but this does not apply to holders of first-
class railpasses. Reservations are suggested for destinations within
France and obligatory for international service. Full meal and
drink service is available in the dining car. The equipment is air-
conditioned and exceptionally comfortable. Most TEE trains are
being phased out in favor of the next category.

IC — *Intercité*. High-speed international trains serving many
towns in France with modern equipment. Both first- and second-
class seating is available. A supplemental fare is charged, but not
to users of railpasses. Reservations can be made if desired.

Turbotrain — These modern, high-speed turbine-operated
trains link Paris with the Normandy coast, and are frequently used
on other major non-electrified lines. Turbotrains carry both first-
and second-class cars, as well as a dining car. Reservations are
desirable due to the limited seating capacity.

Corail — Very modern, air-conditioned locomotive-hauled
express trains carrying both first- and second-class passengers.
Food and beverage service is usually provided, often in the form
of a *"Gril-Express"* cafeteria car, or sometimes a snack bar or
roving push cart. Reservations are available if desired.

A TGV Train at St. Charles Station, Marseille

Corail 200 — As above, but traveling at speeds of up to 125 mph.

Autorail — Self-propelled railcars which may operate as locals or expresses. First class is not always available.

As far as speed is concerned, rail service is divided into the following service categories:

Rapide — This is an overall category for certain high-speed limited expresses. Many of these are of the TGV, Turbotrain or Corail types described above. A supplemental fare, waived for railpass holders, may be charged on some departures. The trains carry both first- and second-class accommodations and usually offer food and beverage service. Seats may be reserved if desired, a requirement on the TGV types.

Express — These trains make more stops and frequently use modern Corail equipment. The category also includes a number of foreign trains which may or may not measure up to French standards of comfort. Food and beverage service is sometimes offered, and both first- and second-class seating is available.

Omnibus — Often not given any particular designation, these locals make many stops and can take you to smaller, off-beat destinations. Much of the equipment is old and sometimes rather quaint, although there are modern omnibus trains. First class is not always offered.

In addition, you may also want to use these services:

RER — Commuter trains operating on a very frequent schedule in and around Paris which connect with the Métro subway system. Some lines are operated by **SNCF** *(railpasses valid, but ask for a free ticket to operate the turnstiles)* and others by **RATP** — Paris Transit Authority *(Paris Sesame Pass valid)*. The equipment is modern and consists of both first- and second-class cars.

Buses — *Autocars,* operated by or for the French National Railroads and marked "SNCF," connect certain rural areas with train stations in larger towns; and fill in for some rail services during off-peak hours. Railpasses are valid on these — *but not other* — buses.

SCHEDULES for all SNCF services are available at the stations. Generally, the easiest way is to ask at the train information window, usually marked *"Renseignements."* The personnel there may not always speak English, but you will have no trouble if you write out the name of your destination and indicate the time you would like to leave. Doing this avoids the confusion caused by towns with similar-sounding names, such as Cannes, Cagnes or Caen. It also prevents misunderstandings of day-to-day variations when, for example, a particular train only runs on Saturdays in summer. At the same time, always be sure to check the return schedule so you don't wind up stranded in some quaint medieval village.

There is now a **telephone number** for **train information in English**. In Paris, dial **43-80-50-50**. From other parts of France, first dial 16, wait for a tone, then continue with 1-43-80-50-50.

All schedules are stated in terms of the 24-hour clock, thus a departure at 3:32 p.m. would be shown as 15.32. Free printed pocket schedules *(Fiches-Horaires)* are available for popular destinations, and schedules are also posted throughout the stations. Be careful of any footnotes on these, as they often refer to variations. The glossary on page 14 will be helpful in making translations, as will a pocket French-English dictionary. The regional schedule books *(Indicateur Officiel),* available at station newsstands, are complete but bulky to use. The smaller **Thomas Cook Continental Timetable**, sold in some travel book stores in America, by mail from the Forsyth Travel Library (P.O. Box 2975, Shawnee Mission, Kansas 66201, phone [913] 384-0496 for credit-card orders), or at Thomas Cook offices in Britain, is very useful although it does not list *every* local service.

RESERVATIONS are required for all TGV trains and can be made up to two months in advance of, and until five minutes before, departure time if seats are still available. There is a nominal charge for this. Travelers who can read French may prefer the handy coin-operated TGV reservation machines in TGV stations, which are valid only for departures within the next hour. You may want to make reservations for other rail trips, particularly on the often-crowded Turbotrains to the Normandy coast in high season, or for some TEE trains. One advantage to reservations is that you can specify a smoking or non-smoking section, and a window or aisle seat. Otherwise, reservations are really not necessary for the daytrips in this book other than those by TGV. Those traveling without them should be careful not to sit in someone else's reserved seat, which is marked by a card at the compartment entrance or above the seat.

PARIS has many train stations, a legacy from the days before nationalization when just about every route was operated by a different company. The map on page 17 shows the general location of those which are of interest to tourists. All of these are connected by the Métro subway system and can be easily reached. An inter-station bus service — free to holders of tickets or passes — is provided by the SNCF. Be sure you know which station you are leaving from before starting out on the day's adventures.

It is always best to arrive at the station (*Gare*) a little early in order to aquaint yourself with its layout. On the departure platform (*Quai*) you will usually find a sign marked *"Composition des Trains"* which shows the make-up of every express leaving from that platform, including the location of each car. This serves two purposes. First, you won't have to make a last-minute dash when you discover that the first-class cars stop at the opposite end of a long platform. Secondly, and more important, it shows which — if any — cars are dropped off en route to your destination.

The routing and final destination of each car is usually shown just outside its door as well as in its vestibule. First-class cars are marked with the numeral "1" near the door, and with a yellow stripe above the windows.

Most express trains offer a **food and beverage service** of some sort, as indicated on the schedules. Riding in a regular dining car, bar car or self-service *"Gril-Express"* car can be a delightful experience, but beware the pushcarts in other cars which sell well-shaken cans of warm beer. You are much better off stocking up on snacks and refreshments at the station and bringing them along with you, as most Europeans do. Establishments offering such take-out service are usually marked with the word *"Emporter."*

A RAIL TRAVELER'S GLOSSARY

Aller . . . . To go one way
Aller et Retour . . . . Round trip
A Partir . . . . From (date) on
Arrêt . . . . Stop, halt
Arrivée . . . . Arrival
Autobus, Autocar . . . . Bus
Autorail . . . . Railcar
Avec Supplément . . . . With surcharge
Banlieue . . . . Suburban (commuter trains)
Billet . . . . Ticket
Billet Simple . . . . Ordinary one-way ticket
Bureau de Change . . . . Currency exchange
Changement . . . . Change (of trains)
Composition des Trains . . . Train make-up
Composteur . . . . Ticket validating machine
Compostez votre Billet . . . Validate your ticket
Consigne . . . . Checkroom, left luggage
Consigne Automatique . . . Luggage locker
Contrôleur . . . . Ticket collector
Correspondence . . . . Connection
Couchette . . . . Inexpensive sleeping car with bunks
Couloir . . . . Aisle (seat)
Dames . . . . Women
Défense de Fumer . . . . No smoking
Demi-Tarif . . . . Half fare
Départ . . . . Departure
Deuxième Classe . . . . Second Class
Douane . . . . Customs
Emporter . . . . To take out, as in items from snack bar
Entrée . . . . Entrance
Entrée Interdite . . . . Do not enter
Faculatif . . . . Optional, on request (train or bus stops)
Fenêtre . . . . Window (seat)
Fêtes . . . . Holidays
Fiches-Horaires . . . . Free pocket-sized timetables
Fumeurs . . . . Smoking
Gare . . . . Train station
Gare Routière . . . . Bus station
Grandes Lignes . . . . Main lines
Gril-Express . . . . Cafeteria car
Guichet . . . . Ticket window
Horaire . . . . Timetable
Jusqu'au . . . . Until (date)
Libre . . . . Free, available
Libre Service . . . . Self service

Ligne	Line
Location de Voitures	Car rental
Métro	Subway
Messieurs	Men
Monter	To board (the train)
Objets Trouvés	Lost-and-found
Occupé	Occupied
Parcotrain	Inexpensive parking lot near station
Place	Seat
Plein Tarif	Full fare
Poste-PTT	Post office, telephone service
Première Classe	First class
Prochain	Next (departure)
Quai	Platform
Quotidien	Daily
RATP	Paris Transit Authority
Renseignements	Information
RER	Paris commuter rail lines
Reseau	Network, system
Réservation	Reservation
Retardé	Delay
Salle d' Attente	Waiting room
Sauf	Except
Sortie	Exit
Sortie de Secours	Emergency exit
SNCF	French National Railroads
Syndicat d' Initiative	Local tourist information office
Tarif	Fare
Tous les Jours	Every day
Train + Vélo	Bicycle rental at station
Trains d' Affaires	Trains favored by businessmen
Voie	Track
Voiture	Car (of train or otherwise)
Voiture Directe	Through car to indicated destination
Voyage	Trip, travel
Voyager	To travel
Voyageur	Traveler, passenger
Wagon	Railroad car
Wagon-Lit	Sleeping car
Wagon-Restaurant	Dining car

DAYS OF THE WEEK:

Lundi	Monday
Mardi	Tuesday
Mercredi	Wednesday
Jeudi	Thursday
Vendredi	Friday
Samedi	Saturday
Dimanche	Sunday
Fêtes	Holidays

SEASONS:

Printemps	Spring
Été	Summer
Automne	Autumn
Hiver	Winter

RAILPASSES can be a phenomenal bargain if you intend to do any real amount of train travel. Ask your travel agent about them before going to France, as they are difficult — but not impossible — to purchase once there. The International Information Office at the center of the ticket corridor in St. Lazare station in Paris does sell them, although the price may be higher. The French National Railroads (**SNCF**) accepts the following passes:

EURAILPASS — the granddaddy of them all, allows unlimited first-class travel throughout 16 European countries, excluding Great Britain. It is available for periods of 15 or 21 days, or 1, 2, or 3 months. The Eurailpass includes a wide variety of fringe benefits, such as rides on many private railroads including the Provence Railroad (see page 249), some buses, several popular lake and river cruises, and a variety of international ferry steamers.

EURAIL YOUTHPASS — This economy version of the Eurailpass is available to anyone under the age of 26 and allows unlimited second-class travel in the same 16 European countries, for periods of one or two months. The fringe benefits are pretty much the same.

The **FRANCE VACANCES PASS** is valid for unlimited travel in France only (also to Monaco and to Geneva via TGV), and offers a substantial saving over the Eurailpass. It is available in both first- and second-class versions, for periods of 7 or 15 days, or for one month. The attractive fringe benefits — *which may be used up to 8 days before or after the period of railpass validity if desired* — include a *Paris Sesame Pass* for 2, 4, or 7 days allowing unlimited use of the Paris Métro along with buses and RER commuter lines operated by the RATP; a free round-trip transfer between Charles de Gaulle or Orly airports and downtown Paris; admission to the Georges Pompidou arts center and museum; and a one-day pass for the private Provence Railroad (see page 249). It also allows discounts on car rentals at more than 200 rail stations in France and discounts on SNCF bus excursions.

In addition, there is a low-cost **InterRail Pass** available to youths under the age of 26 who are bona-fide residents of a European country, including Great Britain. The conditions pertaining to this pass are very different from those given above.

All railpasses must be **validated** at the information window of a train station on the first day of actual use. The first and last days of validity will be entered on the pass at that time.

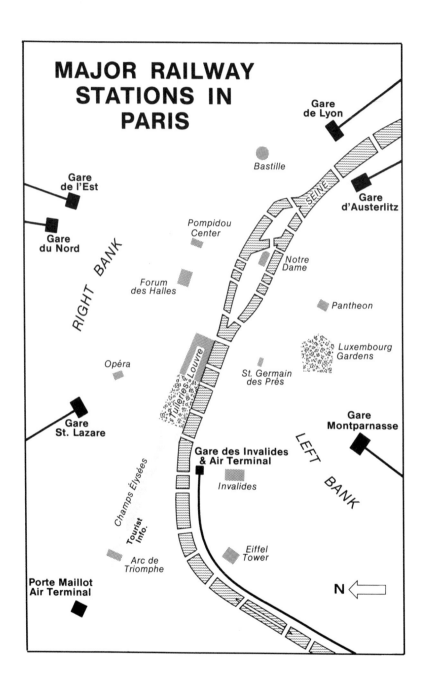

MAJOR RAILWAY STATIONS IN PARIS

Gare de Lyon

Gare de l'Est

Bastille

SEINE

Gare d'Austerlitz

Gare du Nord

Pompidou Center

RIGHT BANK

Notre Dame

Forum des Halles

Pantheon

Louvre

Opéra

Luxembourg Gardens

St. Germain des Prés

Tuileries

Gare Montparnasse

Gare St. Lazare

Gare des Invalides & Air Terminal

Invalides

Champs Élysées

LEFT BANK

Tourist Info.

Eiffel Tower

Arc de Triomphe

Porte Maillot Air Terminal

N

Be certain that you agree with the dates *before* allowing the agent to write them in.

If you intend to take several of the daytrips in this book, and especially if at least one of them is to a distant location such as Lyon, Dijon or Angers, a railpass will probably wind up saving you a considerable amount of money. Even if the savings are less than that the pass should still be considered for the convenience it offers in not having to line up for tickets, and the freedom of just hopping aboard almost any train at whim. Possession of a railpass will also encourage you to become more adventurous, to seek out distant and offbeat destinations.

The Eurailpass, Eurail Youthpass and France Vacances Pass are sold by most travel agents in North America, who also have current information and prices; and by mail from the Forsyth Travel Library mentioned on page 12 . Alternatively, you could contact the nearest French National Railroads office. In North America these are located in New York, Chicago, San Francisco, Beverly Hills CA, Coral Gables FL, Montreal and Vancouver. The address of the New York office is:

FRENCH NATIONAL RAILROADS
SNCF
610 Fifth Avenue
New York, NY 10020
Phone (212) 582-2110

Any of their locations will happily supply you with a free booklet of French and European fares, useful in determining whether to buy a railpass. They also have offices in London and throughout Western Europe.

Those who have decided against a railpass can purchase **tickets** (*billets*) at ticket windows (*guichets*) in the stations, or from automatic vending machines. There is usually no saving to be had by buying a round-trip ticket. Be sure to **validate** your ticket — *compostez votre billet* — before use by inserting it into one of the orange ticket-stamping machines (*composteur*) located near the platforms. Round-trip (*aller et retour*) tickets must also be stamped on the return journey. Failure to validate could result in a fine, since the SNCF operates on an honor system with only a few spot checks made, and unvalidated tickets could be used over and over again or even redeemed for cash.

BY BUS:

Six of the daytrips in this book are to destinations not served by the railroad. To reach them by public transportation, you should first take a train to the nearest town on a rail line and then continue on by connecting bus. Instructions for doing this are given in each case. Railpasses are valid on buses operated by or for the SNCF; others require payment of a modest fare. Buses, often called *Autobus* or *Autocar,* usually depart from a bus station (*gare routière),* most often located next to or near the train station.

BY CAR:

Many tourists prefer to explore France by car, which may be the most economical means of transport when several people are traveling together. Although slower, cars offer a complete freedom from schedules. All of the daytrips in this book can be made this way, with distances and specific road directions provided for each. In addition to a car you will need a valid driver's license and a good regional road map. Those published by Michelin are excellent and highly detailed.

Driving in France is essentially the same as in the U.S.A. or Canada, but attention should be paid to a few points. Seat belts are compulsory at all times for both the driver and front-seat passenger, with children under 10 confined to the rear seat — unless there is none. Failure to heed this rule could result in a fine. Similarly, the penalties for driving while intoxicated can be quite severe. Be particularly wary of the notorious *priorité à droite,* a peculiarly French concept in which vehicles coming from the right have the right-of-way. While there are many exceptions to this rule, you should always be careful and never try to bluff a French driver — they *know* their rights and take them very seriously.

Roads in France are excellent and well marked. *Autoroutes,* designated by the letter "A" preceding their number, are usually limited-access toll roads (*Péage*) with a 130-kph speed limit. This may be lower in some areas, or where there is no toll. Other main roads, known as *Routes Nationales* or "N" roads, are free and most often have a 90-kph limit (60 kph in built-up areas). To get the real flavor of the country, however, you should at least occasionally drive on the *Routes Départementales* (letter "D"), local roads which meander from village to village. The routes suggested in the book for each daytrip are the fastest ones. If you have the time, you might find it more enjoyable to use minor roads instead, following a good local road map.

A DRIVER'S GLOSSARY

Accotement non Stabilisé . . . . Soft shoulder
Allumez vos Phares . . . . Turn on headlights
Arrêt Interdit . . . . No stopping
Attention . . . . Caution
Au Pas . . . . Slow
Autoroute . . . . High-speed limited-access highway, usually toll. Indicated by letter "A" preceding route number
Autres Directions . . . . Other directions
Carte Grise . . . . Car registration papers
Carte Routière . . . . Road map
Céder la Passage . . . . Yield
Centre Ville . . . . To the center of town
Chaussée Déformée . . . . . . Bad road surface
Chantier . . . . Road construction
Chute de Pierres . . . . Falling rocks
Circulation Interdite . . . . . . No thoroughfare
Descente Dangereuse . . . . Steep hill
Déviation . . . . Detour (Diversion)
Douane . . . . Customs
Eau . . . . Water
École . . . . School
Entrée Interdite . . . . No entrance
Essence . . . . Gasoline (Petrol)
Fin d'Interdiction . . . . End of restriction
Fin de Limitation de Vitesse . . . . End of speed restriction
Gravillons . . . . Gravel road surface
Halte . . . . Stop
Hauteur Limitée . . . . Low clearance
Huile . . . . Oil
Impasse . . . . Dead-end road (Cul-de-Sac)
Interdiction de Doubler . . . No passing
Interdiction de Stationner . . . . No parking
Limitation de Vitesse . . . . . Speed restriction
Location de Voitures . . . . . . Car rental (Hire)
Nids de Poule . . . . Pot holes
Passage à Niveau . . . . Grade crossing
Passage Interdit . . . . Entry forbidden, no thoroughfare
Passage Protégé . . . . Right-of-way at intersection ahead
Péage . . . . Toll (road)
Pente Dangereuse . . . . Steep incline

Permis de Conduire....... Driver's license
Piétons .... Pedestrians
Piste Reservée aux
Transports Publics...... Lane reserved for public transport
Pneus..................... Tires
Poids Lourds .... Truck (Lorry) route
Priorité à Droite .... Vehicles coming from the right have the right-of-way
Priorité à Gauche .... Vehicles coming from the left have the right-of-way
Ralentir .... Reduce speed
Rappel.................... Previous sign still applies
Réservé aux Piétons ...... Pedestrians only
Réservée aux Transports
Publics .... (Lane) reserved for public transport
Route Barrée .... Road closed
Route Étroite.............. Narrow road
Route Glissante .... Slippery road
Sauf (Seulement)
Riverains .... (Private road) for residents only
Sens Interdit .... Wrong direction
Sens Unique............... One-way street
Serrez à Droite .... Keep to the right
Serrez à Gauche .... Keep to the left
Sortie .... Exit
Sortie de Camions .... Truck crossing
Stationnement Autorisé... Parking allowed
Stationnement Interdit ... No parking
Tenez vos Distances...... Keep your distance
Toutes Directions .... All directions
Travaux .... Road work
Verglas .... Slippery road
Virages .... Curves ahead
Voie de Dégagement ..... Private entrance
Voie Unique .... Single-lane traffic
Voiture.................... Car, vehicle
Voiture à Louer........... Rental car
Zone Bleue................ Time-indicator disc required for parking
Zone Rouge .... Tow-away zone

APPROXIMATE CONVERSIONS

1 Mile = 1.6 km

1 km = 0.6 miles

1 U.S. Gallon = 3.78 litres

1 litre = 0.26 U.S. Gallons

A brief glossary for drivers is provided on page 20. For more comprehensive automotive terms, you may want to use a pocket-sized phrase book, such as *French for Travellers* by Berlitz.

CAR RENTALS (*Location de Voitures*) can be arranged in advance through your travel agent or one of the major chains such as Hertz, Avis, National, Dollar or Budget. There are also many local firms which might charge less, but which may impose severe restrictions on drop-off possibilities and other conveniences. Among the best deals available are the **fly/drive** plans offered by Air France and some other carriers in conjunction with their transatlantic flights. Check with your travel agent about this as arrangements must be made in advance. Those traveling primarily by train may also want to rent a car on occasion. The **Train + Auto** service operated in connection with SNCF is an excellent way to do this, with discounts for holders of the economical France Vacances Pass (see page 16). If you intend to rent a car for three weeks or longer it will pay to consider leasing — an arrangement offered through your travel agent which is exempt from the stiff 33% tax on car rentals. Finally, in estimating your expenses, remember that gasoline (*essence*) costs roughly twice as much in France as in North America. Before returning a rental car, be sure to fill up the tank to avoid a high refilling charge.

BY AIR:

You may prefer air travel for the long haul between major base cities in France, particularly from Paris to Nice. Both Air France and Air Inter operate frequent flights on this route. Air Inter also has an extensive network of domestic services between all major cities in France, with competition from several regional carriers.

As to transatlantic services, **Air France** offers direct flights from more North American gateway cities to France than any other carrier. These include New York, Chicago, Washington D.C., Houston, Los Angeles, Anchorage, Montreal, Toronto, and Mexico City. Both the wide-body 747 and the supersonic Concorde are used for transatlantic crossings. Four classes of service are available: **Concorde** (the only class on supersonic flights), **Première** (first class, with sleeper seats, on 747s), **Air France Le Club** (business class on 747s), and **Economy**. Passengers bound for Nice will be happy to know that Air France makes quick and easy connections with through luggage checking from North America.

Paris has two major airports, **Charles de Gaulle** *(also called "Roissy")*, north of the city; and **Orly**, to the south. Most transatlantic flights land at Charles de Gaulle, where Air France has its own terminal with convenient connecting flights to other cities in Europe and throughout the world. The airline operates a frequent bus service to both airports. Those going to Charles de Gaulle leave from Porte Maillot in Paris, and those to Orly from Invalides. In either case the travel time is about 30 minutes. They also have buses running directly between the two airports — a 50-minute ride — which is free for connecting passengers. A more convenient way of getting into town is by taxi, which is not too terribly expensive and has the advantage of going directly to your destination. Holders of the "France Vacances" pass described on page 16 may want to take advantage of the combination bus/train services, called "Roissy Rail" and "Orly Rail" respectively, operated by SNCF.

The Nice-Côte d'Azur airport is so close to downtown Nice that taxis are practical for all but the slimmest budgets. There is also a local bus service.

PACKAGE PLANS:

The cost of your trip to France can be cut substantially by selecting one of the many attractive package plans which combine transatlantic airfares with local hotel accommodations and/or car rentals. **Air France** has the widest selection of these, offering a flexible length of stay to fit the needs of independent travelers. These may be combined with a fly/drive arrangement if desired — just choose the elements and make up your own custom package. Similar plans are offered by other carriers. Since the details of these programs, as well as the airfares, change frequently you should consult with a reliable travel agent well ahead of time.

HOLIDAYS:

Legal holidays *(Fêtes Légales)* in France are:

January 1
Easter Monday
May 1 (Labor Day)
May 8 (V-E Day)
Ascension Day
   (40 days after Easter)
Whit Monday (Second
   Monday after Ascension)

July 14 (Bastille Day)
August 15 (Assumption Day)
November 1 (All Saints' Day)
November 11 (Armistice Day)
Christmas

Trains operate on holiday schedules on these days, and some attractions may be closed — see the "When to Go" section for each daytrip. Banks close at noon on the day preceding a holiday. When any of these falls on a Sunday, the following Monday is taken as a holiday.

FOOD AND DRINK:

Several choice restaurants are listed for each destination in this book. Most of these are long-time favorites of experienced travelers and serve French cuisine. Their approximate price range, based on the least expensive complete set meal offered, is indicated as follows:

$ — Inexpensive, but may have fancier dishes available.

$$ — Reasonable. These establishments may also feature daily specials.

$$$ — Luxurious and expensive.

Those who take their dining very seriously should consult an up-to-date restaurant and hotel guide such as the classic red-cover *Michelin France,* issued annually in March.

It is always wise to check the prices posted outside the restaurant before entering. Remember that in France the word *"menu"* refers to a fixed-price set meal, often a daily special, consisting of several courses and possibly wine as well. The use of a pocket-sized translator such as the *Marling Menu Master* will allow you to try unfamiliar dishes without anxiety.

Those in a hurry to get on with their sightseeing will find that there are many low-cost alternatives to restaurant dining. These range from the traditional *pique-nique* lunch made from ingredients purchased at nearby markets to having a *croque-monsieur* or other sandwich at a café; or whatever catches your eye in a self-service cafeteria (the nationwide *Flunch* chain is quite good) or even a French hamburger and *crudités* at one of those ubiquitous fast-food outlets such as *Quick* or *Free Time.*

If you are not completely famished but would still like a traditional French meal, why not stop in at a crêperie? The specialties there include *galettes* (pancakes stuffed with meat, cheese, vegetables or fish), dessert crêpes and hard cider. These places are often quite atmospheric and very inexpensive. Pizzerias are also extremely popular with the French.

SUGGESTED TOURS:

The do-it-yourself walking tours in this book are relatively short and easy to follow. On the assumption that most readers will be traveling by public transportation, they always begin at the local train station or bus stop. Those going by car can make a simple adjustment. Suggested routes are shown by heavy broken lines on the maps, while the circled numbers refer to attractions along the way, with corresponding numbers in the text.

Trying to see all of the sights in a given town could easily become an exhausting marathon. You will certainly enjoy yourself more by being selective and passing up anything that doesn't catch your fancy in favor of a friendly sidewalk café. God will forgive you if you don't visit *every* church.

TOURIST INFORMATION:

Virtually every French town of any tourist interest has its own information office, usually called a *Syndicat d'Initiative* or *Office de Tourisme,* which can help you with specific questions, furnish maps and brochures, or book local accommodations. They almost invariably have at least one person on staff who speaks English. Sometimes these offices are closed on Sundays, holidays, or over the noon meal period.

The location of the offices is shown on the town maps in this book by the word "**info.**," and repeated along with the phone number under the "Tourist Information" section for each trip. To phone ahead from **Paris** to somewhere else in France, first dial 16, wait for a tone, then continue with the complete 8-digit number. To phone from anywhere else in France to anywhere *except* Paris, just dial the 8-digit number. Phone calls to Paris from the rest of France are made by dialing 16, waiting for a tone, then continuing with the prefix 1 and the complete 8-digit Paris number. Calling ahead is useful if the whole reason for your daytrip hinges on seeing a particular sight which might possibly be closed, or perhaps to check the weather.

Most pay phones in France use coins — just load up the slot with small denominations and any which are not used will be returned. The newer type of pilfer-proof pay phones accept no coins but are operated by inserting a *"Carte de Téléphone,"* available at any post office or *"tabac"* shop. The cost of each call is automatically subtracted from the value of the card.

The **Paris Tourist Office** is located at 127, Ave. des Champs-Elysées, phone 47-23-61-72, with branches at the following train stations: Nord, Est, Lyon, and Austerlitz.

ADVANCE PLANNING INFORMATION:

The **French Government Tourist Office** has branches throughout the world which will gladly help you in planning your trip. In North America these are located at:

610 Fifth Ave. *(mail requests only)*
– or –
628 Fifth Ave. *(personal callers)*
New York, NY 10020
Phone (212) 757-1125

645 North Michigan Ave.,
Chicago, IL 60611–2836
Phone (312) 337-6301

9401 Wilshire Blvd.,
Beverly Hills, CA 90212–2967
Phone (213) 271-6665

1 Hallide Plaza, Suite 250
San Francisco, CA 94102–2818
Phone (415) 986-4161

103 World Trade Center
2050 Stemmons Freeway
P.O. Box 58610
Dallas, TX 75258
Phone (214) 742-7011

1981 McGill College, Suite 490
Montreal, P.Q. H3A 3W9
Phone (514) 288-4264

1 Dundas Street West
Suite 2405, Box 8
Toronto, Ont. M5G 1Z3
Phone (416) 593-4723

In England, they are at 178 Piccadilly, **London** WIV OAL, phone (01) 493-65-94.

Section II

Daytrips from Paris

The Ile-de-France

To explore the Ile-de-France is to see the story of a great civilization unfold before your eyes, an experience no visitor to Paris should miss. This central region, without defined borders and existing in the mind almost as much as in reality, is the very heart and soul of France — the royal island from which a remarkable nation emerged.

Roughly speaking, the Ile-de-France is the area within about a fifty-mile radius of Paris. A dense network of rail lines and highways provides easy access to its many attractions. The seven daytrip destinations which follow were chosen for both their high quality and for the broad variety of adventures they offer. Once having sampled these delights, you may want to try other places in the same region — such as St.-Denis, Compiègne, Vaux-le-Vicomte, Barbizon, Rambouillet, St.-Germain-en-Laye, Malmaison or Beauvais.

Paris is by far the most convenient base for one-day excursions into the Ile-de-France, but those wishing to stay outside the city might consider nearby towns with both hotels and fast commuter service. Two excellent choices for this are Versailles and St.-Germain-en-Laye.

Because of the short distances involved, it is sometimes possible to visit two destinations in the same day, albeit at a rather hectic pace. Such pairings which work well in this region are: Versailles with Chartres, Fontainebleau with Moret-sur-Loing, and Chantilly with Senlis.

Those traveling by rail will note that several different train stations in Paris are used for the various trips. The map on page 17 shows the general location of these.

Versailles

By far the most popular daytrip destination in France, Versailles embodies in stone the awesome will of Louis XIV, the "Sun King." A visit to this enormous palace will tell you a great deal about the Age of Absolutism, for Louis XIV did not merely rule a country, he *was* the state.

Versailles was built, in effect, as the seat of government — a place where the king could keep his eye on the treacherous nobility. Begun in 1661, it took over fifty years to complete. Few structures on earth can begin to match its splendor, with so much to see that attempting to do it all could lead to the visual equivalent of indigestion. A more sensible plan is to hit only the highlights of the château, the gardens and the Trianons on the first visit; then plan on returning at some later date. The tour outlined here is limited to the most important features and — with a bit of rushing — could be done in half a day.

Energetic travelers making an early start will find it possible to combine this trip with one to Chartres, the subject of the next chapter.

GETTING THERE:

Trains on the SNCF-RER commuter line C-5 leave very frequently from the underground Invalides station in Paris, located on the left bank of the Seine just across the Alexandre III bridge. These take you to Versailles' Rive Gauche station, a short stroll from the château, in under 30 minutes. Railpasses are valid, but ask at the information office for a free ticket to operate the turnstiles. There are also regular trains from Montparnasse and St.-Lazare stations in Paris which go to other stations in Versailles, farther from the château.

By car, Versailles is about 13 miles southwest of Paris via the A-13 Autoroute or the N-10 road.

WHEN TO GO:

Good weather is necessary to appreciate the marvelous gardens at Versailles. Avoid coming on a Monday or major holiday, when the château is closed.

The Hall of Mirrors

FOOD AND DRINK:
Versailles has a number of fine restaurants, including:
Trois Marches (3 Rue Colbert, by the château), rates two Michelin stars. $$$

Trianon Palace Hotel (1 Blvd. de la Reine, near the Neptune Basin) $$$

Rescatore (27 Ave. de St.-Cloud) $$$

Boule d'Or (25 Rue Mar. Foch, near Notre-Dame Church) $$$

Potager du Roy (1 Rue Mar. Joffre, near St.-Louis Cathedral) $$

TOURIST INFORMATION:
The tourist information office is located at 7 Rue des Réservoirs, near the château. You can phone them at 39-50-36-22.

SUGGESTED TOUR:
Leave the Rive Gauche **train station** (1) and follow the map to nearby Place d'Armes. The **Palace of Versailles** *(Château)* (2), opening before you, was originally a hunting lodge of Louis XIII. His son, Louis XIV, greatly expanded this to create a sumptuous new palace where the court could be consolidated under one roof, far from the intrigues of Paris. The most noted architects of the time, Louis Le Vau and, later, Jules Hardouin-Mansart, were engaged along with the celebrated landscape gardener André Le

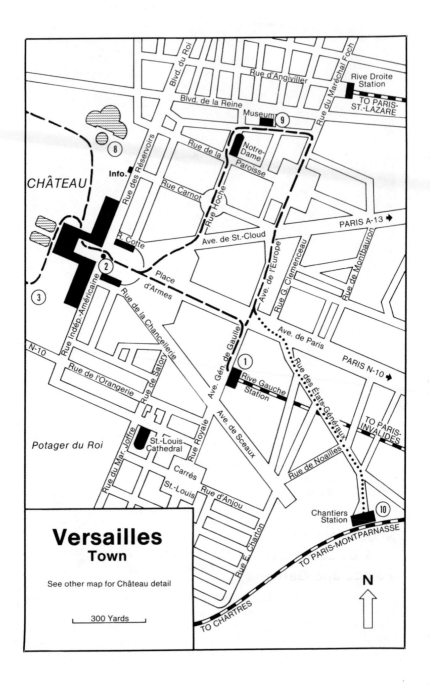

Versailles
Town

See other map for Château detail

300 Yards

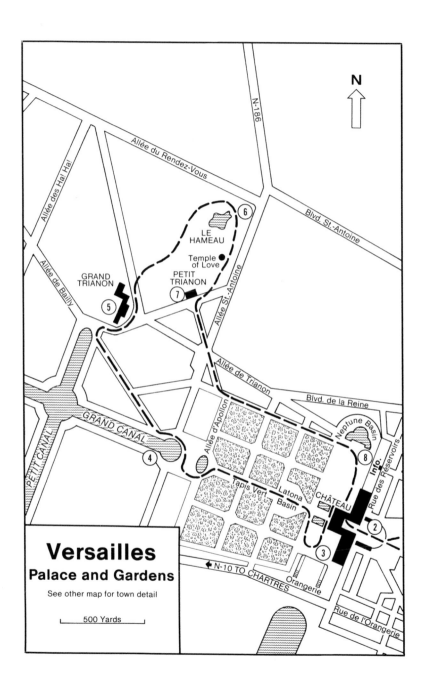

N

Le Hameau

Temple of Love

Grand Trianon

Petit Trianon

Allée du Rendez-Vous

Allée des Hai Hai

Allée de Bailly

N-186

Blvd. St.-Antoine

Allée St.-Antoine

Allée de Trianon

Blvd. de la Reine

PETIT CANAL

GRAND CANAL

Allée d'Apollon

Neptune Basin

Rue des Réservoirs

Info.

Tapis Vert

Latona Basin

CHÂTEAU

Orangerie

N-10 TO CHARTRES

Rue de l'Orangerie

Versailles
Palace and Gardens

See other map for town detail

500 Yards

The Palace of Versailles

Nôtre and the great decorator Charles Le Brun. Together they directed a vast army of workers who drained the marshes, leveled hills and moved forests. A full half-century of monumental labor went into the Versailles you see today. After the death of Louis XIV in 1715, the château continued to be used by his successors until the French Revolution, during which it was ransacked and nearly fell to ruin. Since then, much of it has been magnificently restored, with work continuing to this day.

Enter the château and visit the **State Apartments**, which include the famous **Hall of Mirrors**, the Chapel, the King's Suite and the Queen's Suite. An illustrated guide booklet in English is available at the entrance, which is quite useful since you'll be wandering through on your own. Other parts of the palace, including the **Private Apartments** and the **Royal Opera**, may be seen on guided tours only. The château is open from 9:45 a.m. to 5 p.m., every day except Mondays and some holidays. The great garden fountains are operated between 4 and 5 p.m. on certain Sundays from May to October, while spectacular night festivals are held occasionally during the summer. Ask at the tourist office for current schedules.

No visit to Versailles is complete without a stroll through the fabulous gardens. Begin with the **Parterres du Midi** (3), over-looking the **Orangerie**. Walk over to the Latona Basin and follow the Tapis Vert, a long green avenue between some enchanting

A Corner of Le Hameau

hidden groves, to the **Grand Canal** (4), where boats may be hired.

Continue on to the **Grand Trianon** (5), a smaller château built in 1687 to avoid the formalities of court life. After the Revolution it was used by Napoleon and is furnished in the Empire style. Opening times are the same as those for the main palace.

Now follow the map to **Le Hameau** (6), a thoroughly delightful little hamlet where the unfortunate Marie Antoinette played at being a peasant. Paths from here lead past the Temple of Love to the **Petit Trianon** (7), an elegant small château erected by Louis XV and later used by Marie Antoinette. It is open from 2–5 p.m., except on Mondays and some holidays. Return to the main palace by way of the **Neptune Basin** (8).

Before heading back to Paris, you may want to explore a bit of the town of Versailles. An interesting short walk can be made by following the map past the Church of Notre-Dame to the pleasant **Lambinet Museum** (9), which specializes in 18th-century art. Those intrepid souls intent on continuing on to Chartres by rail should depart from Versailles' **Chantiers station** (10).

Chartres

Rising majestically above the Beauce plain, the Cathedral of Chartres is one of the greatest legacies of the Middle Ages and the quintessential Gothic cathedral. Pilgrims and tourists from all over the world are drawn to it by the thousands, yet most overlook the charms of the town itself. And that's a pity — for Chartres is one of those rare French *villes* which kept its essentially medieval character intact.

It may seem surprising that a town as small as Chartres should possess one of the largest cathedrals on earth. The place, however, appears to have a long history of religious significance. Ancient Druids probably worshipped at the well under the cathedral crypt. Later the capital of the Gallic Carnutes, it was called *Autricum* by the Romans, who built a temple on the same site. Early Christians replaced this with a basilica, saving the statue of the Roman goddess whom they took to be the Virgin. Five subsequent churches were built on the spot, culminating in the present 13th-century masterpiece. A precious relic believed to be a garment worn by the Virgin Mary, which has been in the cathedral since 876, is responsible for Chartres being a place of pilgrimage for over a thousand years.

Indefatigable travelers may want to combine a daytrip to Chartres with one to Versailles (see page 28), which is entirely possible by train or car but not especially recommended.

GETTING THERE:

Trains leave Montparnasse station in Paris fairly frequently for the one-hour trip to Chartres. Return service operates until late evening. These trains also stop at Versailles.

By car, the fastest route is via the A-10 and A-11 Autoroutes, a distance of 55 miles. A slower but more interesting route is to take the N-10 through Versailles and Rambouillet.

WHEN TO GO:

Try to visit Chartres in good weather, when sunshine illuminates the incredible stained-glass windows to best effect. The art museum is closed on Tuesdays and major holidays.

Chartres Cathedral

FOOD AND DRINK:

Chartres has many restaurants which cater primarily to tourists. Among the better choices are:

Henri IV (31 Rue Soleil d'Or, a block south of the cathedral) Very well known, awarded one Michelin star. $$$

Grand Monarque (22 Pl. Épars, on the N-10 a few blocks southwest of the cathedral) Nouvelle cuisine. $$$

La Vieille Maison (5 Rue au Lait, near the cathedral) $$$

Normand (24 Pl. Épars, on the N-10 a few minutes southwest of the cathedral) $

Café Serpente (2 Cloître Notre-Dame, facing the cathedral) $$

Le Biniou (7 Rue Serpente, a block south of the cathedral) Crêpes in a Breton atmosphere. $

TOURIST INFORMATION:

Make inquiries at the Office du Tourisme, facing the cathedral. The phone number is 37-21-54-03.

SUGGESTED TOUR:

From the **train station** (1) you will have a clear view of the cathedral. Follow the map to its fascinating **West Front** (2), much of which survives from an earlier 12th-century structure largely destroyed by fire in 1194. The two asymmetrical towers make a dramatic study in architectural evolution. On the right is the Old Tower, representing the fullest development of the Romanesque style. The New Tower, to the left, is capped with a 16th-century spire, a masterpiece of the Flamboyant Gothic. Between them stands the Royal Portal, three arched doorways from the 12th century. Look carefully at the stunning *Christ in Majesty* carving above the center door. The figures over the right portal depict the Nativity, while those on the left are of the Ascension.

Step inside and witness the true glory of **Chartres Cathedral** — its miraculous **stained-glass windows**. Almost all of these are original, mostly 13th-century with some dating from the 12th. Replacements account for less than six percent of the total 26,000 square feet, making this the largest collection of medieval glass in the world.

Guided tours of the interior are available — those in English being particularly good — or you can pick up a printed guide and explore on your own. Binoculars can be a great help for studying the biblical stories depicted in the windows. Be sure to visit the **Treasury**, behind the Choir, which displays the venerated garment thought to have been worn by the Virgin Mary.

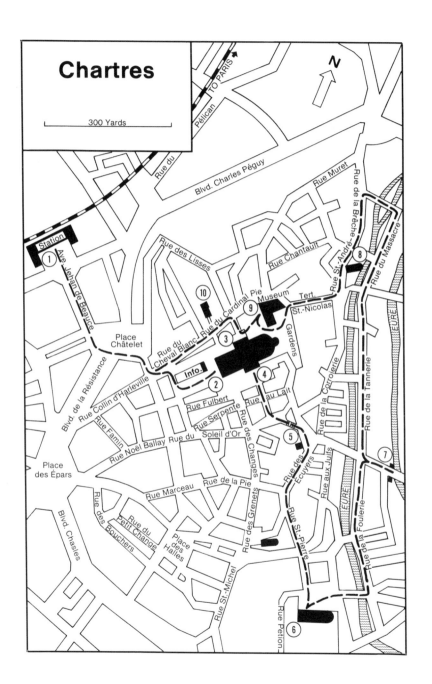

Chartres

300 Yards

TO PARIS

N

Rue du Pélican

Blvd. Charles Péguy

Rue Muret

Rue de la Brèche

Rue du Massacre

Station

1

Rue des Lisses

Rue Chantault

Rue St.-André

8

EURE

Ave. Jehan de Beauce

10

Rue du Cardinal Pie

Museum

9

Tert. St.-Nicolas

Place Châtelet

Rue du Cheval Blanc

3

Gardens

Rue de la Corroierie

Rue de la Tannerie

Blvd. de la Résistance

Info.

2

4

Rue Fulbert

Rue au Lait

Rue Collin d'Harleville

Rue Serpente

Rue des Changes

5

7

Rue Famin

Rue du Soleil d'Or

Rue des Écuyers

EURE

Rue Noël Ballay

Place des Épars

Rue de la Pie

Rue aux Juifs

Rue de la Foulerie

Rue Marceau

Blvd. Chasles

Rue des Bouchers

Rue du Petit Change

Place des Halles

Rue des Grenets

Rue St.-Pierre

Rue St.-Michel

Rue Pétion

6

A climb to the top of the **North Tower** will reward you with spectacular views. The entrance to this is by the door in the **North Transept** (3). Another sight not to be missed is the ancient **Crypt** of the original church, which can be visited on special guided tours only. These depart, oddly enough, from a souvenir shop *(Maison des Clercs)* just outside the **South Transept** (4).

Leave the cathedral and follow the map to the Rue des Écuyers. On the right, at number 35, you will find a curious old house with a 16th-century turret staircase of carved oak known as the **Escalier de la Reine Berthe** (5). Continue on to the **Church of St.-Pierre** (6). If its great cathedral did not exist, Chartres would still be noted for this magnificent medieval structure, whose flying buttresses and original stained glass are truly impressive.

Stroll over to the Eure stream and cross it. There is a nice view of the cathedral from here. Turn left on Rue de la Foulerie and follow along to **Porte Guillaume** (7) to see what little remains of the old town walls. Return to the stream and walk along Rue de la Tannerie, passing several delightful old waterside buildings. Across the Eure stands the 12th-century **Church of St.-André** (8), a Romanesque structure whose choir once spanned the stream on a daring arch, long since destroyed.

Continue by following the map to the **Beaux-Arts Museum** (9), reached via the steep Tertre Saint-Nicolas steps which open into lovely gardens. The museum, housed in the former Bishop's Palace, contains a superb collection of paintings (particularly those by Vlaminck), enamels, tapestries, furniture and artifacts of regional history. It is open from 10 a.m. to noon and 2–6 p.m. (5 p.m. in winter) every day except Tuesdays and holidays.

Another attraction you may want to visit is the **Cellier de Loëns** (10) at number 5 Rue du Cardinal Pie. This 13th-century cellar once stored tithes and is now the International Stained-Glass Center, offering rotating exhibits of the art which made Chartres famous.

Fontainebleau

Haunted by memories of François I and Napoleon Bonaparte, the Château of Fontainebleau beguiles with its marvelously haphazard layout and intimate atmosphere. Many prefer it to Versailles. This was a real home for the rulers of France, from the 12th century right down to Napoleon III in the 19th.

The palace as it stands today is mostly the result of an extensive reconstruction carried out in the 16th century by François I, the king most credited with bringing the Renaissance to France. Only the keep *(donjon)* in the Oval Court survives from the Middle Ages. Later kings, including Louis XIV, made frequent use of the château, drawn primarily by the sporting opportunities of the surrounding forest. Fontainebleau became the favorite residence of Napoleon I, who had it thoroughly redecorated. It was also the scene, in 1814, of his abdication and departure for Elba.

The Forest of Fontainebleau is exceptionally lovely with its wide variety of wild, natural beauty. Those with cars may want to pick up a map at the tourist office and go exploring, particularly to the charming village of Barbizon. This trip can easily be combined in the same day with one to Moret-sur-Loing, subject of the next chapter, which is only six miles away on the same rail line.

GETTING THERE:

Trains depart Gare de Lyon station in Paris almost hourly for Fontainebleau-Avon, less than 45 minutes away. These are met by a bus marked "Château," which goes to the palace. Return trains run until mid-evening.

By car, the fastest way is via the A-6 Autoroute, followed by the N-7E and N-7 roads; a total distance from Paris of 40 miles.

WHEN TO GO:

The château is closed on Tuesdays and some major holidays. Pleasant weather will make a walk in the gardens more enjoyable.

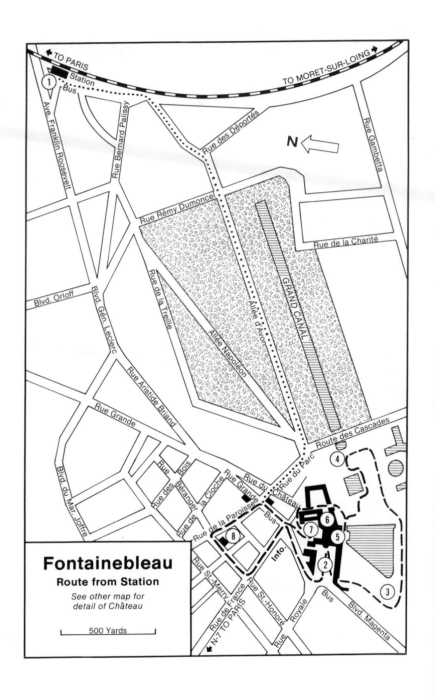

TO PARIS

TO MORET-SUR-LOING

Station

Bus

N

Ave. Franklin Roosevelt

Rue Bernard Palissy

Rue des Déportés

Rue Gambetta

Rue Rémy Dumoncel

Rue de la Charité

Blvd. Orloff

Blvd. Gén. Leclerc

Rue de la Treille

Allée d'Avon

Allée Napoléon

GRAND CANAL

Rue Aristide Briand

Rue Grande

Route des Cascades

Blvd. du Mar. Joffre

Rue des Bois

Rue Béranger

Rue de la Cloche

Rue Grande

Rue du Château

Rue du Parc

Route des Cascades

Rue de la Paroisse

Bus

Info.

Bus

Blvd. Magenta

Rue Royale

Rue St-Honoré

Rue de France

Rue St-Merry

N-7 TO PARIS

Fontainebleau
Route from Station

*See other map for
detail of Château*

500 Yards

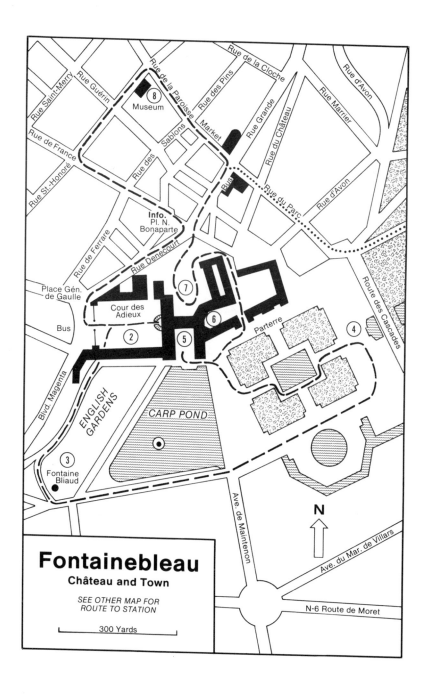

Fontainebleau

Château and Town

*SEE OTHER MAP FOR
ROUTE TO STATION*

300 Yards

FOOD AND DRINK:

The town of Fontainebleau has a great many restaurants and cafés in all price ranges, particularly on and near Rue Grande and Place Général de Gaulle. Among the better choices are:

Aigle Noir (27 Place Napoléon Bonaparte, near the château) Elegant hotel with two restaurants, $$$ and $$

Londres (Place Gén. de Gaulle, opposite the château). $$

François I (3 Rue Royale, opposite the château) $$

Filet de Sole (5 Rue Coq-Gris, near the tourist office) $$

Le Dauphin (24 Rue Grande, near the tourist office) $

Le Grillardin (12 Rue Pins, near Rue Grande) $

TOURIST INFORMATION:

The tourist information office, phone 64-22-25-68, is located at 31 Place Napoléon Bonaparte, near the château.

SUGGESTED TOUR:

The Fontainebleau-Avon **train station** (1) is nearly two miles from the palace. Get there by one of the frequent buses marked "Château," or on foot through the park.

Enter the **Château** (2) via the White Horse Courtyard, also known as the **Cour des Adieux**, where Napoleon I bid a tearful farewell to his troops in 1814 as he went into exile. You may stroll through the **Grand Apartments** at your own leisure, following a well-marked route. In order to understand what you're seeing, however, it will help to purchase an illustrated guide in English or rent one of the taped-commentary cassette players. Both are available at the entrance. The most outstanding sights are the 16th-century **Galerie François I**, the **King's Staircase**, the **Ballroom**, the **Royal Apartments** and **Napoleon's Apartments**. To see the more intimate **Petit Apartments** requires taking a guided tour. The château is open every day except Tuesdays and some holidays; from 9:30 a.m. to 12:30 p.m. and again from 2–5 p.m. In either case, be sure to arrive at least an hour before closing time to avoid being rushed.

Leave the château and follow the map through a passage in the south wing to an intriguing 16th-century grotto. This opens into the informal **English Gardens** (Jardin Anglais) (3) laid out by Napoleon. Continue on past the original spring, the **Fontaine Bliaud**, from which the name of the palace and town derives. Next to this is the **Carp Pond** with its delightful little island pavilion.

You are now in the formal gardens, the Parterre designed for Louis XIV by the architect Le Vau, which offers marvelous views of the château. Stroll down to the **Cascades** (4) and look out

The Château of Fontainebleau

over the Grand Canal, a center of pageantry in the time of the Sun King, then return to the palace. Horse carriage rides are usually available along here.

The **Cour de la Fontaine** (5) is a beautiful courtyard overlooking the carp pond. Take an admiring glance, then follow around past the ancient **Oval Court** (6) with its 12th-century keep — used by François I as his bedroom. This is usually locked, but you can peek in through the grill. Continue on past the 17th-century Cour des Offices and visit the **Jardin de Diane** (7), a wonderfully romantic garden noted for its elegant fountain dating from 1603.

Those who would like to see some of the town should exit onto Rue Grande and turn right. A left on Rue Paroisse leads past a market place to the interesting **Napoleonic Museum of Art and Military History** (8) on Rue St.-Honoré. Noted for its fine collection of swords, it is open from 2–5 p.m., daily except on Sundays, Mondays, and holidays.

Return to Place Général de Gaulle, facing the entrance of the château. From here you can get a bus back to the train station.

Moret-sur-Loing

Although it has long been a favorite weekend retreat for Parisians, Moret-sur-Loing has yet to be discovered by foreign visitors. This deliciously picturesque old town on the meandering Loing river looks like a scene from an Impressionist painting, and in fact is one. The noted artist Alfred Sisley spent the latter years of his life here, immortalizing for all time its narrow streets, quaint church, delightful bridge and charming watermills.

Moret was a strategically important border fortress as early as the 12th century, when it protected the Ile-de-France from the counts of Champagne. Many of its original structures still exist, preserved amid a medieval atmosphere virtually unmatched elsewhere in the region.

A daytrip to Moret can be combined quite easily with one to Fontainebleau, just six miles away on the same rail line. If you are driving, you could visit Vaux-le-Vicomte, a fabulous château just outside Melun, instead. Those who are going to Moret only will find that it makes a good afternoon trip.

GETTING THERE:

Trains leave Gare de Lyon station in Paris almost hourly for Moret-Véneux-les-Sablons station, usually stopping at Fontainebleau en route. The trip takes less than one hour. Return service operates until mid-evening. Although Moret is a very small town, it is also an important rail junction, with trains to and from Paris using different, widely spaced platforms. Be careful to note the correct one on the departure board.

By car, the quickest route is to follow the directions to Fontainebleau (page 39), then take the N-6 into Moret, which is about 48 miles from Paris.

WHEN TO GO:

Moret can be enjoyed at any time in good weather, particularly on weekends. If you plan to visit Clemenceau's house or the castle keep you should note the very limited opening times. *Son et Lumière* spectacles are held on Saturday nights in summer — check the tourist office for details.

Porte de Bourgogne Gate and the Bridge

FOOD AND DRINK:

There are a number of charming restaurants, mostly located near the bridge. Some choices are:

Auberge de la Terrasse (40 Rue de la Pêcherie, near the river. $$

Bon Abri (90 Ave. Fontainebleau in nearby Véneux-les-Sablons, not far from the train station) $$

TOURIST INFORMATION:

A tourist information office is located on Place de Samois, next to the Porte de Samois. You can call them at 60-70-41-66.

SUGGESTED TOUR:

The Moret-Véneux-les-Sablons **train station** (1) is nearly a mile from the town proper. You could call for a taxi, although the walk is rather pleasant. Enter the Old Town through the 12th-century **Porte de Samois** gate (2), next to the tourist office. Continue down Rue Grande where, at number 24, opposite the war memorial park, you will pass the house where Napoleon spent the last night on his return from Elba. Turn right into a passageway leading to a courtyard behind the town hall. Here stands the so-called **Maison François I** (3), a splendid Renaissance façade of unknown origin. Back on the Rue Grande there are two fine Renaissance houses at numbers 28 and 30.

Stroll straight ahead through the venerable 12th-century **Porte de Bourgogne** gate (4). From here a famous bridge spans the Loing river. Midstream, on either side, are two striking old mills, now private residences. Once across, make a left into the **park** (5) on the river's edge where you can enjoy the romantic view captured in Sisley's renowned painting *"The Bridge at Moret,"* displayed in the Impressionist museum of the Louvre in Paris.

Follow the map past a set of locks on the Burgundy Canal to the **Georges Clemenceau Museum** (6). Designed as a retirement place by the eminent French premier shortly before his death, this intimate, very personal and extremely charming small house was occupied by his son until 1964. It is now open to the public on Saturdays, Sundays and holidays from 2:30–6 p.m. between Palm Sunday and the end of November. Don't miss seeing it.

Return across the bridge and follow Rue de la Tannerie to the ancient **Castle Keep** (Donjon) (7) on Rue du Château. Built in 1128, it was used for several months as a prison for Nicolas Fouquet, Louis XIV's finance minister who amassed a great fortune at the State's expense. The keep is open on Sundays and holidays from 2:30–6 p.m. between Easter and the end of September.

At number 9 Rue du Château is the **house** (8) where the artist Alfred Sisley spent the last years of his life. One of the pioneers of Impressionism, he showed little aptitude in promoting his work and died in poverty. Ironically, his paintings now hang in the world's greatest museums.

Stroll through the evocative narrow alleyways in the immediate area, then continue on to the magnificent Gothic **Church of Notre-Dame** (9). Begun in 1166 on ground consecrated by Thomas à Becket, the Archbishop of Canterbury, construction continued until the 15th century, when its Flamboyant porch was added. The church is quite interesting to visit — its flying buttresses dramatic in their upward surge. To the right of the church, in an old timbered house, nuns still sell the famous *Sucres d'Orge,* the barley-sugar specialty of Moret.

Follow the map via Rue Grande and make the first possible turn through an old building to the river's edge. Wander along to some **old fortifications** (10) which are now parts of houses, then return to Rue Grande and the station.

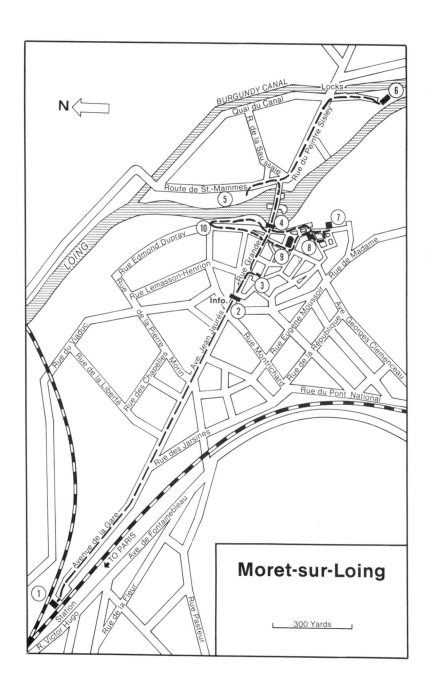

N

BURGUNDY CANAL   Locks

Quai du Canal

R. de la Saussaie

Rue du Peintre Sisley

6

Route de St.-Mammes

5

4

7

LOING

Rue Edmond Dupray

10

Rue Grande

9

8

Rue de Madame

Rue Lemasson-Henrion

Rue de la Pierre Morin

3

Info.

2

Rue Eugène Moussoir

Ave. Georges Clemenceau

Rue du Viaduc

Rue de la Liberté

Rue des Chapelles

Ave. Jean Jaurès

Rue Montrichard

Rue de la République

Rue du Pont National

Rue des Jarsines

Avenue de la Gare

TO PARIS

Ave. de Fontainebleau

1

Station

R. Victor Hugo

Rue de la Fleur

Rue Pasteur

Moret-sur-Loing

300 Yards

Provins

Another one of those intriguing medieval towns that somehow get overlooked by tourists, Provins can be a real charmer. Once the third-largest city in France (after Paris and Rouen), it is now a pleasant backwater with distant echoes of a long-ago past. This is a place for quiet contemplation far from the madding crowds, where vestiges of the early Middle Ages have survived intact.

The town's decline began as early as the 14th century. Before that, Provins was the capital of Brie, seat of the counts of Champagne and the site of major fairs famed throughout Europe. It has a curious connection with English history. During the 13th century it was ruled by Edmund, duke of Lancaster, who adopted as his own the famous red rose of Provins — later to become a symbol in the War of the Roses. Both the plague and the Hundred Years War took their toll, but it was perhaps the growing importance of nearby Paris which contributed most to the downfall of this once-great city.

Provins is built on two levels. The lower town (*Ville Basse*) is reawakening with renewed prosperity, while the upper town (*Ville Haute*), perched high on a promontory overlooking the Brie plain, slumbers on amid ruined memories. Both have their fascinations, and both are covered on the suggested walking tour.

GETTING THERE:

Trains depart Gare de l'Est station in Paris in the morning and again around noon for Longueville, where you change to a connecting local for the short ride to Provins. The total journey takes a bit over one hour. Return service operates until early evening. Study the schedules carefully to avoid a wait at Longueville, not exactly the most scintillating place in France.

By car, it's the N-19 all the way from Paris, 53 miles away. A more complex but probably faster route is to leave Paris on the A-4, switching quickly to the N-4, then finally the D-231 into Provins.

The Tour de César

WHEN TO GO:

Good weather is essential for this largely outdoor trip. The famous Tour de César is open every day except Christmas and New Year's, but some other attractions tend to operate only on Sundays and holidays.

FOOD AND DRINK:

Provins offers a nice variety of restaurants along the walking route. Some suggestions, in the order you will pass or come close to them, are:

Le Médiéval (Place Honoré de Balzac, in the lower town) $$

Le Croix d'Or (1 Rue des Capucins, in the lower town, near the Durteint stream) $$

Aux Vieux Remparts (3 Rue Couverte, in the upper town, near the Grange aux Dîmes) Good location. $$

La Fontaine (10 Rue Victor Arnoul, in the lower town, near St.-Ayoul) $$

Le Berri (17 Rue Hugues Legrand, in the lower town, near St.-Ayoul) $

TOURIST INFORMATION:

The tourist information office, phone 64-00-16-65, is at the Tour de César, in the upper town.

SUGGESTED TOUR:

Leave the **train station** (1) and follow the map past several streams in the colorful lower town. The climb to the upper town is rather steep, but manageable and highly worthwhile. Once there, step into the **Jardin des Brébans** for a nice view, then stroll over to the **Tour de César** (2). Dating from the 12th century, this massive octagonal tower was erected on the site of a Roman fortress and is still in magnificent condition. Its circular base was built by the English during the Hundred Years War as a platform for their artillery. Enter the tower and climb its narrow staircases, which get somewhat spooky as you ascend to the very top for a fantastic panorama of the entire region. The tower is open every day except Christmas and New Year's Day, from 9:30 a.m. to noon and 2–6 p.m., closing at 5 p.m. in the winter season. At its base is the tourist information office.

The **Church of St.-Quiriace** (3), equally ancient, is just a few steps away. Originally planned to be much larger, its choir, apse and transepts were the only parts completed before the days of prosperity ran out for Provins. Its interior, however, is quite impressive and should not be missed. The church is open on weekends and holidays; otherwise see the tourist office for entry.

Stroll over to the **Maison Romane** (4) on Rue du Palais. This partly 10th-century house now contains an interesting museum of local archaeology, usually open in the afternoons on Sundays and holidays during the season. Return to the Tour de César and continue along the footpath at its base to Rue de l'Ormerie, following that to Place du Châtel.

The **Grange aux Dîmes** (5), a curious 12th-century tithe barn now housing a museum of medieval artifacts, can be visited daily between 9:30 a.m. and 6 p.m., except on some major holidays. In the basement there is an entrance to a large network of underground passageways.

Now follow Rue de Jouy to the **Porte de Jouy** (6), a medieval gate in the still-extant town walls. Turn right and follow the insides of the ramparts for a short distance, then return and go through the gate. A left on a delightful country lane leads along the massive fortifications past the **Brèche des Anglais** (7), a hole through which the English invaded the town in 1432.

Re-enter the town through the 12th-century **Porte St.-Jean** (8), another fortified gate, and return on Rue St.-Jean to Place du Châtel. From here, walk downhill on Rue St.-Thibault to the **Hôtel Dieu** (9). Once the palace of the countess of Champagne, this heavily reconstructed medieval building has an entrance to the mysterious, enigmatic subterranean passages *(Souterrains)* of

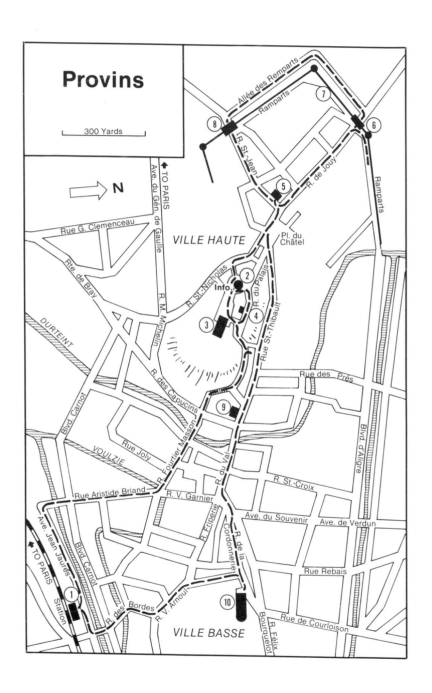

Provins

300 Yards

→ N

TO PARIS

Ave. du Gén. de Gaulle

Rue G. Clemenceau

VILLE HAUTE

Rte. de Bray

DURTEINT

R. M. Michelin

R. St.-Nicholas

Info.

Allée des Remparts

Ramparts

R. St.-Jean

R. de Jouy

Remparts

Pl. du Châtel

R. du Palais

Rue St.-Thibault

Rue des Prés

R. des Capucins

Blvd. Carnot

VOULZIE

Rue Joly

R. Fournier Masson

R. du Val

R. St.-Croix

Blvd. d'Aigre

Rue Aristide Briand

R. V. Garnier

R. Friperie

R. de la Cordonnerie

Ave. du Souvenir

Ave. de Verdun

Ave. Jean Jaurès

TO PARIS

Blvd. Carnot

Station

R. des Bordes

R. V. Arnoul

R. Félix Bourquelot

Rue Rebais

Rue de Courloison

VILLE BASSE

1 2 3 4 5 6 7 8 9 10

A Corner of the Ramparts

Provins, some of which may date from the time of the Franks. These can be seen on guided tours — ask at the tourist office for details.

You have now returned to the lower town. Stroll along Rue du Val and Rue de la Cordonnerie to the **Church of St.-Ayoul** (10), once the center of a cult around which the *Ville Basse* developed. Destroyed by fire in the 12th century, the church was soon rebuilt and features some truly outstanding sculptures along with other works of art. From here it is a short walk back to the station.

Chantilly

The Ile-de-France region is justly renowned for its many splendid châteaux. Some of these, especially Versailles, are monumental in scope while others, such as Fontainebleau, leave the visitor endowed with an immensely satisfying sense of history. For sheer beauty, however, the dream-like Château of Chantilly is by far the most outstanding. Many even consider it to be the loveliest in all France. This is surely reason enough to make the easy daytrip, but Chantilly gilds the lily with yet more sumptuous attractions. There are enchanted gardens, a magnificent forest, one of the nation's best art museums, stables which resemble a palace, a world-famous racetrack and — of course — the delicious whipped cream and black lace for which the town is noted.

Chantilly has an illustrious history going back to a Roman named Cantilius. The present château — actually two separate châteaux joined by a common entrance — is the fifth on the same site. Its larger part, the impossibly romantic Grand Château, is a late-19th-century pastiche while the older Petit Château dates from the 16th century. It was here that a well-known event (or story?) occurred in 1671, when Louis XIV came calling for a three-day visit — along with five thousand of his retainers. The greatest chef in France at the time, François Vatel, was employed at the château and had to feed all those hungry mouths on virtually no notice. Things went wrong and finally, when the promised fish failed to arrive in time, the overwrought Vatel ended it all with a sword thrust through his body.

By getting off to an early start, a trip to Chantilly could easily be combined in the same day with one to Senlis (see page 58), just five miles away by bus from the train station, or by car. Alternatively, you could visit Compiègne instead.

GETTING THERE:

Trains leave Nord station in Paris almost hourly for the 30-minute ride to Chantilly. Return service operates until early evening.

By car, leave Paris on the A-1 Autoroute, switching to the N-1 near St.-Denis and then to the N-16. Chantilly is about 25 miles from Paris.

WHEN TO GO:

Good weather is essential for a visit to Chantilly. Avoid coming on a Tuesday, when everything is closed. Two bonus sights, the Maison de Sylvie and the Jeu de Paume, are open in the afternoon on Saturdays, Sundays and holidays between March 1st and November 15th.

FOOD AND DRINK:

There are a few good restaurants between the train station and the château. The best choices are:

Relais Condé (42 Ave. Mar. Joffre, near the station) $$
Quatre Saisons (9 Ave. Gén. Leclerc, near the station) $$
Tipperary (6 Ave. Mar. Joffre, on the way to town) $$
Château (22 Rue Connétable, near the Grandes Ecuries) $$

In addition to the above, there are several inexpensive restaurants and cafés around the station and in town. No food or drinks are available at the château or on its grounds.

TOURIST INFORMATION:

The tourist information office is located on Ave. Maréchal Joffre a block from the train station. You may want to call them first to avoid coming on a crowded race day, usually held on certain Sundays in June. The number is 44-57-08-58.

SUGGESTED TOUR:

Leave the **train station** (1) and follow the map past the tourist office to the **Racetrack** (2), where the prestigious *Prix de Diane* and *Prix du Jockey Club* races are run each June. This beautifully-situated course has been attracting Paris society since 1836.

Continue on to the **Château** (3), rising from the middle of a tiny lake like a fantastic scene from a fairytale. One single admission covers both the castle and its grounds. Cross the bridge and enter the **Condé Museum**, which occupies the entire château. The sumptuous collection of art, along with the estate, was bequeathed to the *Institut de France* in 1897 by its last owner, the Duke of Aumale, fifth son of Louis-Philippe, the last king of France. A small guide brochure in English is available at the entrance.

The rooms to your right, in the **Grand Château**, contain the picture galleries and may be seen at your own leisure. Laid out in a charming 19th-century style, the walls are covered from top to bottom with an amazingly good collection of canvases. To see the rest of the château you will have to take a guided tour, included in the admission price. Don't miss the private apartments in the **Petit Château**, especially the Chapel and the Library,

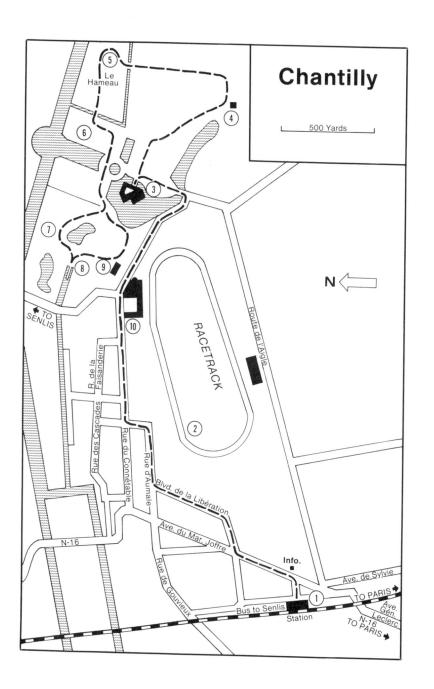

Chantilly

500 Yards

N ⟵

5 Le Hameau

4

6

3

7

8 9

RACETRACK

Route de l'Aigle

TO SENLIS

10

R. de la Faisanderie

Rue des Cascades

Rue du Connétable

Rue d'Aumale

Blvd. de la Libération

2

N-16

Ave. du Mar. Joffre

Info.

Rue de Gouvieux

Ave. de Sylvie

Bus to Senlis Station

1

TO PARIS

Ave. Gén. Leclerc

N-16 TO PARIS

The Château of Chantilly

whose greatest treasure is the *Très Riches Heures du Duc de Berry,* one of the great masterpieces of the Middle Ages. Because of its fragile condition this is rarely exhibited, but copies are on display. The château is open every day except Tuesdays, from 10:30 a.m. to 6 p.m., closing at 5 p.m. in winter.

Leave the castle and walk straight ahead into the park. Once in the woods, turn right and follow the map past the tiny chapel of St.-Paul to the **Maison de Sylvie** (4), a house with a long history of romantic affairs. The paths now lead through an enchanted forest, complete with statuary in little clearings, to **Le Hameau** (5), a rustic hamlet where the nobility played at being peasants. This was the prototype for Marie Antoinette's famous *hameau* at Versailles. Continue around to the formal **gardens** and **waterways** (6) designed by that great landscape artist, André Le Nôtre, who was also largely responsible for the gardens at Versailles.

The picturesque **English Gardens** (7) come as a great contrast. Stroll through them to the **Ile d'Amour** (8), an idyllic little

In the Forest

island, then continue on to the **Jeu de Paume** (9), which is sometimes open.

One last sight remains in Chantilly, just outside the palace precincts. This is the **Grandes Écuries** (10), a stable built like a fabulous palace. The story is told about the Duke of Bourbon, owner of the château during the early 18th century, having this luxurious barn erected because he expected to be reincarnated as a horse and wanted to assure his future comfort. Whether this event actually occurred is not known, but the posh interiors are now open to visitors as the **Living Museum of the Horse**. Demonstrations of dressage, a great treat, are given several times daily. The stables are open every day except on Tuesdays and Christmas.

Senlis

Permeated with a distinctly medieval atmosphere, Senlis has almost totally escaped the turmoils of history. Its ancient twisting lanes remain largely as they were during the Middle Ages, when the long line of French royalty began there in 987 with the election of Hugues Capet as the first true king of France. Senlis was old even then, having been built on the foundations of a Gallo-Roman settlement.

The town continued as a seat of kings, at least on a part-time basis, until the reign of Henri IV in the 16th century. After that, royalty no longer came and Senlis entered a long period of slumber, interrupted only now and then by a few wars, the French Revolution, and a close brush with total destruction at the hands of invading Germans in 1914.

Much of the town's fascinating past is still intact, steeped in an aura of charm and ready to be enjoyed today. You may want to combine this visit with one to nearby Chantilly (page 53), quite easily done by getting off to an early start.

GETTING THERE:

Trains depart Nord station in Paris almost hourly for the 30-minute ride to Chantilly, where you change to a bus for Senlis. These buses, leaving from the north side of the Chantilly station, are operated by the railroad and accept train tickets or passes. The distance is only five miles. Upon arrival at the Senlis bus station, check the posted schedule of return buses to Chantilly, from which trains to Paris operate until early evening.

By car, take the A-1 Autoroute north from Paris to the Senlis exit, a distance of 32 miles.

WHEN TO GO:

Avoid coming on a Tuesday, when the ancient Royal Palace and the museums are closed.

FOOD AND DRINK:

Senlis has a fair selection of restaurants, the best choices being:

Hostellerie Bellon (51 Rue Bellon, near the bus station) $$
Chalet de Sylvie (1 Place Verdun, near the bus station) $$
Le Formanoir (17 Rue Châtel, two blocks from the cathedral) $$

The Cathedral of Notre-Dame

Le Saint-Aignan (9 Rue Léon Fautrat, near the town hall)
Crêperie. $

TOURIST INFORMATION:

The tourist information office, phone 44-53-06-40, is located
on Place du Parvis-Notre-Dame, in front of the cathedral.

SUGGESTED TOUR:

Leave the **bus station** (1) and follow the map to the **Jardin
du Roi** (2), a lovely park built along the remains of the original
Gallo-Roman fortifications.

Retrace your steps and turn right on Rue de Villevert to Place
du Parvis. This engaging little square facing the cathedral is home
to the small but charming **Museum of Fine Arts** (*Musée
Vermandois*) (3), which also features an interesting audio-visual
presentation. It is open during the same times as the other
museums in town. The tourist office, on the west side of the
square, can furnish you with information for making a possible
side trip to the Gallo-Roman Amphitheatre (8).

The 12th-century **Cathedral of Notre-Dame** (4) is one of
the earliest Gothic structures in France. Although rather small,
it projects an immense aura of charm. Examine the carvings over

the main portal, which relate to the life of the Virgin, then enter through the splendid south transept, added after a disastrous 16th-century fire. The interior, altered many times throughout the centuries, is noted for its exceptionally beautiful balcony running above the side aisles.

Stroll over to what remains of the **Château Royal** (5), a complex of ancient buildings which were once a principal residence for the early kings of France, particularly during the Merovingian and Carolingian eras. The last king to use the castle was Henri II, while still a 16th-century prince. Following that, the château deteriorated badly and was finally ruined during the Revolution. Enough has survived, however, to be of interest. Against the city wall, on the north side of the grounds, stand the foundations of the original keep, incorporating parts of a Roman tower.

Also within the castle precincts is the intriguing **Museum of the Hunt** (Musée de la Vénerie), located in the 18th-century Priory of St.-Maurice. Displays of this most royal of sports include costumes, artifacts, paintings and literally thousands of antlers. It may be seen only on guided tours, which begin hourly with an audio-visual show in an adjacent building. Tickets are sold at the entrance to the Château Royal, along with tickets to the grounds alone — take your choice. Both the castle ruins and the museum are open every day except on Tuesdays and on Wednesday mornings; from 10 a.m. to noon and 2–6 p.m., closing an hour earlier on Mondays and during the winter season.

From here, a delightful walk can be made by following the map along colorful old streets and through the ancient **Fausse Porte** (6), a remnant of the original walls. Continue on to the 15th-century **Town Hall** (Hôtel de Ville) (7) on Place Henri IV. It is possible to take an interesting side trip to the relics of a **Gallo-Roman Amphitheatre** (Arènes) (8) unearthed in 1863, but ask about this at the tourist office first.

Return to the cathedral via Rue de la Tonnellerie and Rue St.-Frambourg. Along the way you will pass the 12th-century **Church of St.-Frambourg** (9), recently restored by the Hungarian pianist Georges Cziffra as a concert hall (Auditorium Franz Liszt).

The former Bishop's Palace (10) next to the cathedral now houses the **Museum of Art and Archaeology** (Musée des Saphis), worth a short visit before returning to the bus station. Its hours are the same as those of the Museum of the Hunt.

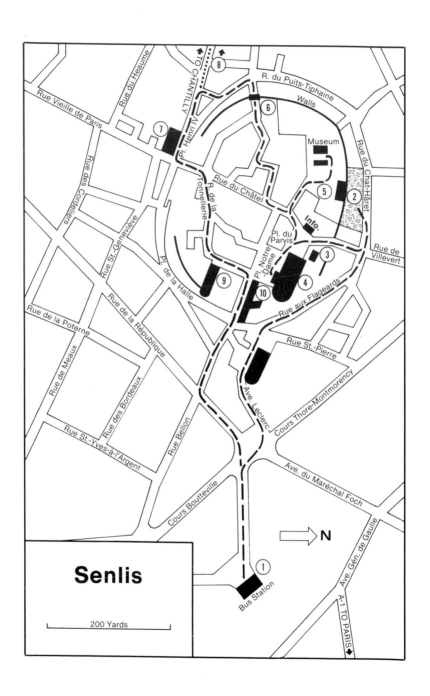

Senlis

200 Yards

Section III

Daytrips from Paris

Normandy and the North

Normandy, an ancient province lying between the Ile-de-France and the English Channel, is truly a land apart. Molded by its unique history, it offers an amazingly wide variety of sights ranging from some of the prettiest countryside in Europe to dynamic cities, from quaint fishing villages to luxurious seaside resorts. Although the distances are fairly great, an efficient transportation network brings many of its best attractions within comfortable daytrip range of Paris.

Throughout its often turbulent history, Normandy has been a battleground — a place conquered and reconquered by forces outside the mainstream of the French experience. At various times it was held by the Celts, the Romans, the Germanic tribes and, most important of all, the Norsemen — Vikings from Scandinavia — who in the ninth century settled this land for good, thus accounting for the preponderance of tall, blue-eyed Normans today. It was their renowned leader, William the Conqueror, who defeated the English near Hastings in 1066 — an event which forever changed the course of European history. As a result, much of our own heritage derives from Norman tradition.

During most of the Middle Ages, Normandy was at best only marginally under the control of French kings. For long periods it was ruled by the English, and its semi-autonomy ended only with the French Revolution. In our own century the Germans again occupied the land, being driven out by the Battle of Normandy in 1944.

The six daytrips in this section can easily be made by trains departing from St.-Lazare station in Paris. By car, the region is well served via its high-speed lifeline, the A-13 *"Autoroute de Normandie."* Those with more time may prefer to stay over and explore its outer fringes, especially the near-magical Mont St.-Michel, a miraculous sight which sadly lies beyond any reasonable daytrip range of Paris.

Outside Normandy itself, this section also includes a daytrip to Amiens, a singularly impressive city in the largely dreary industrial north.

Giverny and Vernon

Born in 1840, the celebrated French painter Claude Monet was one of the founding fathers of Impressionism and a vital force in the modern art movement it led to. After a long period of ridicule and poverty, his talent finally received broad public recognition. Now fairly prosperous, Monet in 1883 created for himself and his family a lovely home surrounded by lush gardens near the Seine, in the tiny hamlet of Giverny. It was in this serene environment that his greatest works were achieved.

Following Monet's death in 1926, the property deteriorated badly until 1966, when it was willed to the *Institut de France* by his son Michel. Generous donations, primarily from the United States, have made possible a stunning restoration of this extraordinary place. Ever since its public opening in 1980 as the Claude Monet Museum, the gardens — along with his remarkably charming house and cavernous studio — have become an extremely popular daytrip destination, indeed a pilgrimage, for art lovers and tourists alike.

Organized bus tours to Giverny are offered by several firms in Paris, which are certainly a convenient way to reach this secluded spot. They have the disadvantage, however, of limiting the amount of time you can spend savoring its enchanting atmosphere. They also overlook nearby Vernon, an ancient town of considerable charm, worthy of a trip in itself. With a little bit of effort it is entirely possible to see both by either train or private car. Giverny, by the way, makes a fine half-day trip, leaving Paris at noon.

GETTING THERE:

Trains depart St.-Lazare station in Paris several times daily for Vernon, less than an hour away. From here you can take a taxi the three-mile distance to Giverny. It is also possible to walk or rent a bicycle *(Train + Vélo)* at the Vernon station. To make the return easier, there is a public phone at the museum with numbers for the local taxi service posted. Return trains run until early evening.

By car, take the A-13 Autoroute to the Bonnières-Vernon exit, then the N-15 into Vernon, cross the Seine and follow signs to the Monet Museum. It is about 50 miles from Paris.

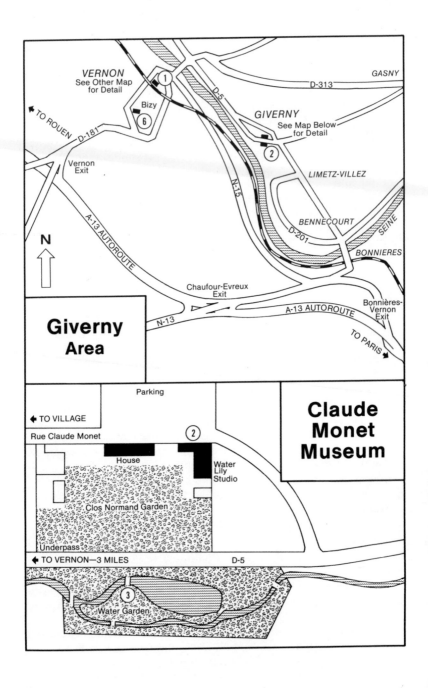

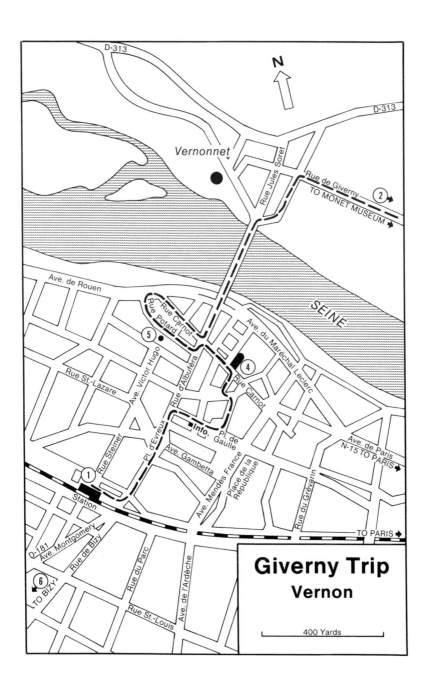

D-313

N

D-313

Vernonnet

Rue Jules Soret

Rue de Giverny

TO MONET MUSEUM

②

SEINE

Ave. de Rouen

Rue Carnot

Rue Potard

⑤

Ave. du Maréchal Leclerc

Rue St-Lazare

Ave. Victor Hugo

Rue d'Albuféra

④

Rue Carnot

Rue Steiner

Pl. d'Evreux

Info.

Pl. de Gaulle

Ave. Gambetta

Ave. de Paris
N-15 TO PARIS

Ave. Mendès France

Place de la République

Rue du Grévarin

①

Station

TO PARIS

D-181

Ave. Montgomery

Rue de Bizy

Rue du Parc

Ave. de l'Ardèche

⑥

TO BIZY

Rue St.-Louis

Giverny Trip
Vernon

400 Yards

Inside the Water Lily Studio

WHEN TO GO:

The Monet gardens and house are open between April 1st and October 31st, daily except Mondays. Hours for the gardens are from 10 a.m. to 6 p.m., while the house closes between noon and 2 p.m. You will have the place more to yourself in the mornings, before the tour buses arrive. Avoid coming on a rainy day.

FOOD AND DRINK:

There are several simple eating places in Giverny — ask at the museum about this. You could also take along a picnic lunch to enjoy in the gardens. The town of Vernon offers a much wider selection of restaurants, some choices being:

Évreux (7 Place Évreux, two blocks from the station) $$

Strasbourg (6 Place Évreux, two blocks from the station) $

Beau Rivage (13 Ave. M. Leclerc, near the river) $$

Les Fleurs (71 Rue Carnot, near the Archives Tower) $$

TOURIST INFORMATION:

The tourist information office in Vernon is located in Passage Pasteur, phone 32-51-39-60. You can also call the Monet Museum at 32-51-28-21. They speak English.

SUGGESTED TOUR:

From the Vernon **train station** (1) you can take a taxi or drive to the *Musée Monet* in Giverny, a trip of nearly three miles. Walking is also possible by following the map, or you can rent a bicycle at the station. The route is quite level, but often has heavy traffic.

Monet's House at Giverny

Arriving at the **Claude Monet Museum** (2), you will have a choice of purchasing a ticket for the studio and gardens alone or a combination which includes the house. Buy the latter — it's worth it. Visits begin in the huge **Water Lily Studio**, built in 1916 to accommodate large canvases. The paintings on the wall are, of course, copies; the originals being in leading museums.

Stroll over to the painstakingly restored **house**, surfaced in pink crushed brick with green doors and shutters. Its exquisite interior, looking like the pages from a fashionable architectural magazine, is perhaps a bit too tidy for the home of an artist, but very beautiful nonetheless. It was here that Monet entertained his closest friends, including the French premier Georges Clemenceau and fellow artists Renoir, Degas, Rodin and Cézanne, among others.

The **Clos Normand Garden**, facing the house, is totally French in concept. Monet loved gardens, and as his fortunes improved he employed several gardeners to maintain them. From here, a tunnel leads under the public road to the famous **Water Garden** (3), which he created by diverting a nearby stream. This part of the property exudes a distinctly Oriental aura. Much of it seems familiar, especially the wisteria-entwined **Japanese Bridge**, a subject for many of his best-known paintings, around

The Japanese Bridge in the Water Garden

which clusters of water lilies float on the pond. It was in this miniature universe that Monet, always an innovator, made the stylistic transition beyond Impressionism and came very close to the abstract art of later years.

Returning to **Vernon**, you will have a beautiful view from its bridge of the town, the Seine and the woods beyond. Visit the 12th-century **Church of Notre-Dame** (4), noted for its splendid west-front rose window and lavish interiors. In the immediate vicinity stand a number of medieval half-timbered houses, lending atmosphere to this ancient settlement founded by Rollo, the first duke of Normandy, in the ninth century. Stroll along Rue Carnot and Rue Potard. The **Archives Tower** (5) is all that remains of a massive castle built in 1123 by King Henry I of England. From here it is a short walk back to the train station.

NEARBY SIGHT:

The **Château of Bizy** (6), an 18th-century mansion set in a charming park, may also be visited. Its interior contains many superb pieces in the Empire style along with Napoleonic souvenirs. The château is open from 10 a.m. to noon and 2–6:30 p.m., daily except Fridays, between April 1st and the end of October. To get there, follow the D-181 for one mile southwest of Vernon.

Rouen

One of the best-preserved medieval cities in all of Europe, Rouen is also a thriving modern commercial center. This unusual combination of past and present results from a deliberate decision on the part of local government to strip away decades of "modernization" in the old part of town and restore its ancient features. At the same time, cars were banned from many of the streets, creating an unusually pleasant — and very beguiling — pedestrian shopping zone. If ever there was a city designed to be explored on foot, Rouen is it.

Over two thousand years ago, Rouen was already in existence as a Celtic encampment on the banks of the Seine. This evolved into a market town known as *Ratuma* to the Gauls and later as *Rotomagus* to the Romans. Its real history, however, begins with an invasion by the Vikings from Scandinavia, who made it the capital of their Norman duchy in 912. The brilliant Norse leader Rollo established an able administration which did much to develop the local economy. His linear descendant, William the Bastard, known to history as the Conqueror, defeated the English near Hastings in 1066 and became king of England, bringing Norman civilization to that island country.

Centuries later it was the English who invaded Normandy. During the Hundred Years War a strange leader arose among the French, Joan of Arc, who persuaded the king to allow her to lead troops in battle. Eventually she was captured by the Burgundians and sold to the English, who brought her to Rouen in 1431 for a mockery of a trial — after which she was burned at the stake in the town's market place.

In the years that followed the reestablishment of French rule, Rouen blossomed into a beautiful and prosperous city with many fine Renaissance buildings. Although it suffered badly during the 16th-century Wars of Religion and again during World War II, it has today regained its place as one of the great cities of France.

There is far more to Rouen than can be comfortably seen in one day. For your own sake, be selective and follow your interests. Time spent leisurely watching the passing parade from a café can be just as rewarding as seeing every last museum.

GETTING THERE:

Trains leave St. Lazare station in Paris frequently for Rouen's Rive Droite station, a trip of about 70 minutes. Return service operates until mid-evening.

By car, Rouen is 86 miles from Paris via the A-13 Autoroute. Don't even *think* of driving in the inner city.

WHEN TO GO:

Rouen may be enjoyed in any season, but avoid coming on a Tuesday if you plan on visiting any of the major museums.

FOOD AND DRINK:

The city offers an extraordinarily wide range of excellent restaurants, most of which specialize in the rich, highly caloric Norman cuisine. Some good choices, in the order you will pass or come close to them along the walking route, are:

La Grillade (121 Rue Jeanne d'Arc, by the station) $

Havre (27 Rue Verte, by the station) $

Pascaline (5 Rue Poterne, behind the Palace of Justice) $$

Couronne (31 Place Vieux Marché) 14th-century house, Norman specialties, especially duck. $$$

Bertrand Warin (9 Rue Pie, off the Place Vieux Marché) Rates one Michelin star, Norman dishes. $$$

Auberge l'Ecu de France (Place Vieux Marché) $$

Bois Chenu (23 Place de la Pucelle, near the Place Vieux Marché) $$

La Vieille Auberge (37 Rue St.-Étienne-des-Tonneliers, near the river) $

Reverbère (5 Place République, near the river) $$

Dufour (67 Rue St.-Nicolas, near the cathedral) $$

Beffroy (15 Rue Beffroy, near the Fine Arts Museum) Awarded one Michelin star, Norman cuisine. $$$

La Marmite (100 Rue Ganterie, near the Fine Arts Museum) $$

La Galette (168 Rue Beauvoisine, near the Fine Arts Museum) Crêperie. $

TOURIST INFORMATION:

The friendly tourist office, phone 35-71-41-77, is in front of the cathedral.

SUGGESTED TOUR:

Follow the map from Rouen's Rive Droite **train station** (1) to Place de la Cathédrale, where the tourist information office is housed in an elegant 16th-century Renaissance building. Along the way you will pass many examples of old half-timbered houses which have been put to modern use while still retaining the town's medieval atmosphere.

The **Cathedral of Notre-Dame** (2), one of the finest Gothic structures in existence, is familiar to art lovers as the subject for a series of Impressionist paintings by Monet which captured its spirit under changing atmospheric conditions. Its **west front** displays at a glance the entire history of Gothic cathedral construction. The base of the left tower dates from the early 12th century and, along with two doors, is the only portion of the church which survived the devastating fire of 1200. On the right is the so-called **Butter Tower**, supposedly financed by the sale of indulgences allowing the faithful to eat butter during Lent. This flamboyant structure was erected in the 15th century. The next hundred years saw the addition of the central portal and rose window. Construction continued through the 19th century, when the delicate open-ironwork spire, the tallest in France, was completed.

A stroll through the cathedral's majestic interior is impressive. Note in particular the **Booksellers' Staircase** in the north transept and the **tombs** of several historical figures, including those of Rollo, the first duke of Normandy and Richard the Lionhearted, king of England. Guided tours are conducted through the fascinating 11th-century **crypt** and the ambulatory, several times daily during the summer season, and on weekends and some holidays the rest of the year.

Walk down Rue du Gros-Horloge, a pedestrians-only shopping street of well-preserved houses, many of them half-timbered. The **Great Clock** (*Gros-Horloge*) (3), a famous symbol of Rouen, was relocated here in 1527. Its adjoining 14th-century belfry may be climbed between Palm Sunday and mid-September, from 10 a.m. to noon and 2:30–5:30 p.m., but not on Tuesdays or on Wednesday mornings. The ticket is also valid for the Fine Arts, Wrought Iron, and Ceramics museums. Splendid views of the old city from its platform make the climb very worthwhile.

Stroll over to the magnificent **Palace of Justice** (4), one of the great civic structures of Europe. Originally built in the 16th century and later modified, its Gothic façade becomes increasingly flamboyant as it rises above the ground floor. You can visit its Prosecutors' Room, reached via the left wing staircase, on weekdays. Recent excavations in the courtyard have unearthed an underground 12th-century synagogue or yeshiva, which can be seen by arrangement with the tourist office.

On May 30th, 1431, Joan of Arc was burned at the stake in

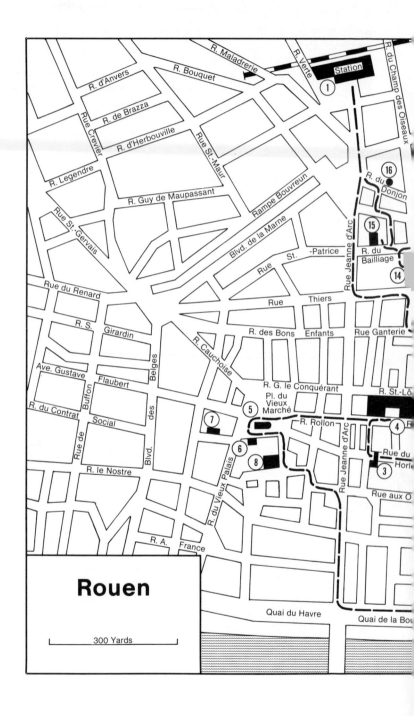

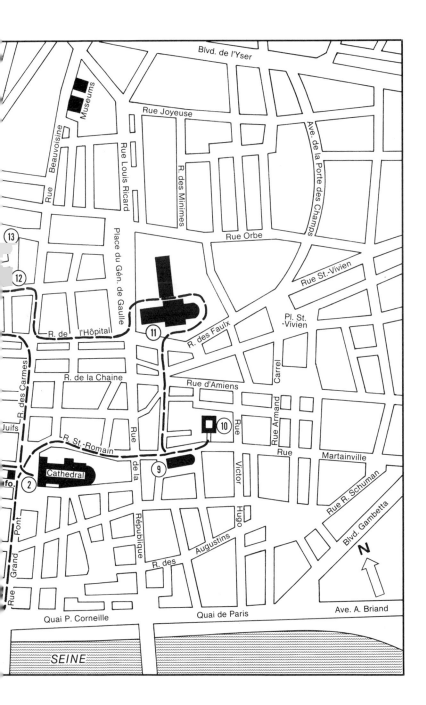

The Great Clock on Rue du Gros-Horloge

Rouen's **Market Place** *(Place du Vieux Marché)* (5), the next stop on the walking tour. A huge cross now marks the spot where she met her fiery end. The strikingly contemporary **Joan of Arc Church**, adjacent to this, was consecrated in 1979 and contains a large area of marvelous 16th-century stained-glass windows from a previous church on the site. Also in the square is a modern covered marketplace, several inviting outdoor cafés, and the tiny but fascinating **Joan of Arc Museum** (6), a commercial enterprise crammed with re-created scenes from the life of the Maid of Orléans. Another nearby sight which may be of interest is the **Pierre Corneille Museum** (7) on the Rue de la Pie, where the famous French playwright was born in 1606 and where he lived most of his life.

It is only a few steps to the Place de la Pucelle, site of the elegant **Hôtel de Bourgtheroulde** (8). This sumptuous 16th-century mansion, now a bank, combines Gothic with early Renaissance elements. Step into the courtyard to admire the decorations,

Inside the Aître St.-Maclou

some of which depict the meeting of François I and England's Henry VIII at the Field of the Cloth of Gold in 1520. Weekend visitors should ring for entrance.

Return to the cathedral via the route shown on the map, which takes you along the right bank of the Seine. Colorful Rue St.-Romain, lined with picturesque half-timbered medieval and Renaissance houses, leads past the **Archbishop's Palace**. It was here that Joan of Arc was sentenced to death and, twenty-five years after the execution, at last found innocent.

The **Church of St.-Maclou** (9) is perhaps the most striking example of Flamboyant Gothic architecture in France. Badly damaged in World War II, it is now slowly being restored. Parts of its lovely interior are now open and should not be missed, particularly the remarkable organ loft.

Another absolute "must" sight in Rouen is the **Aître St.-Maclou** (10), a 16th-century cloister which once served as a plague cemetery. Its ossuary galleries, now occupied by an art school, are carved with exceptionally macabre figures of death. Go in for a peek.

Return to the church and follow the gorgeous Rue Damiette to the **Abbey Church of St.-Ouen** (11). This enormous structure, dating mostly from the 14th century, replaces earlier churches on the same site since the seventh century. Stroll through the gardens behind it and return through the City Hall (*Hôtel de Ville*).

Now follow the map to the **Le Secq des Tournelles Museum** (12), located in a desanctified former church. Its vast collection of wrought iron objects dating from the third through the 19th centuries is totally fascinating. The opening times are the same as those for the Fine Arts Museum described below, and the same ticket applies. Continue on to the nearby **Church of St.-Godard** (13), a late-15th-century structure noted for its unusual wooden roof and outstanding stained-glass windows, especially the one depicting the Tree of Jesse at the choir end of the south aisle.

The **Fine Arts Museum** (*Musée des Beaux-Arts*) (14) has one of the best provincial collections in France. There are paintings by Gérard David, Rubens, Ingres, Delacroix, Velázquez, Corot and many others, along with those by native-son Géricault. Impressionism is well represented by Sisley and Monet (*Rouen Cathedral*). There are also several rooms of contemporary art including one devoted to the local Duchamp family. The museum is open daily except on Tuesdays; from 10 a.m. to noon and 2–6 p.m., but closed on Wednesday mornings. The same ticket is also valid for the Wrought Iron and Ceramics museums, and for the Clock Tower.

Rouen's latest attraction, the splendid **Ceramics Museum** (15) is located in a former mansion just one block away. The opening times and ticket are the same as for the Fine Arts Museum.

Before leaving Rouen, it would be altogether fitting to visit the **Joan of Arc Tower** (16) near the train station. This former keep is all that remains of a 13th-century castle, and is the place where the Maid of Orléans was confronted with the instruments of torture. You can climb to its top for a nice view.

The city offers several other first-rate museums, details of which can be obtained from the tourist office in front of the cathedral.

Caen

Just enough of old Caen survived the terrible devastation of World War II to make it an attractive daytrip destination. The three monumental structures associated with William the Conqueror remained miraculously intact while the rest of the city has been largely rebuilt in the contemporary mold, with broad boulevards, pedestrian malls and open green spaces.

Caen had virtually no history before Duke William of Normandy, also known as "the Bastard" and "the Conqueror," made it his capital and favorite residence in the 11th century. During the years that followed it developed into both a seaport and a university town, sometimes under English rule. World War II brought ferocious destruction — over three quarters of the city lay in total ruin after a lengthy battle beginning in June of 1944. Many of its citizens found shelter in the important historical structures, which were spared by the Allies after receiving this information from the Resistance. What has emerged since then is an unusually pleasant, if not very dramatic, city where modern architecture has blended in well with what remains of the past.

GETTING THERE:

Trains depart St. Lazare station in Paris almost hourly for the two-hour run to Caen. Many of these are Turbotrains with somewhat limited capacity, so it will pay to claim your seat early or make reservations, especially during peak periods. Return service operates until mid-evening.

By car, it's the A-13 Autoroute all the way, 150 miles from Paris.

WHEN TO GO:

Good weather is important for this largely outdoor trip. The two museums are closed on Tuesdays and major holidays.

FOOD AND DRINK:

Some choice restaurants, in the order you will pass or come close to them on the walking tour, are:

Poêle d'Or (7 Rue Laplace, near the Orne River) $

A la Pomme d'Api (127 Rue St.-Jean) $

Les Quatre Vents (116 Blvd. Mar. Leclerc, in the Hôtel Moderne) $$

Relais des Gourmets (15 Rue Geôle, near the castle) Rates one Michelin star. $$$

La Bourride (15 Rue Vaugueux, near the castle) Awarded one Michelin star. $$$

Le Dauphin (29 Rue Gemare, near the castle) $$$

Les Echevins (36 Rue Ecuyère, near the Abbaye aux Hommes) $$$

Alcide (1 Place Courtonne, near the old port) $

Relais Normandy (by the train station) $$

In addition, there are a number of restaurants and cafés of all descriptions in the shopping zone between Place St.-Pierre and Place de la République.

TOURIST INFORMATION:

The Tourist information office, phone 31-86-27-65, is located in a lovely Renaissance mansion on Place St.-Pierre, near the castle.

SUGGESTED TOUR:

The **train station** (1) is nearly a mile from Place St.-Pierre, the center of town. You could take a bus or a taxi there, although the walk is both level and very pleasant. Along the way you will pass the remarkable **Church of St.-Jean** (2), a 15th-century Flamboyant Gothic structure whose unfinished west tower tilts ever so slightly.

Continue on to Place St.-Pierre. The tourist office occupies a splendid 16th-century mansion, the **Hôtel d'Escoville**, whose richly decorated courtyard should be seen. This feeling of luxury, a reflection of Caen's prosperous past, is mirrored in the **Church of St.-Pierre** (3). Its ornate, almost lush, interior is among the most outstanding in Normandy.

The enormous **Castle** (4) begun by William the Conqueror still dominates the city. Stroll up to the massive ramparts, built between the 12th and 15th centuries, cross the moat and climb up on the fortifications for a stunning view of Caen. Little remains of the original structures within the walls, most of them having been replaced with later buildings.

The most recent addition to the castle grounds is the **Fine Arts Museum** (*Musée des Beaux-Arts*) (5), whose discreet contemporary architecture harmonizes with its ancient surroundings. A rarity among French provincial museums, its superb collections are exceptionally well lit and displayed. They were begun in the early 19th century when both the Revolution and the Napoleonic conquests made large quantities of great art, formerly belonging to the Church and aristocracy as well as to foreign countries, available to public institutions. Artists represented include Van

The Abbaye aux Hommes

der Weyden, Breughel, Tintoretto, Poussin, Rubens, Van Dyck, Tiepolo and Géricault, among many others. The museum is open every day except on Tuesdays and major holidays; from 10 a.m. to noon and 2–6 p.m., closing an hour earlier in winter.

Stroll over past the 12th-century **St.-Georges Chapel** to the **Normandy Museum** (6), also within the castle precincts. Displays here are primarily concerned with local everyday life, particularly during the last century, and with regional arts and crafts along with archaeological finds. The opening times are the same as those for the Fine Arts Museum.

Wander around to the rear of the castle enclosure for a look at the so-called **Exchequer House** — a rare example of early 12th-century domestic architecture — and at the ruins of an equally old square **keep**, both built by Henry I, king of England and son of the Conqueror.

Now follow the map to the interesting Gothic and Renaissance **Church of St.-Sauveur** (7) and the picturesque Rue Froide. Return on Rue St.-Pierre and turn right down Rue Hamon, continuing through a modern pedestrian shopping district with pleasant cafés to Place de la République.

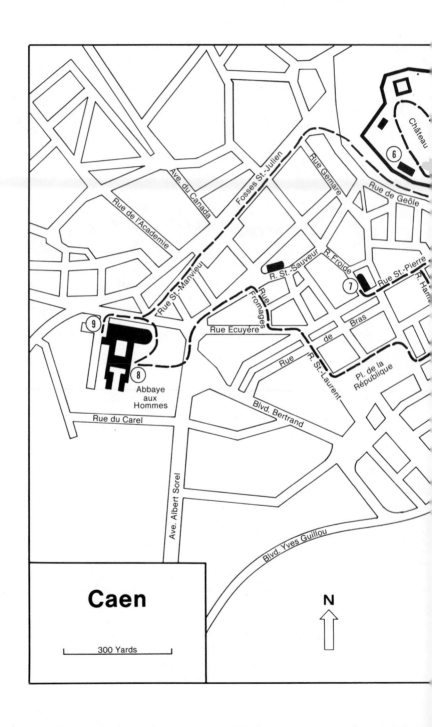

Caen

300 Yards

N

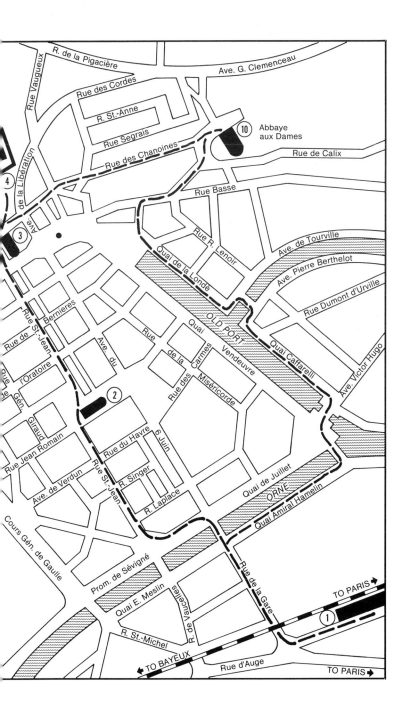

From here the map leads the way through a colorful neighborhood to Caen's premier attraction, the famous **Abbaye aux Hommes**, whose conventual buildings now incorporate the **City Hall** (Hôtel de Ville) (8). The esplanade in front of this provides a marvelous sight for sore eyes. Interesting guided tours of the old abbey buildings, reconstructed in the 18th century, depart hourly from the City Hall entrance.

Walk around to the rear of the complex and visit the **Church of St.-Étienne** (9), the original church of the abbey. This magnificent structure was founded in the 11th century by William the Conqueror — an illegitimate son of Duke Robert the Devil — as penance for the sin of having married his distant cousin Matilda. Not that the lady was willing — she had in fact made it perfectly clear that she would rather be a nun than marry a bastard. William, feeling his oats, dragged her by the hair and beat her into submission. Both were excommunicated as a result, and later reinstated by the Pope only after promising to build two abbeys and four hospitals. The union actually turned out well, with Matilda becoming queen of England in 1068.

Step inside to visit William's **tomb**, in front of the high altar. His burial was as tempestuous as his life. When he died in 1087 at Rouen, his heirs made a mad scramble for the spoils and neglected his body, which rotted for days before being ignominiously put in the grave after payment of an extortion fee. It did not lie there in peace either. During the 16th century his bones were scattered by rebellious Protestants, later recovered, and again dispersed during the Revolution. Some parts may still be there, but no one is sure.

Return to the castle area via Rue St.-Manvieu and Fossés St.-Julien, then follow the map to the **Abbaye aux Dames** (10), the other abbey founded as a result of the illicit marriage. Its **Church of La Trinité** is more richly ornamented than its male counterpart and has an interesting 11th-century **crypt** which can be reached from the south transept. Matilda was buried here, in the choir, and like that of her husband William, her tomb was desecrated during the Wars of Religion and again in the Revolution.

The suggested route back to the train station, shown on the map, takes you past the old port (Bassin St.-Pierre), connected to the sea via the Orne and a canal. It is now used for pleasure craft, with larger ships docking at the new harbor to the east.

Bayeux

One of the greatest chronicles of the Middle Ages — the famous "Bayeux Tapestry" — is an incredibly lucid history lesson embroidered in cloth. You have surely seen reproductions of it, but to experience the real thing you will have to come to Bayeux, a thoroughly delightful town that is well worth the trip.

Known as the cradle of the Norman dynasty, the town has roots going back much further than the Viking invasions. In Gallo-Roman times it was called *Augustodurum,* and became a bishopric as early as the fourth century. Rollo the Dane, a progenitor of William the Conqueror, married the daughter of the town's ruler early in the tenth century, thus creating the line that gave England some of its most notorious kings. The Norse language continued to be spoken here long after the rest of Normandy adopted French culture, an early sign of Bayeux's stubborn resistance to change. Centuries later, in June of 1944, it was the first town to be liberated by the Allies during the Battle of Normandy, and miraculously suffered no damage.

Bayeux today remains a remarkably well-preserved medieval town whose narrow streets and ancient buildings continue to enchant thousands of visitors. Although well geared to the modern tourist trade, it seems to be amazingly unaffected by it.

GETTING THERE:

Trains *(marked for Cherbourg)* leave St. Lazare station in Paris several times in the morning for Bayeux, a run of about two and a half hours. Most of these are Turbotrains with limited seating capacity during peak periods, so either make a reservation, claim your seat early, or ride in the dining car. Return service operates until early evening. Check the schedules carefully.

By car, take the A-13 Autoroute to Caen, then the N-13 into Bayeux. The distance from Paris is 167 miles.

WHEN TO GO:

Bayeux's major attractions are open daily, except that the Battle of Normandy Museum closes on weekdays from November through March. Good weather will make the trip more enjoyable.

FOOD AND DRINK:

As an important tourist center, Bayeux has restaurants and cafés in all price ranges. Some of the better choices are:

Lion d'Or (71 Rue St.-Jean, near the watermill) A famous old inn, awarded one Michelin star. $$$

Luxembourg (25 Rue Bouchers, two blocks northwest of the tourist office. $$

Crêperie Duhomme (3 Rue Genas-Duhomme, two blocks northwest of the tourist office) Crêpes menu. $

Les Gourmets (Place St.-Patrice, five blocks northwest of the tourist office) $

TOURIST INFORMATION:

The tourist information office, phone 31-92-16-26, is located in a charming half-timbered medieval house at 1 Rue des Cuisiniers, one block north of the cathedral.

SUGGESTED TOUR:

Leave the **train station** (1) and follow the map to the **William the Conqueror Center** (Guillaume le Conquérant) (2), located in a courtyard just off Rue de Nesmond. This is where the world-famous **Bayeux Tapestry**, one of the greatest legacies of the Middle Ages, is displayed. Also known as La Tapisserie de la Reine Mathilde, it has long been the subject of two popular misconceptions. First, this is not a tapestry at all, but actually an embroidery on linen. Second, it was almost certainly not made by Queen Matilda herself since the style strongly suggests Saxon craftsmanship, probably commissioned by William's half-brother, Bishop Odo of Bayeux, as a decoration for his cathedral. That it survived at all is a miracle. In 1792, when revolutionary zealots were stripping the churches bare, an observant army officer rescued it from the ignominious fate of being used as a wagon tarpaulin. Seeing its propaganda value, Napoleon had it widely exhibited to drum up support for his planned invasion of England.

The 231-foot-long 11th-century embroidery resembles nothing so much as a gigantic comic strip, and would not look out of place in our Sunday newspapers. Its 58 scenes graphically depict the events leading up to the Norman Conquest of 1066, as well as the Battle of Hastings itself — one of the major turning points in the annals of western civilization. Of course, the story is seen through Norman eyes; victors do have a way of controlling history.

Be sure to rent one of the earphone devices, which give an engrossing blow-by-blow account in English of the entire complex saga. Without this it is very difficult to understand. You can move along at your own pace, taking plenty of time to absorb it all. The center is open every day, from 9 a.m. to 7 p.m. between June 1st and September 30th; from 9 a.m. to noon and 2–6 p.m. between October 1st and March 31st; and from 9 a.m. to 12:30

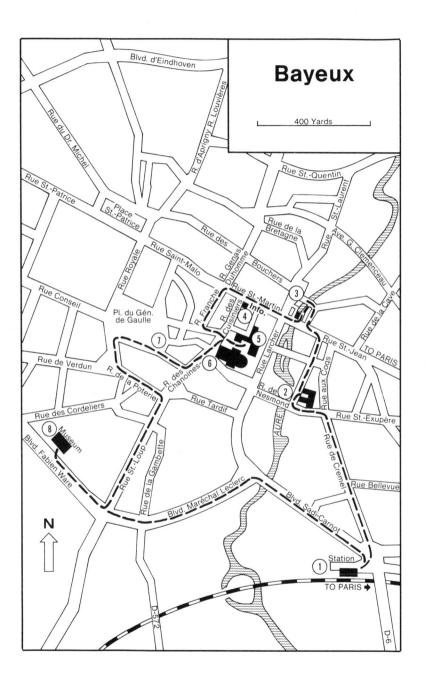

Bayeux

400 Yards

Blvd. d'Eindhoven

Rue du Dr. Michel

R. d'Aprigny

R. Louvières

Rue St.-Quentin

Rue St.-Patrice

Place St.-Patrice

Rue de la Bretagne

Rue St.-Laurent

Ave. G. Clémenceau

Rue des

Rue Saint-Malo

Rue Royale

Rue Genas Duhomme

Bouchers

Rue St.-Martin

3

Rue de la Cave

Rue Conseil

Pl. du Gén. de Gaulle

R. Franche

R. des Cuisiniers

Info.

4

5

7

Rue de Verdun

R. de la Poterie

R. des Chanoines

6

Rue Larcher

Rue St.-Jean

TO PARIS

Rue Tardif

R. de Nesmond

2

Rue aux Coqs

Rue des Cordeliers

Rue St.-Loup

Rue de la Gambette

L'AURE

Rue St.-Exupère

8 Museum

Blvd. Fabien Ware

Blvd. Maréchal Leclerc

Blvd. Sadi-Carnot

Rue de Cremel

Rue Bellevue

N

1 Station

TO PARIS ➡

D-572

D-6

The Covered Fish Market and Old Mill

p.m. and 2–6:30 p.m. between April 1st and May 31st. Tickets are also valid for the Baron Gérard Museum.

Continue on through the grounds of an ancient hospital and follow the map to the Aure stream. Just across this is the **Lace-Making Center** (3), where yesterday's crafts are still practiced, and where you are welcome to stop in for a look. Walk along the water's edge past a charming old mill for a truly gorgeous view with the cathedral's towers rising in the background. The former Covered Fish Market, now a cultural center, is at the corner of Rue St.-Jean. Turn right here and follow Rue St.-Martin to the **Tourist Information Office** (4), located in a lovely 14th-century house.

The walking route now takes you through a picturesque neighborhood to the **Baron Gérard Museum** (5), in the former Bishop's Palace, which displays a fascinating collection of local ceramics and lace along with faience from Rouen, furniture and paintings. The latter includes several Italian Primitives, Flemish and French works. Opening hours are the same as those for the Bayeux Tapestry, and the same ticket applies.

Next to this stands the very impressive **Cathedral of Notre-Dame** (6). Parts of it date from the 11th century, when the cathedral was consecrated by Bishop Odo in the presence of the

Museum of the Battle of Normandy

Conqueror. Most of the original church was destroyed in 1105 by William's son, Henry I *(Beauclerc)* of England, and rebuilt in later centuries. The carvings above the west front doors depict the Passion and the Last Judgement, while those on the south transept tell the story of Thomas à Becket's murder in Canterbury Cathedral. Step inside for a look at the magnificent interior and to visit the 11th-century crypt.

Now follow the route on the map past **Place du Général de Gaulle** (7), a charming square where the famous wartime leader made his first speech on liberated soil in June of 1944.

Continue on to the **Memorial Museum of the Battle of Normandy** (8). This modern structure, surrounded by armor from the participating nations, commemorates the D-Day landings with intriguing displays of the soldiers' lives throughout the conflict. Little touches like cigarette packages and newspaper clippings make the human drama an unforgettable experience. Don't miss seeing this. The museum is open daily from 9:30 a.m. to 7 p.m. during July and August; and 10 a.m. to 12:30 p.m. and 2–6:30 p.m. during the rest of the year, except that between November 1st and March 31st it is open on weekends only. The British military cemetery is nearby.

Deauville and Trouville

Aristocratic Deauville is Normandy's most elegant seaside resort, while its more down-to-earth neighbor Trouville possesses a charm distinctly its own. A daytrip here in the high season offers a chance to watch the Beautiful People at play. Things quiet down during the rest of the year, but enough activity remains to make the trip interesting.

Trouville is an old resort along the Normandy coast, with a popularity dating from the 1830s when sea bathing first came into vogue. The court of Napoleon III flocked here, as did a number of famous writers and artists — especially the Impressionists. Its *belle époque* atmosphere lingers on amid the unspoiled ambiance of the simple fishing port it once was.

Just across the narrow Touques River, Deauville was developed by speculators in the mid-19th century as an elitist watering place for the smart set, who were presumably tired of plebeian Trouville. Sometimes called the "Twenty-first *arrondissement* of Paris," its aura of chic sophistication has remained pretty much intact to this day.

This trip can easily be combined in the same day with one to the utterly delightful fishing village of Honfleur, described on page 92.

GETTING THERE:

Trains for Trouville-Deauville depart St. Lazare station in Paris several times in the morning. Check at the information office as a change at Lisieux may be necessary and schedule variations are common. Turbotrains are frequently used, making reservations desirable. Travel time averages about two hours. Return service runs until early evening.

By car, Deauville is 129 miles from Paris via the A-13 Autoroute.

WHEN TO GO:

Deauville's high season lasts from July until the end of August, with somewhat less activity during the summer months before and after this. Crowds are at their maximum on weekends. Trouville can be enjoyed any time during the warm season, provided the weather is good. Its art museum is closed on Tuesdays,

Port Deauville

on weekdays between April and mid-June, and also between October and March.

FOOD AND DRINK:

Most restaurants in Deauville and Trouville specialize in seafood, and many have outdoor café tables. Some excellent choices are:

Ciro's   (Promenade des Planches in Deauville, right on the beach) The "in" place. $$$

Saratoga (1 Ave. Gén. de Gaulle, Deauville, near the casino) $$$

Chez Camillo   (13 Rue Désiré le Hoc, Deauville, three blocks from the station) $$$

Chez Miocque   (81 Rue Eugène Colas, Deauville, near the tourist office) $$

Carmen   (24 Rue Carnot, Trouville, near the casino) $

La Petit Auberge (7 Rue Carnot, Trouville, near the casino) $

Les Vapeurs   (160 Blvd. F.-Moureaux, Trouville, by the old port) $$

A good selection of less expensive restaurants can be found in both towns, particularly in Trouville.

TOURIST INFORMATION:

The tourist information office in Deauville, phone 31-88-21-43, is located on Place Mairie, two blocks from the Casino d'Été. Its counterpart in Trouville is in that town's casino. You can phone them at 31-88-36-19.

SUGGESTED TOUR:

Leave the Trouville-Deauville **train station** (1), which is shared by both towns, and follow the map past the Floating Basin and the tourist office to the **Casino d'Été** (2). Open from mid-March through mid-September, this is the "summer" casino — there is a "winter" casino (d'Hiver) close by, so you can gamble all year round.

Wander around the opulent shops which fill the neighborhood, then stroll down Rue Gontaut-Biron to the **Promenade des Planches**, a wooden boardwalk where the famous and the infamous come to see and be seen. Follow this to the new marina development of **Port Deauville** (3). A walk out on the breakwater will reward you with some marvelous views.

Return to the Planches and follow elegant Blvd. Eugène Cornuché to the yacht basin, where a tiny pedestrian **ferry** (Bac Piétons) (4) crosses the harbor to Trouville. At times of low tide a small footbridge is swung across the river in its place.

Trouville's **Casino** (5), built in 1912 in the grand belle époque manner, still reflects the days when such notables as Marcel Proust frequented the town — before high society drifted across the river to posher Deauville.

Once again, there is a Promenade des Planches. Stroll along this or on the beach, then follow the map to the **Municipal Museum** (6) in Villa Montebello on Rue Général Leclerc. Paintings by the early Impressionist Eugène Boudin and others, exhibited here, have captured the spirit of Trouville during its halcyon years.

Return via rues Pasteur, de la Chapelle and Victor Hugo to the old town. Unlike Deauville, Trouville exists in its own right as a fishing village and remains active all year round. Much of the charming bustle can be enjoyed along its riverside quay, the Blvd. Fernand Moureaux. From here, the **Pont des Belges** (7) leads across the river to the train station.

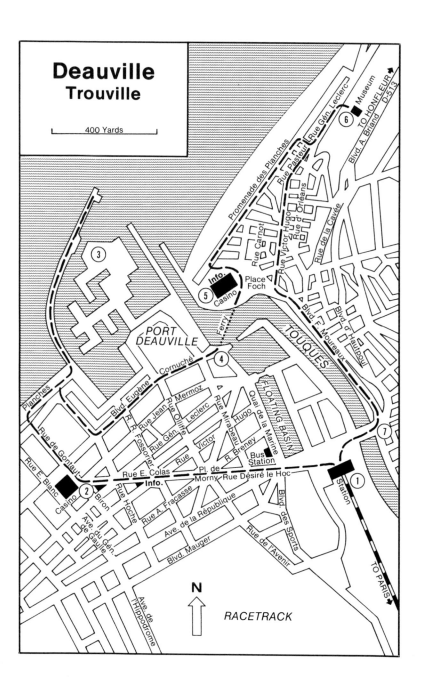

Honfleur

If a contest were held to determine the loveliest fishing port in France, Honfleur would certainly be among the top contenders. Its old harbor is so astonishingly picturesque that it defies description. The wonder of it all is that this is not just a tourist attraction but a hard-working port which somehow escaped the march of time. Perhaps this is because Le Havre, just across the bay, has long ago captured the heavy shipping industry, and also simply because Honfleur has no beach to speak of.

Located at the mouth of the Seine estuary, Honfleur was an important port ever since the 14th century, falling into English hands on several occasions. It was from here that Samuel Champlain set sail for the New World in the early 17th century, a voyage which resulted in the founding of Québec as a French colony. Later, during the 19th century, it became popular with artists, particularly with the followers of locally-born Eugène Boudin, including Jongkind and Monet. The attraction still holds, as can be seen by the number of easels lined up along the old port on a nice day.

This trip can be combined in the same day with one to Deauville and Trouville (see page 88).

GETTING THERE:

Trains depart St. Lazare station in Paris several times in the morning for Trouville-Deauville. See page 88 for more information. From there, transfer to a local bus for the nine-mile ride to Honfleur. The bus stop (*Gare Routière*) in Deauville, shown on the map on page 91, is two blocks from the train station. You could also take a taxi. Return trains operate until early evening.

There are also buses to and from Lisieux or Évreux, both of which have train service to Paris. Check the schedules carefully.

By car, take the A-13 Autoroute to the Beuzeville exit, then the D-22 and D-580 into Honfleur. The total distance from Paris is 120 miles.

WHEN TO GO:

Honfleur may be visited at any time in good weather, but note that the art museum is closed on Tuesdays and major holi-

Place Thiers near the Old Port

days, and that some attractions are either closed or have limited hours during the off season.

FOOD AND DRINK:

Many visitors are drawn to Honfleur for its beauty and charm. As a result, the village has quite a few good restaurants and cafés, mostly around the two ports. Some of the better selections are:

Ferme St.-Siméon (on the D-513 road to Trouville, less than a mile from the old harbor, uphill)   Very famous. Reservations needed, phone 31-89-23-61. $$$

Au Vieux Honfleur (13 Quai St.-Étienne, by the old port) $$

Cheval Blanc (2 Quai des Passagers, by the Avant Port) In an ancient house. $$

L'Absinthe (10 Quai de la Quarantaine, by the Avant Port) $$

Écluse (2 Quai de la Quarantaine, by the Avant Port) $$

Deaux Ponts (20 Quai de la Quarantaine, by the Avant Port) $$

Hostellerie Lechat (3 Place St.-Catherine, near the church) $$

TOURIST INFORMATION:

The tourist information office, phone 31-89-23-30, is at 33 Cours des Fossés, by the bus station.

SUGGESTED TOUR:

The **bus stop** (1) is on Place de la Porte de Rouen, close to the tourist office. Stroll over to the exceedingly picturesque **Old Port** (*Vieux Bassin*) (2), whose quays are lined with quaint houses of wood and slate. The present tidal basin was begun in the 17th century to accommodate the growing maritime development of Honfleur; other harbors being added in the 19th century.

Just a few steps away, the former Church of St.-Étienne, dating from the 14th and 15th centuries, now houses the **Museum of Old Honfleur** (3). Displays here are concerned with the town's illustrious maritime past, going back as far as Gallo-Roman times. Next to this, on the Rue de la Prison, the small **Museum of Ethnography and Folk Art** (4) features reproductions of local room interiors. Both museums are open from 10 a.m. to noon and 3–6 p.m.; closed on Fridays and some major holidays. The maritime museum is also closed on weekdays out of season. One ticket covers both.

Continue around the tiny street, little changed since the 16th century. All about you are ancient slate-roofed houses which recall life in a small Norman town many centuries ago. Back at the quay, make a right to Place de l'Hôtel de Ville, a spot favored by amateur painters trying to recapture scenes made famous by the Impressionists of the 19th century.

Beyond the tidal locks lies **La Lieutenance** (5), a jumble of 16th-century buildings which was once home to the governor of Honfleur. Part of the 13th-century town walls, the Porte de Caen, is incorporated in the side overlooking the square. On your right is the Avant Port, anchorage of the town's fishing fleet.

Follow the map to the **Church of St.-Catherine** (6), a very strange sight in this part of Europe. It may well remind you more of Norway than Normandy. Built completely of wood by 15th-century shipwrights immediately after the Hundred Years War, this double-naved masterpiece has withstood five centuries of continued threat from fire and decay. Its interior is astonishing. Just opposite the church is its detached **bell tower**, also built of wood around the same time. A visit inside will only take a few moments and is quite interesting. The admission ticket is also valid for the Boudin Museum.

Continue on to the **Eugène Boudin Museum** (7). A native of Honfleur, Boudin provided the original inspiration for the Impressionist painters, especially for his friends Jongkind and Monet. Outstanding works by these and other artists, as well as 20th-century painters such as Villon and Dufy, are very well dis-

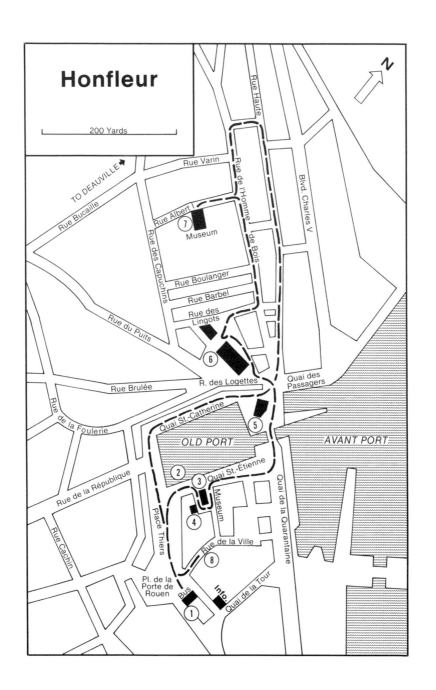

Honfleur

200 Yards

TO DEAUVILLE →

Rue Varin

Rue Bucaille

Rue Albert

Rue des Capuchins

⑦ Museum

Rue de l'Homme de Bois

Rue Haute

Blvd. Charles V

Rue Boulanger

Rue Barbel

Rue du Puits

Rue des Lingots

⑥

R. des Logettes

Quai des Passagers

Rue Brulée

Quai St-Catherine

Rue de la Foulerie

OLD PORT

AVANT PORT

⑤

②

③ Quai St.-Étienne

Rue de la République

④ Museum

Quai de la Quarantaine

Rue de la Ville

⑧

Place Thiers

Rue Cachin

Pl. de la Porte de Rouen

Bus

Info.

Quai de la Tour

①

The Old Port and La Lieutenance

played in a contemporary setting. The museum is open from 10 a.m. to noon and 2–6 p.m., every day except Tuesdays and major holidays, between Easter and the end of September. During the rest of the year it is open in the afternoons only, as well as on Saturday and Sunday mornings.

Now follow the map to the charming Rue Haute. The house at number 90 was the birthplace in 1866 of the composer Erik Satie. Return to the Old Port and stroll around it to Place Thiers. The **Rue de la Ville** (8) has two interesting 17th-century salt houses. From here it is only a few steps to the bus stop.

Amiens

Relatively few tourists venture into the often-bleak industrial north of France. This region does, however, have some outstanding attractions that make interesting daytrip destinations for experienced travelers in search of the unusual. By far the best of these is Amiens, an ancient riverside city which boasts the largest — and the most perfect — cathedral in all of France. The easy journey there provides an opportunity to experience yet another facet of this complex nation, and to see some sights unique to this town alone.

Throughout much of its long and turbulent history, Amiens was a battlefield lying in the path of invading armies. Once the capital of the Celtic Ambiani tribe, it was subjugated by Julius Caesar in the first century B.C. and again by the ninth-century Normans. During the Franco-Prussian War of 1870 Amiens was occupied by German forces, who returned in World War I and left it largely destroyed. The Second World War brought enormous losses as sixty percent of the city was reduced to rubble. Somehow, through all of this, the magnificent cathedral — along with a few other architectural gems — managed to survive unscathed. Postwar reconstruction has added a few interesting, if not exactly beautiful, structures, while current restoration efforts in the medieval quarter by the river are making the town attractive once again.

GETTING THERE:

Trains bound for Amiens leave Nord station in Paris several times in the morning, the trip taking a little over one hour. Return service operates until mid-evening.

By car, Amiens is 92 miles north of Paris via the A-1 Autoroute and the D-934 and N-29 roads. There is a somewhat shorter route taking the N-1 all the way, but traffic may be heavy.

WHEN TO GO:

Amiens may be visited at any time, noting that the Picardy Museum is closed on Mondays and some major holidays.

FOOD AND DRINK:
There is a fine selection of restaurants in Amiens. Some good choices, in the order you will pass or come close to them on the walking tour, are:

> **Carlton Belfort** (42 Rue de Noyon, near the train station) Hotel. $$
>
> **Joséphine** (20 Rue Sire Firmin Leroux, three blocks south of the cathedral) $$
>
> **La Mangeoire** (3 Rue des Sergents, two blocks southwest of the cathedral) Crêperie. $
>
> **Nord-Sud** (11 Rue Gresset, near the City Hall) $$
>
> **Petit Chef** (8 Rue Jean Catelas, near the tourist office) $$
>
> **Mermoz** (7 Rue Jean Mermoz, three blocks north of the train station) $$

TOURIST INFORMATION:
The tourist information office, phone 22-91-79-28, is located in the Maison de la Culture at the foot of Rue Jean Catelas. Ask them about boat trips in the famous *Hortillonnages*.

SUGGESTED TOUR:
Leave the **train station** (1) and amble over to the **Tour Perret** (2), a curious 26-story mini-skyscraper of truly inspired ugliness. At the time of its construction in 1952 it ranked as the tallest building in Europe. You can ascend to its top for a splendid view of the cathedral and the water gardens, and at the same time not have to look at the building itself.

The route on the map leads through a busy shopping district past the beautiful façade of an 18th-century theatre. Turn right into the Passage du Logis du Roi, where you will see the 16th-century brick-and-stone Logis du Roi alongside a fine Renaissance façade. Opposite this stands the imposing Palace of Justice.

Continue on to the **Cathedral of Notre-Dame** (3), regarded by many to be the most perfect example of a pure Gothic structure on earth. Its richly carved **west front** merits a long and careful examination, especially the 13th-century statue of Christ and the superb relief of the Last Judgement; both by the central doorway. The two towers flanking the rose window, of unequal height, are later additions. Amiens Cathedral was begun in 1220 and pretty much completed in record time, thus accounting for the truly remarkable architectural unity. A reflection of the town's medieval prosperity, it is the largest cathedral in France.

Step inside to witness its astonishing proportions and noble use of space. Of particular note are the 16th-century **choir stalls**, whose oak carvings depict both religious and secular life,

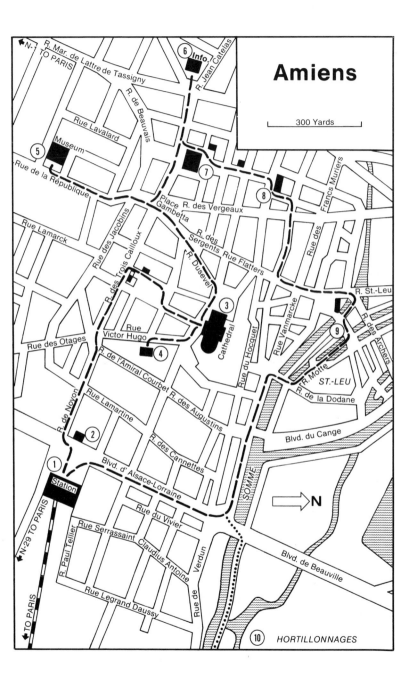

Amiens

300 Yards

The Cathedral of Notre-Dame

the latter often satirically. Stroll around the ambulatory to admire the marvelous choir screen. The cathedral is open daily from 10 a.m. to noon and 2–6 p.m.

Walk around to the rear of the cathedral, then visit the **Art and Regional History Museum** (4) in a superb 17th-century mansion, the Hôtel de Berny. The furniture and room settings are quite interesting, as are items relating to the author Jules Verne, who lived most of his life in Amiens.

Now follow the map to the **Picardy Museum** (5), which features an excellent collection of art focussing on the 18th-century French style — particularly paintings by Quentin de la Tour and Fragonard. There are also representative works of the Flemish and Dutch schools along with other European masters. The ground floor is devoted to archaeological exhibits. Visits may be made from 10 a.m. to noon and 2–6 p.m., but not on Mondays, major holidays, or Sunday afternoons.

The St.-Leu Quarter

Return to Place Gambetta and turn left to the Tourist Information Office in the modern **Maison de la Culture** (6). You may want to ask here about boat trips in the *Hortillonnages* (10), an interesting experience unique to Amiens, which are available at specific times during the high season.

Retrace your steps as far as the 17th-century **City Hall** *(Hôtel de Ville)* (7). A left here leads past the 16th-century Bailliage (note the dormer windows and Renaissance façade), the equally-old square Beffroi tower, and the **Church of St.-Germain** (8) in the Flamboyant Gothic style.

The medieval **St.-Leu Quarter** (9), cut through with numerous canals, still exudes an aura of the Middle Ages. Much of this area has become quite seedy, but recent efforts at gentrification, including the restoration of many fine old houses, are already yielding results. Stroll through its evocative narrow streets, noting in particular the picturesque 15th-century Church of St.-Leu.

From here you can return to the station following the route on the map. Along the way you may want to make a side trip to the extraordinary **Hortillonnages** (10), a curious area of market gardens surrounded by irrigation canals, which have been cultivated since the Middle Ages. To get more than a fleeting glimpse of them requires exploring by boat. Current information concerning boat trips and rentals can be had at the tourist office.

Section IV

Daytrips from Paris

Champagne, Burgundy and Beyond

Wine lovers in particular will savor the five delicious daytrips in this section. Each destination offers a golden opportunity to sample some of France's best vintages right in their own region and return to your Paris base the same evening. But you don't really need a passion for liquid treasures to enjoy the area; even teetotalers will delight in its captivating old towns.

The Champagne district, where all of the world's true champagnes are made, centers on the ancient historical city of Reims. Once you've seen that, you may want to visit other places in the area. Épernay is an especially good choice for its champagne cellars alone, although the town itself is almost without interest.

Throughout most of its long history, Burgundy (*Bourgogne*) has been a land apart; one whose borders remain vague and undefined. Not until the 15th century was it absorbed into France. Much of its colorful past is still highly visible in Auxerre, Dijon and Beaune, the three daytrip destinations chosen to best represent this ancient wine region. Travelers with more time may want to stay over for a few days and explore some of its other attractions, such as Sens, Vézelay, Autun, Nevers or Cluny.

And beyond? That's Lyon — which makes no wine of its own but as the gastronomic capital of France certainly consumes enough; so much so that in fact it is reputed to lie at the junction of not two but three rivers — the Rhône, the Saône, and the Beaujolais.

As an alternative to Paris, Dijon with its excellent rail and highway connections makes a convenient base city for one-day forays throughout Burgundy and to Lyon. Those with cars might also consider staying in Beaune.

Reims

World renowned for its magnificent cathedral, traditionally the coronation site for the kings of France, Reims is also one of the two leading centers of the champagne trade. What better place could there possibly be to sample the bubbly while exploring an intriguing old city?

Reims' grandiose and often turbulent history goes back over two thousand years. Its name derives from a Celtic tribe, the Remi, who lived there long before the Romans changed it to *Durocortorum*. Clovis, king of the Franks, was baptized in a predecessor of its cathedral in A.D. 496, which resulted in the conversion of the Franks to Christianity. Since then, practically every French king received his crown in Reims, the last being Charles X in 1825.

During World War I the city found itself in the middle of a battle zone, being subjected to intense bombardment for four long years. Miraculously, the splendid 13th-century cathedral survived, wounded but still intact, although three-quarters of Reims was reduced to rubble. The Second World War brought great destruction as well, along with another place in history. It was here that the unconditional surrender of the Third Reich was signed in 1945, putting an end to that terrible conflict.

Postwar reconstruction and the restoration of ancient monuments has made Reims once again the fascinating place that it was in the past. Often spelled as "Rheims," the city's name is pronounced as "Rrans," more or less rhyming with *dance*.

It is possible to combine a visit to Reims with one to nearby Épernay, the other major champagne producer, as they are both on the same rail line. The only sights to see there are the champagne *caves*, which are world-famous and absolutely first rate. Ask at the tourist office near the train station for details.

GETTING THERE:

Trains depart Gare de l'Est station in Paris several times in the morning for the 90-minute run to Reims. Some require a change at Épernay. Return service operates until mid-evening.

By car, Reims is 88 miles northeast of Paris on the A-4 Autoroute.

WHEN TO GO:

Reims may be enjoyed at any time, but note that the St.-Denis Museum is closed on Tuesdays and holidays. Some of the champagne cellars are closed on weekends and during the winter.

FOOD AND DRINK:

Being a major wine center, Reims offers an extraordinarily high level of cuisine. Some choice restaurants, in the order you will pass or come close to them along the walking tour, are:

Le Florence (43 Blvd. Foch, near the train station) Rates one Michelin star. $$$

Foch (37 Blvd. Foch, near the train station) $$$

Continental (95 Place Drouet d'Erlon, near the train station) $$

Flamm Steak (17 Rue Libergier, near the front of the cathedral) Crêpes, among other items. $

Le Vigneron (13 Rue de l'Université, near the rear of the cathedral) In an old house. $$

Boyer "Les Crayères" (64 Blvd. Vasnier, not far from the St.-Remi Basilica, near the champagne caves.) Very *haute cuisine,* awarded *three* Michelin stars, reservations needed, phone 26-82-80-80. $$$

Le Forum (34 Place du Forum, near the Museum of Old Reims) $

TOURIST INFORMATION:

The tourist information office, phone 26-47-04-60, is located at 1 Rue Jadart, behind the St.-Denis Museum, with a part-time branch by the cathedral. Ask them about visits to the champagne cellars.

SUGGESTED TOUR:

Leave the **train station** (1) and follow the map to the **Cathedral** (2). Nearly all of the kings of France were crowned here following a precedent set in 496 by Clovis, king of the Franks. The present cathedral, along with those of Paris, Chartres and Amiens, is a perfect example of the French Gothic style's golden age. It was begun in 1211 and essentially completed within a century, thus accounting for its remarkable stylistic unity.

The richly decorated **west front** with its three deeply recessed doorways recalls the stories of the Bible in carved stone. Its central portal is dedicated to the Virgin, while the right doorway, flanked by the prophets, represents the Last Judgement. Perhaps the most famous symbol of Reims is the enigmatic "smiling

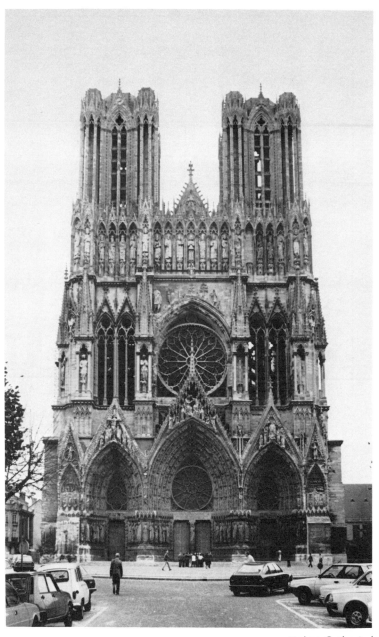

Reims Cathedral

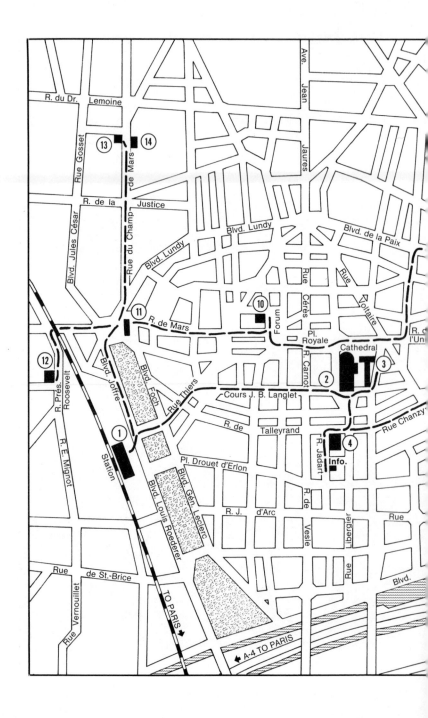

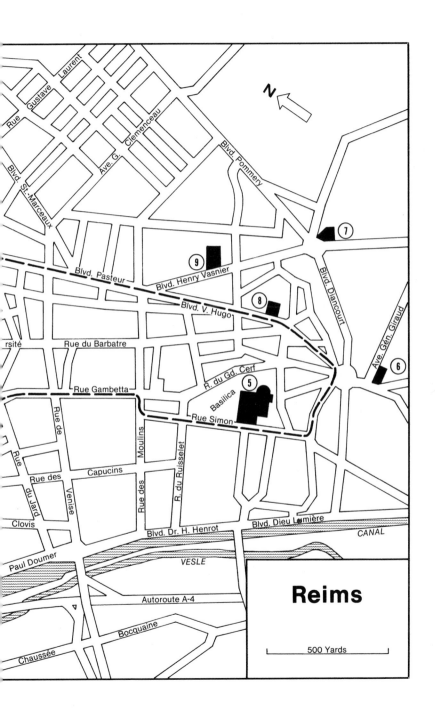

Reims

500 Yards

angel" in the left doorway, easily worth the small effort of singling out.

Step inside to admire the **stained-glass windows**, some of which are 13th-century originals. Of particular note is the fabulous rose window at the west end. There are also some wonderful modern stained-glass windows by the artist Marc Chagall in the Lady Chapel, installed in 1974. Seventeen marvelous tapestries depicting the life of the Virgin are displayed during the summer months.

Leave the cathedral and stroll around to the rear to witness the almost weightless elegance of its flying buttresses. Next to it is the former **Archbishop's Palace** (*Palais du Tau*) (3), once the residence of the king during coronations and now a museum of the cathedral's treasures. It may be visited any day except Tuesdays and major holidays; between 10 a.m. and noon and 2–6 p.m., closing an hour earlier in winter.

The **Museum of Fine Arts** (*Musée St.-Denis*) (4) is located in a former abbey just two blocks from the cathedral. Its collections include an outstanding series of 16th-century portrait drawings by both Lucas Cranach the Elder and his son the Younger. Among the other treasures are two cycles of medieval tapestries and wall hangings, no less than twenty-five landscapes by Corot, and a marvelous gathering of 19th- and early-20th-century French paintings. The museum is open every day except Tuesdays and holidays; from 10 a.m. to noon and 2–6 p.m.

Stop in at the nearby tourist office to find out which champagne cellars are open, then follow the map to the **Basilica of St.-Remi** (5) on Rue Simon. This is the oldest church in Reims, dating from the first half of the 11th century. Much of it is in the Romanesque style, while the huge 12th-century choir makes a tentative transition into the early Gothic. Behind the altar lies the reconstructed tomb of Saint Remi, a 5th-century archbishop who established the importance of Reims by baptizing Clovis as a Christian and anointing him king of the Franks.

Adjoining the church on the north side is its former abbey, now housing the city's **Archaeological Museum** (*Musée Abbaye St.-Remi*). Displays here include fascinating artifacts from prehistoric times to the late Middle Ages, along with notable tapestries illustrating the life of Saint Remi. It is open during the same times as the Fine Arts Museum.

Now for a real treat — the famous **champagne cellars**, many of which are located in this part of town. The leading ones which offer public tours without prior arrangement are shown on the map. Those in the immediate vicinity are:

Veuve Clicquot-Ponsardin (6). These *caves* date from Gallo-Roman times.

Pommery (7). An elegant and fascinating tour through ancient pits below the city.   •

Taittinger (8). A somewhat spooky amble in the crypts of a former abbey, preceded by an excellent audio-visual show.

Piper-Heidsieck (9). Ride a little electric train through the cellars.

All of the tours are free, but do not necessarily offer free samples. You may, of course, buy some bottles of the bubbly. Visits are usually conducted in English, French and German. A jacket or sweater is helpful as the *cave* temperatures hover around the 50-degree mark. Times of operation vary with each house, so check first with the tourist office for current information.

Return to the cathedral area via the route on the map. Continuing on, you will pass the restored **Place Royale** with its statue of Louis XV. From here it is only a few steps to **Place du Forum**, where parts of the original Roman forum are visible. The **Museum of Old Reims** (*Musée-Hôtel le Vergeur*) (10), on its north side, displays a splendid collection of antique furniture and art, including a noted set of engravings by Albrecht Dürer of the Apocalypse and Christ's Passion.

The route now leads past several outstanding mansions and the City Hall to the third-century **Mars Gate** (*Porte Mars*) (11), the largest monument left in Reims from the Roman era.

Before returning to the nearby train station you may want to visit a few other interesting sights. The **Salle de Guerre** (12), located in a technical school at 12 Rue Franklin Roosevelt, is the room in which Germany unconditionally surrendered to the Allies on May 7, 1945. It has been left exactly as it was on that momentous day, when it was a part of General Eisenhower's headquarters. Visits may be made any day except Tuesdays and holidays; from 9 a.m. to noon and 2–6 p.m.; but not between the middle of November and the middle of March.

Another worthwhile sight is the strikingly modern **Foujita Chapel** (13), designed by the Japanese artist Léonard-Tsugouharu Foujita after his conversion to Catholicism in Reims. Just across the street is another champagne house, **Mumm** (14), which also offers a splendid tour of its cellars.

Auxerre

You won't find a great many tourists in Auxerre, but that's their loss. This marvelously atmospheric holdover from the Middle Ages is the capital of lower Burgundy and center of the Chablis wine growing region. The town, as you approach it along the banks of the Yonne river, makes an exceptionally handsome sight with its church spires piercing the skyline above a huddle of ancient houses.

Inhabited since Celtic times, Auxerre was later a Roman fortress called *Autessiodurum,* from which its name derives. The town, converted to Christianity, became the seat of a bishop as early as the third century, and later an important scholastic center. Its medieval heart is today one of the best-preserved in France — an exceptionally attractive place where you can enjoy strolling around the winding, narrow lanes and exploring its picturesque old structures in peace. Auxerre, incidentally, is pronounced *"Ausserre."*

GETTING THERE:

Trains leave Gare de Lyon station in Paris several times in the morning for Auxerre's St.-Gervais station, less than two hours away. Some of these require a change at Laroche-Migennes. Return service operates until early evening.

By car, take the A-6 Autoroute and enter Auxerre on the N-6 road, a total distance from Paris of 105 miles.

WHEN TO GO:

A trip to Auxerre can be made at almost any time, but avoid coming on a Tuesday or holiday when its major attractions are closed.

FOOD AND DRINK:

Some fine restaurants, in the order that you will pass or come close to them, are listed below. Naturally, you will probably want to sip Chablis, the local wine.

> **Restaurant Maxime** (5 Quai de la Marine, by the river, below the cathedral) Attractive location. $$

> **Jardin Gourmand** (56 Blvd. Vauban, not far from the St.-Germain Abbey) Received one star from Michelin. $$

Auxerre from the Yonne River

La Grilladerie (45 bis Blvd. Vauban, not far from the
   St.-Germain Abbey) $$

La Marmite (34 Rue du Pont, near St.-Pierre Church) $

St.-Hubert (3 Rue de la Poterne, off Quai de la
   République, between the two bridges) $

TOURIST INFORMATION:

The tourist information office, phone 86-52-06-19, is located
along the Quai de la République, by the river, below the cathedral.

SUGGESTED TOUR:

Leave the **train station** (1) and follow the map to the Yonne
river, from which you get a splendid view of the old town. A
right here leads to a footbridge. Cross this and, passing the tourist
office, walk uphill to the **Cathedral of St.-Étienne** (2), a re-
markable structure in the Flamboyant Gothic style begun in the
13th century but not completed until the 16th. This was the
scene, in 1422, of a fateful meeting in which the English and
the Burgundians plotted against the French. In 1429 it was visited
by a disguised Joan of Arc on her way to meet the dauphin at
Chinon. After defeating the English at Orléans she returned here
with Charles VII en route to his coronation at Reims. Another
historical event took place in front of the cathedral in 1815 when
Napoleon, returning from exile, conspired with Marshal Ney
against Louis XVIII, for which Ney was later shot.

The cathedral's interior features some very fine medieval stained-glass windows along with an admirable Gothic choir. Be sure to visit its 11th-century **crypt**, the sole remaining part of an earlier cathedral on the same site. There you will see the famous *Christ on Horseback* fresco, the only one of its kind in the world. Other sights in the church include its treasury of illuminated manuscripts and the **north tower**, which may be climbed for a closeup view of the town.

Now carefully follow the map through a maze of ancient streets to **Place St.-Nicholas** (3), a delightful square in the old marine quarter. Continue on past a handsome 16th-century half-timbered house to the **Abbey of St.-Germain** (4), founded in the sixth century by Queen Clothilde, wife of Clovis, above the tomb of Auxerre's fifth-century bishop and native son, Saint Germain. Rebuilt in later years, the church itself is of minor interest, but the **crypts** are another story. Some of these date from as early as the fifth century. The ninth-century Carolingian chambers contain several fabulous frescoes, among the very earliest yet discovered in France, depicting the martyrdom of Saint Stephen. In the Merovingian part of the crypt there are some oak beams that are over 1,100 years old. The crypts may be visited — with a guide — every day except Tuesdays and holidays, from 9 a.m. to noon and 2–6 p.m. Save the ticket — it is also valid for the Leblanc-Duvernoy Museum.

Continue on to the **Lapidary Museum** (5) in the former Chapel of the Nuns of the Visitation. Its Gallo-Roman stone sculptures and other archaeological finds may be seen between July 1st and September 15th, every day except Tuesdays, from 10 a.m. to noon and 2–6 p.m.

Rue de Paris and Rue d'Eglény lead to the **Leblanc-Duvernoy Museum** (6), installed in an elegant 18th-century mansion. The magnificent collection of Beauvais tapestries, porcelains, furniture and other items of the 18th-century decorative arts should not be missed. It is open daily from 10:30 a.m. to noon and 2–5:30 p.m., except on Tuesdays and holidays.

The route goes past the **Church of St.-Eusèbe** (7), noted for its 12th-century Romanesque tower, and winds its way around to Auxerre's famous 15th-century **Clock Tower** (*Tour de l'Horloge*) (8), opposite the Town Hall. This delightfully animated part of town, now pedestrianized, is also its commercial center. All around the tower stand ancient houses, many of them half-timbered, which serve as luxurious shops.

Returning to the station, you will pass the **Church of St.-**

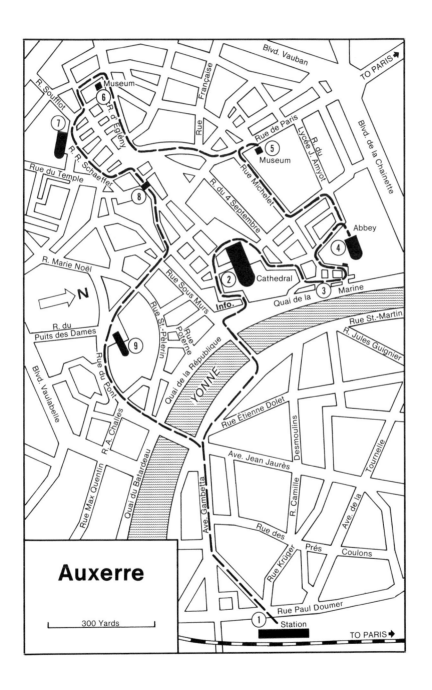

Blvd. Vauban

TO PARIS ➡

R. Soufflot

Museum

6

R. d'Eglény

7

Rue Française

Rue de Paris

R. du Lycée J. Amyot

Blvd. de la Chainette

R. R. Schaeffer

Rue du Temple

8

Museum

5

Rue Michelet

R. du 4 Septembre

Abbey

4

R. Marie Noël

Cathedral

2

3

Marine

R. du Puits des Dames

Rue Sous Murs

Info.

Quai de la

Rue St.-Martin

R. Jules Guignier

Rue St.-Pèlerin

Rue Poterne

9

Quai de la République

YONNE

Blvd. Vaulabelle

Rue du Pont

R. A. Challes

Rue Étienne Dolet

Desmoulins

Rue de la Tournelle

Ave. Jean Jaurès

R. Camille

Quai du Batardeau

Rue Max Quentin

Ave. Gambetta

Rue des

Prés

Coulons

Rue Krüger

Ave. de la

Auxerre

300 Yards

Rue Paul Doumer

1

Station

TO PARIS ➡

The Clock Tower

Pierre (9) with its highly impressive Renaissance façade. Continue on downhill to the Paul-Bert Bridge for a last look at Auxerre mirrored in the waters of the Yonne before returning to Paris.

Dijon

There is a lot to see in Dijon — if you can just tear yourself away from the pleasures of the table long enough to feast the eyes as well as the palate. Long renowned as the region's gastronomic center, this ancient city is also the traditional capital of Burgundy. Its rulers left behind a rich heritage which today makes it a veritable treasury of the arts. Dijon is an exceedingly likeable place, and an eminently walkable one as well.

Originally a Roman encampment on the military road linking Lyon with Mainz, *Divio,* as Dijon was then known, became the capital of the Burgundian kingdom during the Dark Ages, only to be destroyed by fire in 1137. The late 12th century saw its reconstruction as a fortified city, while the Cathedral of St.-Bénigne was begun a hundred years later.

Philip the Bold, son of King John II of France, inherited Burgundy in 1364, thus starting the powerful line of Valois dukes whose loyalty to the Kingdom of France wavered with each succeeding generation. During this time Burgundy was greatly expanded, making Dijon in effect the capital of what is now the Netherlands, Belgium, Alsace and Lorraine as well as the present region of *Bourgogne.* This enormous growth coincided with the beginning of the Renaissance, attracting many leading artists to Dijon, where there was both work and money. The golden days came to an end in 1477 when Duke Charles the Bold was killed fighting Louis XI, thus reunifying Burgundy with France.

GETTING THERE:

Trains for Dijon leave Gare de Lyon station in Paris fairly frequently. The speedy TGVs *(reservations required)* make the run in about 100 minutes; others take somewhat longer. Return service operates until mid-evening.

By car, Dijon is 195 miles from Paris via the A-6 Autoroute. This is a bit too far for a daytrip, although Dijon makes an excellent stopover en route between Paris and Provence or the Riviera.

WHEN TO GO:

Dijon may be visited at any time of the year since the walk is short and much of your time will be spent indoors. Most of the major sights are closed on Tuesdays and holidays.

FOOD AND DRINK:

The overall quality of dining in Dijon is exceptionally high, with such local specialties as *boeuf bourguignon* and *coq au vin* being international favorites. Start your meal with a *kir*, an apéritif made from white wine and blackcurrant liqueur, named after the city's onetime mayor. Burgundy's fabulous Côte d'Or begins just south of Dijon, assuring a plentiful supply of world-class wines at reasonable prices. The city is also very famous for its mustard, a jar of which makes a nice souvenir.

Some outstanding restaurants, in trip sequence, are:

Les Caves de la Cloche (14 Place Darcy, under the Hôtel Cloche) $$$

Hôtel du Nord (2 Rue de la Liberté, near Place Darcy) $$

Moulin à Vent (8 Place François Rude) $

Restaurant le Dôme (16 Rue Quentin, one block west of Notre-Dame Church) $

La Chouette (Breuil) (1 Rue de la Chouette, one block east of Notre-Dame Church) Awarded one Michelin star. $$$

Pré aux Clercs et Trois-Faisans (13 Place de la Libération, near the Ducal Palace) $$

Le Rallye (39 Rue Chabot-Charny, near the Palace of Justice) Received one Michelin star. $$

Pierre Fillion (39 Rue Buffon, three blocks southeast of the Palace of Justice) $

La Toison d'Or (Les Oenophiles) (18 Rue Ste.-Anne, three blocks southwest of the Palace of Justice) In an old mansion, with ancient wine caves and museum. $$

Le Vinarium (23 Place Bossuet, three blocks east of the cathedral) $$

Chapeau Rouge (5 Rue Michelet, behind the cathedral) Rates one Michelin star, reservations needed, phone 80-30-28-10. $$$

Thibert (38 Rue Crebillon, south of the cathedral) $$

TOURIST INFORMATION:

The tourist information office, phone 80-43-42-12, is located at Place Darcy (2), not far from the train station. There is another office at 34 Rue des Forges, phone 80-30-35-39, near the Church of Notre-Dame.

SUGGESTED TOUR:

Leave the **train station** (1) and follow the map to **Place Darcy** (2), an attractive square with a branch of the tourist office, a small park and an 18th-century triumphal arch. Continue on

Place François Rude

Rue de la Liberté past the venerable Grey Poupon mustard store — which has an exhibit of antique jars on display — to **Place François Rude** (3). In the center of this lively square there is a fountain which once ran with new wine at harvest time, topped by a statue of a naked youth treading the grapes. The central market *(Les Halles),* two blocks north of this, bustles with activity on Tuesdays, Fridays and Saturdays.

Follow the narrow Rue des Forges past several exquisite old houses, the most notable being the 15th-century **Hôtel Morel-Sauvegrain** at number 56; the 13th-century exchange — much restored — at number 40; and the **Maison Milsand** dating from 1561, at number 38. The 15th-century **Hôtel Chambellan** at number 34 houses the main tourist office upstairs. A left at Place Notre-Dame leads to the **Church of Our Lady** *(Eglise Notre-Dame)* (4), a unique jewel of 13th-century Gothic architecture. Its façade is literally covered with hideous gargoyles, while from the roof rises the Jacquemart, a mechanical chiming clock which Philip the Bold brought back as war booty from the Flemish town of Courtrai in 1389. Visit the remarkably harmonious interior, noted for its ancient stained-glass windows and an 11th-century Black Virgin carved in wood.

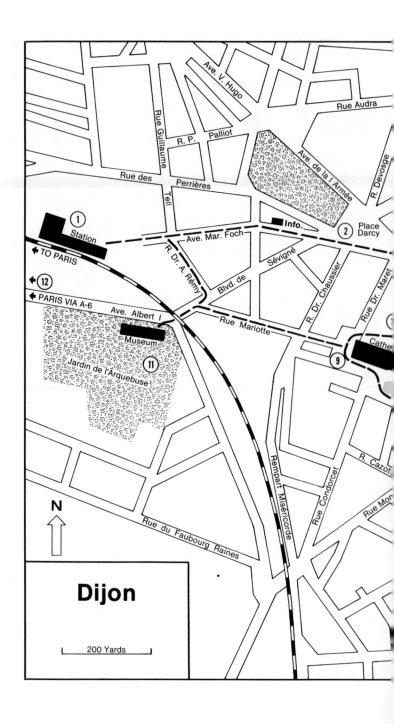

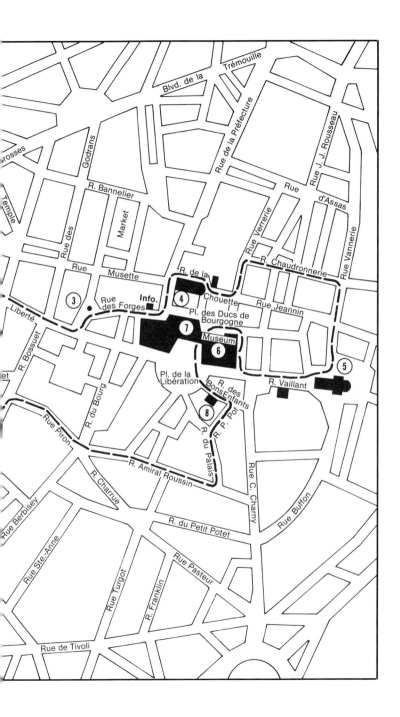

Along Rue de la Liberté

Stroll around to the rear of the church on Rue de la Chouette. At number 8 you will pass the **Hôtel de Vogüé**, a lovely residence in the Renaissance style dating from 1614. Make a left onto Rue Verrerie, and the next right on Rue Chaudronnerie, followed by another right on Rue Vannerie — a short walk taking you down three very picturesque streets lined with medieval buildings. At the end you will come to the **Church of St.-Michel** (5), a curious mixture of Gothic and Renaissance styles built during the 15th and 16th centuries.

The major attraction of Dijon, besides its food and wine, is the **Palace of the Dukes of Burgundy** (6). Begun in the 14th century, it was continually enlarged and modified until the 19th, with much of its classical façade designed by Louis XIV's architect, Jules Hardouin-Mansart of Versailles fame. This enormous complex of structures now houses both the City Hall *(Hôtel de Ville)*, which may be strolled through, and the world-famous **Fine Arts Museum** *(Musée des Beaux-Arts)*, one of the very best in all France.

The entrance to the museum is on Place de la Ste.-Chapelle. Allow plenty of time for a visit — an hour at the very least — and carefully study the posted layout maps as it is quite easy to get disoriented and risk missing some of its best treasures. These include the ducal kitchens, the **tombs** of Philip the Bold and John the Fearless; Italian, Swiss, Flemish and German as well as French paintings and sculptures; and, of course, the outstanding galleries of modern and regional art. The museum is open every day except Tuesdays and major holidays, from 10 a.m. to 6 p.m.

Now stroll into Place des Ducs-de-Bourgogne, a charming square facing the original parts of the palace. A portal at the corner leads back into the palace complex, from which you can climb up the **Tour Philippe-le-Bon** (7) for an excellent view of the city, the mountains beyond and the beginnings of the Burgundy wine district. It is a steep 150 feet to the top of this 15th-century tower, but well worth the effort.

Follow the map through the elegant Place de la Libération to the **Magnin Museum** (8), housed in a fine 17th-century mansion, the Hôtel Lantin on Rue des Bons-Enfants. Step inside to view a sumptuous collection of paintings displayed in the gorgeous environment of original room settings reflecting period bourgeois life. It is open from 9 a.m. to noon and 2–6 p.m., daily except on Tuesdays, Easter and Christmas.

Continue on past the Palace of Justice and turn right on Rue Amiral Roussin. The route now leads through a colorful old part of town to the **Cathedral of St.-Bénigne** (9), a 13th-century example of the Burgundian Gothic style. You can make an interesting visit to its unusual circular crypt, dating from 1007 with some 9th-century segments, which survives from an earlier basilica on the same site.

Next to this is the **Archaeological Museum** (10), housed in the dormitory of a former Benedictine abbey. Displays here include some fascinating Gallo-Roman and medieval artifacts. The museum is open every day except Tuesdays, from 10 a.m. to 6 p.m. during the summer season and from 9 a.m. to noon and 2–6 p.m. the rest of the year.

On the way back to the train station you may want to stop at the **Jardin de l'Arquebuse** (11), a large and very lovely garden which also houses the Natural History Museum. Those with a bit more time can make a short excursion of less than a mile to the famous **Chartreuse de Champmol** (12) *(off the map)*. Originally the burial place of the dukes of Burgundy, this 14th-century monastery was destroyed in the Revolution and the site is now occupied by a mental hospital. Some of its fabulous sculptures by the noted medieval master Claus Sluter are still there, and deserve to be seen by anyone interested in the art of the Middle Ages.

Beaune

Beaune is a mecca for wine lovers the world over, and long the center of Burgundy's liquid trade. Its major sight, the 15th-century Hôtel-Dieu, is surely one of the most extraordinary medieval structures in France, or in all of Europe for that matter. Visitors by the thousands are also attracted to its numerous *caves*, where the wines of Burgundy can be sampled in congenial surroundings.

Wine was not always Beaune's sole *raison d'être*. The 14th-century ramparts, still more or less complete, enclose a remarkably well-preserved town that dates from the time of the ancient Gauls. It remained an important political center of the duchy long after the dukes themselves moved to Dijon, with a strategic location between the once-powerful strongholds of warring nobles. All of this changed in the 17th century, when the local citizens finally turned their full attention to wine. That happy development has brought about a prosperity lasting to this day. Beaune (pronounced *Bone*) is indeed a joyful place to visit.

GETTING THERE:

Trains depart Gare de Lyon station in Paris frequently for Dijon, with the TGV types making the run in about 100 minutes. From there take a connecting local to Beaune, a trip of 22 minutes. There is also frequent bus service between the two towns. Some TGV trains run directly from Paris to Beaune, but at rather odd hours. Return service operates until early evening.

By car, Beaune is 196 miles southeast of Paris on the A-6 Autoroute. A daytrip by car is rather impractical, but the town makes an excellent stopover for those driving between Paris and Provence or the Riviera.

WHEN TO GO:

Beaune may be enjoyed at any time. Even if it is raining, the underground *caves* stay dry — at least as far as precipitation is concerned.

FOOD AND DRINK:

As an important tourist attraction, Beaune offers a great many restaurants and cafés in all price ranges. Some particularly good choices in the center of town are:

The Courtyard of the Hôtel-Dieu

Auberge St.-Vincent (Place de la Halle, near the tourist office) $$

Les Gourmets (17 Rue Monge, near the tourist office) $$

Au Petit Pressoir (15 Place Fleury, near the Hôtel-Dieu) $$

Central Hôtel (2 Rue Victor-Millot, near the Hôtel-Dieu) $$

Relais de Saulx (6 Rue Louis-Véry, near the Hôtel-Dieu) Awarded one Michelin star, reservations suggested, phone 80-22-01-35. $$

And just outside the ramparts are:

Hôtel de la Poste (3 Blvd. Clemenceau, not far from the Hôtel-Dieu) $$$

Chez Maxime (3 Place Madeleine, between the station and the Hôtel-Dieu) $

Auberge Bourguignonne (4 Place Madeleine, between the station and the Hôtel-Dieu) $$

TOURIST INFORMATION:

The tourist information office, phone 80-22-24-51, is next to the Hôtel-Dieu. Be sure to ask them for current information concerning visits to the wine caves.

SUGGESTED TOUR:

Leave the **train station** (1) and follow the map through some colorful old streets to the **tourist information office** (2). Here you can get an up-to-date list of the wine *caves* in town which offer tours or tastings *(dégustation)*. Many of these are located in ancient cellars dating from as far back as the 13th century and make intriguing places to visit. Some are free while others — often with better vintages — charge a nominal admission. Since the old part of Beaune is quite small you will be able to visit the cellars at your leisure anytime along the walking route. The locations of five of the better-known *caves* are shown on the map as circled numbers. They are:

Marché aux Vins, near the Hôtel-Dieu (8).

Caves des Cordeliers, near the Hôtel-Dieu (9).

Maison Calvet, 6 Blvd. Perpreuil, by the town walls (10).

La Halle aux Vins, facing Square des Lions on Blvd. Foch (11).

Maison Patriarche Père et Fils, on Rue du Collège (12).

Now for Beaune's major attraction, the **Hôtel-Dieu** (also known as the *Hospices de Beaune*) (3). This exquisite structure — a major architectural achievement of the 15th century — was founded in 1443 by the chancellor of Burgundy, Nicholas Rolin, as a charity hospital to alleviate the misery of much of the town's population. This was perhaps only too fitting since it was Rolin — acting as tax collector for the dukes — who reduced them to poverty to begin with. Its use as a hospital continued until 1971, with much of it still functioning as an old age home. Guided tours are conducted through it at very frequent intervals, every day from 9 a.m. to 11:30 a.m. and 2–6 p.m., with slightly shorter hours during the winter season. These end in a small art gallery featuring one of the most fabulous paintings from the Middle Ages, Roger Van der Weyden's great polyptych of the *Last Judgement*.

The Hôtel-Dieu is supported primarily by revenues from the 32 *Côte de Beaune* vineyards it owns, whose wines are sold at its famous auction, held on the third Sunday of each November. These tend to establish the prices for all Burgundy wines of the same vintage. The *Hospices de Beaune* label is highly regarded among lovers of fine wines.

Continue on to the **Collegiate Church of Notre-Dame** (4), begun during the 12th century in the Cluniac tradition. Some of its works of art are truly astonishing — particularly the 15th-century tapestries depicting the life of the Virgin, displayed behind the altar between April and November.

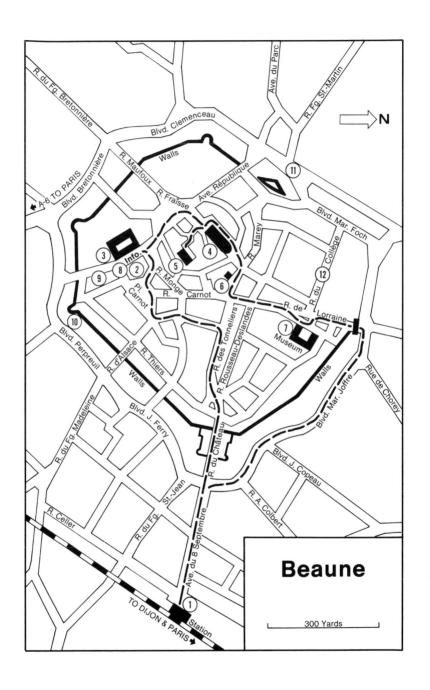

N

R. du Fg. Bretonnière

R. du Parc

R. Fg. St-Martin

Blvd. Clemenceau

Walls

A-6 TO PARIS

Blvd. Bretonnière

R. Maufoux

R. Fraisse

Ave. République

Blvd. Mar. Foch

R. Marey

3

Info.

8   2

9

R. Monge

5

4

6

R. du Collège

12

Pl. Carnot

R. Carnot

R.

R. de

Lorraine

10

R. d'Alsace

R. Thiers

Walls

Blvd. Perpreuil

R. des Tonneliers

R. Rousseau-Deslandes

1

Museum

Walls

Rue de Chorey

Blvd. Mar. Joffre

Blvd. J. Ferry

R. du Fg. Madeleine

St.-Jean

R. du Château

Blvd. J. Copeau

11

Blvd. J. Copeau

R. A. Colbert

R. Celler

R. du Fg.

Ave. du 8 Septembre

TO DIJON & PARIS

1

Station

Beaune

300 Yards

The Collegiate Church of Notre-Dame

Oenophiles — as well as normal folk — will appreciate the **Burgundy Wine Museum** *(Musée du Vin de Bourgogne)* (5), located in the medieval mansion of the dukes of Burgundy. Its many interesting displays cover the history and lore of local wine making from ancient times to the early 20th century. Don't miss the adjacent 14th-century press house *(cuverie)*. The museum is open daily from 9 a.m. to noon and 2–5 p.m.

The walk now winds around past the picturesque 15th-century **Belfry** (6) of the former town hall to the **Museum of Fine Arts** *(Musée des Beaux-Arts)* (7). The rather miscellaneous collections, including some Gallo-Roman archaeological finds, are enlivened by a splendid group of paintings by the 19th-century romantic landscapist, Félix Ziem, a native son of Beaune. Another local lad, Étienne-Jules Marey, a 19th-century scientist who pioneered the principles of motion picture photography, has a separate gallery devoted to his work. Visits may be made from 9 a.m. to noon and 2–5:30 p.m. daily, but not on Tuesdays or between November and Easter.

From here you can return to the station by walking along the ancient ramparts or, better still, return to town for another glass of wine.

Lyon

Until recently, a daytrip to Lyon would have been nearly unthinkable as the second city of France lies some 288 miles southeast of Paris. All of that changed with the introduction of high-speed TGV trains which cover the distance in an astonishing two hours flat. This is a good excursion for railpass holders — you really get your money's worth — and an excellent reason to purchase one of these bargains (see Section I).

Strangely, Lyon has never been much of a tourist attraction. Visitors yes — about five million a year, nearly all on business — but travelers in search of pleasure have largely avoided it; put off, perhaps, by its image as a large, sprawling industrial center. Lyon deserves better than that. Its older sections are surprisingly beautiful, full of life, and endowed with enough first-rate attractions to make just about any other city in France besides Paris pale by comparison.

And then there is the food. Lyon is usually regarded as the gastronomic capital of all France, which in practical terms means that it probably has the best cooking in the world. You could make a trip here just to eat, especially if your object was to indulge in one of the legendary temples of *haute cuisine* the area is famous for.

Over two thousand years old, Lyon was founded in 43 B.C. as the Roman colony of *Lugdunum*. Even before then, the site at the confluence of two rivers had long been occupied by Celts and other people. Under the emperor Augustus it became the capital of Gaul and later, in A.D. 478, the capital of the Burgundians. The city's strategic situation at the crossroads of trade routes favored its development as a mercantile center, a position it still holds. Textile manufacturing took root in the early 16th century, establishing a strong economic base along with banking and printing. Although Lyon — sometimes spelled *Lyons* in English — is now a very modern city with well over a million people in its urban area, the walking tour suggested below is limited to the handsome and very well-preserved older parts of town.

GETTING THERE:

TGV trains (see page 10) depart Gare de Lyon station in Paris frequently for the two-hour run (or flight?) to Lyon. *Do not* get off at Lyon's Part-Dieu station, which is the first stop in the city. Instead, wait for its second stop, a few minutes later, at Lyon's Perrache station. Return service operates until early evening.

By car, the distance from Paris is too great for a daytrip. You may, however, want to make a stopover en route to or from Provence or the Riviera. Lyon is 288 miles from Paris via the A-6 Autoroute.

WHEN TO GO:

Some of the major attractions are closed on Mondays, some on Tuesdays, and others on both days. Good weather will make your trip much more enjoyable.

FOOD AND DRINK:

Lyon abounds in superb restaurants and friendly cafés. The selections listed below are limited to those along or near the suggested walking route. If gastronomic pleasure means more to you than sightseeing, you may prefer dining at a top-rated restaurant such as **Paul Bocuse** in nearby Collonges-au-Mont-d'Or, at **La Pyramide** in Vienne, 18 miles south by car or train, or at one of the fine establishments in other parts of Lyon. Consult an up-to-date restaurant guide such as the *Michelin France* (red cover) for suggestions and details. The city, by the way, lies just between Burgundy and the Côtes du Rhône and is awash in both their wines, particularly Beaujolais. In trip sequence, some choice restaurants are:

L'Alsacienne (20 Place Carnot, in front of the station) $$

La Mère Vittet-Brasserie Lyonnaise (26 Cours de Verdun, down from the concourse between the rail and bus stations at Perrache) Always open. $$

Vettard (7 Place Bellecour) Elegant, rates two Michelin stars, $$$, with next-door branch, Café Neuf at $$

Bourillot (8 Place des Célestins, near Place Bellecour) Awarded one Michelin star. $$$

La Voûte (Chez Léa) (11 Place Antonin-Gourju, near Place Bellecour) Traditional Lyonnais. $$

Tour Rose (16 Rue du Boeuf in Old Lyon near the cathedral) 17th-century townhouse, one Michelin star, nouvelle cuisine. $$$

Boeuf d'Argent (29 Rue du Boeuf, in Old Lyon near the cathedral) $

Le Comptoir du Boeuf (3 Place Neuve St.-Jean, in Old Lyon near the cathedral) $

Les Ardechois (31 Rue St.-Jean, in Old Lyon near the cathedral) $

La Mère Brazier (12 Rue Royale, Les Traboules district, near the Rhône) One Michelin star. $$$

Chevallier (40 Rue du Sergent-Blandan in Les Traboules district) $$

Pied de Cochon (9 Rue St.-Polycarpe, in Les Traboules district) $$

Léon de Lyon (1 Rue Pleney, behind the Fine Arts Museum) Awarded two Michelin stars. $$$

Daniel et Denise (2 Rue Tupin, in the center between Place Bellecour and the Fine Arts Museum) Rates one Michelin star. $$

Nandron (26 Quai Jean Moulin, by the Rhône) Two Michelin stars. $$$

Les Fantasques (47 Rue de la Bourse, near Pont Lafayette on the Rhône) Superb seafood, one Michelin star. $$$

Tante Alice (22 Rue des Remparts-d'Ainay, near the Textile Museum) $$

La Tassée (20 Rue de la Charité, near the Textile Museum) Traditional Lyonnais cooking. $$

TOURIST INFORMATION:

The main tourist information office, phone 78-42-25-75, is located in Place Bellecour (2); with a branch office in the Perrache train station, phone 78-42-22-07. Ask them about guide maps for the Les Traboules district.

SUGGESTED TOUR:

Leave the Perrache **train station** (1), a huge modern complex including a bus terminal, and descend the escalators to Place Carnot. From here the pedestrians-only Rue Victor Hugo leads through a lively shopping district to **Place Bellecour** (2), a vast open space with a flower market, the main tourist office, and an equestrian statue of Louis XIV. Turn left and cross the Pont Bonaparte , a bridge spanning the Saône. Continue straight ahead to the funicular station, buy a ticket from the vending machine, and board the car on the right-hand side marked for Fourvière. This will take you to the top of a very steep hill, from which there is a wonderful panoramic view of Lyon.

The monstrous **Basilica of Notre-Dame de Fourvière** (3), at the top of the funicular and overlooking the city, has to be seen to be believed. This marvelously hideous edifice, a curious *mélange* of architectural styles, was begun in 1870 as thanks to

Lyon

400 Yards

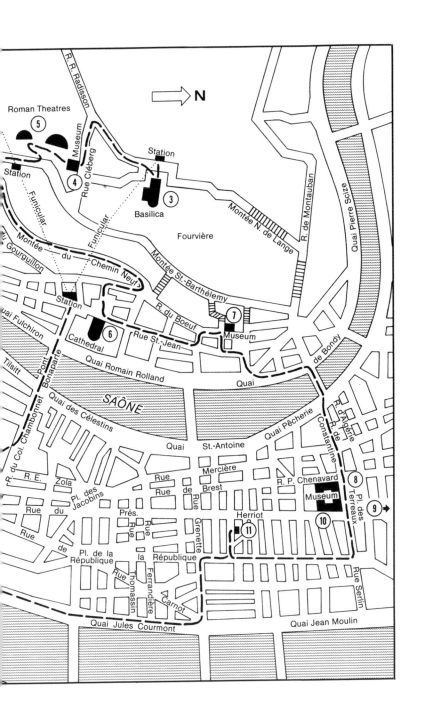

Remains of a Roman Theatre

the Virgin for saving Lyon from the Germans during the Franco-Prussian War. Step inside for a look at the elaborate stained-glass windows, mosaics and the crypt. A tower on the left affords an even better view of the city.

The Fourvière hill was the site of the original Roman settlement and is rich in archaeological finds. Follow the map to the **Gallo-Roman Museum** (4), a superb modern structure, mostly underground, which spirals its way down part of the hillside. As you descend its ramps you will pass many fascinating artifacts from Lyon's ancient past. A descriptive booklet in English is available at the entrance. Visits may be made from 9:30 a.m. to noon and 2–6 p.m., daily except on Mondays and Tuesdays.

Leave the museum from its lowest level and stroll over to the two **Roman Theatres** (5), unearthed in the 1930s. The larger of these is the oldest in France and was built by the emperor Augustus in 15 B.C. It is now used for occasional festival performances.

Continue down the hill via Montée du Chemin Neuf to the **Cathedral of St.-Jean** (6). Begun in the 12th century, it displays a mixture of styles ranging from Romanesque to Flamboyant Gothic. The interior is noted for its 13th-century stained-glass in the choir, apse and rose windows of the transepts. In the north

The Basilica of Notre-Dame-de-Fourvière

transept there is an interesting 14th-century **astronomical clock** which puts on a show at noon, 1, 2, and 3 p.m. Don't miss the **Chapel of the Bourbons** on the north side of the nave. The **Treasury**, to the right of the entrance, exhibits rare pieces of religious art daily except on Tuesdays, from 2–6 p.m.

Adjacent to the cathedral, on its north side, is an outdoor archaeological garden with excavations of earlier churches. Stroll down Rue St.-Jean and turn left to the **Hôtel de Gadagne** (7), a magnificent 16th-century Renaissance mansion now housing both the Historical Museum of Lyon and the intriguing **Marionette Museum**. Puppets have been a tradition of the city since the late 18th century when one Laurent Mourguet, an unemployed silkworker who lost his job after the Revolution made silk un-democratic, created a satirical marionette character named Guignol. The plays, larded with broad humor in the local dialect, are still very popular. Ask at the tourist office for details of performances given in various theatres. Besides the classic

Guignol characters, the museum also has puppets from all over the world, notably those from Cambodia. It is open from 10 a.m. to noon and 2–6 p.m., daily except on Tuesdays.

While still in this colorful area, known as Old (Vieux) Lyon, you should take the opportunity to explore its numerous tiny streets and alleyways. For many years this was a notorious slum, but recent restoration has made it fashionable once again. Some of its narrowest passages, known as traboules, make interior connections between the ancient buildings and adjacent streets, and were used by members of the Resistance during World War II to hide from the Nazis. Maps guiding you through these mazes are available at the tourist office and elsewhere.

Now follow the map across the river to **Place des Terreaux** (8) with its grandiose fountain by the 19th-century sculptor Frédéric Bartholdi, who also created the Statue of Liberty in New York. Those with boundless energy may want to head north up the Croix-Rousse hill and into the evocative quarter of **Les Traboules** (9), off the map, which offers endless possibilities to trabouler, as the sport of exploring the tiny passageways is known. As in Old Lyon, these architectural eccentricities are best seen with a specialized and highly detailed map. Don't get lost.

The **Fine Arts Museum** (Musée des Beaux-Arts) (10), facing Place des Terreaux, has one of the best collections in France. Originally a Benedictine nunnery, the building is somewhat seedy, although not without charm. Its many rooms contain major works covering just about the entire scope of Western art. It is open from 10:45 a.m. to 6 p.m., daily except on Tuesdays.

Continue on, following the map down the pedestrianized Rue de la République, to the **Printing and Banking Museum** (Musée de l'Imprimerie et de la Banque) (11), installed in a 15th-century mansion on Rue de la Poulaillerie. This is a splendid place to visit if the subject holds any interest to you.

The walking route now swings over to the banks of the Rhône, then leads past Place Bellecour (2) to two more attractions. The **Decorative Arts Museum** (12) and its next-door neighbor, the **Historical Museum of Textiles** (Musée Historique des Tissus), share the same admission ticket. As its name implies, the Decorative Arts Museum features exquisite room settings, primarily of the 18th century. If you like fabrics you will love the Textile Museum, which has the largest collection in the world. Both are open from 10 a.m. to noon and 2–5:30 p.m., daily except on Mondays and holidays. From here it is only a short walk back to Perrache station.

The Loire Valley

Few regions of France are as quietly seductive as the Loire Valley. This huge area, whose prime attractions begin about one hundred miles southwest of Paris and extend westward for another hundred, is among the most satisfying tourist destinations in the country. Drained by a broad, lazy river, the "Garden of France" offers a fine climate, bucolic scenery, unusual wines, a deep sense of history and, best of all, many of the very finest châteaux in the land. Some of these are massive fortifications dating from the Middle Ages, when the Loire Valley was a frequent battleground in the struggles between the French and the English. Others were built in more peaceful times and reflect the unparalleled luxury to which the Renaissance nobility had become accustomed.

Distance and the relative seclusion of many of its attractions do combine to make daytrips from Paris to this enchanting region somewhat of a problem. Fortunately, there are some notable exceptions. Angers, Blois and Amboise not only sit squarely on major rail lines and highways, but they also rate high among the most fascinating destinations in the area.

Those who would like to explore the valley in greater depth, visiting the fabulous châteaux of Chambord, Chenonceau, Azay-le-Rideau, Loches, Chinon, Saumur and others, should plan on stopping over for a few days. The most convenient base for daytrips in the region is Tours, from which daily bus excursions are offered to the famous sights. You could also rent a car there, which is certainly the ideal way to reach the more remote châteaux.

The Loire Valley is famous, in France at least, for its splendid variety of wines. Not particularly well known in North America, these charming country vintages provide fresh opportunities for new adventures in tasting. Some of the best are Vouvray, Anjou, Chinon, Muscadet and Pouilly-Fumé.

Also included in this section is that quintessential French provincial town, Bourges. Although it lies a bit outside the region itself, it shares many of its characteristics and is served by the same rail line.

Angers

Situated on the Maine river, just north of the Loire, the ancient capital of Anjou attracts visitors with its mighty fortress — one of the most impressive feudal structures in France — and fine cathedral. Angers is a fairly large and quite animated city which has managed to preserve much of its illustrious past despite heavy wartime damage.

Known to the Romans as *Juliomagus* and later conquered by the Normans, Angers had its true time of glory in the Middle Ages. Between the tenth and twelfth centuries its counts had acquired power exceeding that of even the kings of France. One of these Angevin rulers, Henri Plantagenet, became Henry II of England in 1154 and fathered both Richard the Lionhearted and bad King John — a story of intrigue that makes for fascinating reading. Henry's wife, Eleanor of Aquitaine, had previously been married to Louis VII of France, thus making her queen of both countries at different times. Another local ruler, born in Angers early in the 15th century, was Good King René, duke of Anjou, count of Provence and king of Sicily. This remarkable man, among the most brilliant thinkers of his age, was largely responsible for the artistic tradition of Angers which continues to this day.

GETTING THERE:

Trains leave Montparnasse station in Paris several times in the morning for Angers' St.-Laud station, a trip of about two and a half hours. Return service operates until early evening.

By car, Angers is 180 miles southwest of Paris. Take the A-10 and A-11 Autoroutes to Le Mans, then the N-23 into Angers.

WHEN TO GO:

Avoid coming on a Monday or major holiday, when the museums are closed. The castle is open every day except for a few major holidays.

Within the Castle Grounds

FOOD AND DRINK:

Angers has an excellent selection of restaurants and cafés. Some good choices, in the order you will pass or come close to them on the walking route, are:

Plantagenets (8 Place de la Gare, in the Hôtel France, opposite the train station) $$

Le Vert d'Eau (9 Blvd. Gaston Dumesnil, just across the river from the castle) Classic cuisine, specializes in Loire wines. $$

Le Toussaint (7 Rue Toussaint, near the rear of the cathedral) Rates one Michelin star. Reservations suggested, phone 41-87-46-20. $$

Le Logis (17 Rue St.-Laud, near the Hôtel Pincé) Given one Michelin star, noted for seafood. $$

Petit St.-Germain (3 Rue St.-Laud, near the Hôtel Pincé) $$

Les Gauottes (corner of Rue des Poëliers and Rue du Mail, two blocks behind the Hôtel Pincé) Crêpes. $

Le Quéré (9 Place du Ralliement, near the Hôtel Pincé) $$

L'Entr'acte (9 Rue Louis de Romain, near the Hôtel Pincé) $$

TOURIST INFORMATION:

The tourist information office, phone 41-88-69-93, is on Place Prés. Kennedy opposite the castle — with a branch, phone 41-87-72-50, across from the train station.

SUGGESTED TOUR:

Leave the Angers St.-Laud **train station** (1) and head straight for the **Castle** (*Château*) (2), passing both branches of the tourist office along the way. The forbidding bastion facing you was built in the 13th century by Louis IX, known to history as Saint Louis for his famous sense of moral authority. Previous fortresses had existed on the same site since 851; a 12th-century structure having been used by the Plantagenets. The thick curtain wall, over a half-mile in circumference, links seventeen massive towers along a deep dry moat in which deer now roam.

With a design based on the crusaders' castles in the Holy Land, this citadel was among the most powerful in the kingdom, and was never successfully taken by assault. It came close to being destroyed in the 16th-century Wars of Religion, however, not by attack but by an order from Henri III to dismantle the fortress before it could fall into enemy hands. Fortunately for us, the demolition went very slowly and before much damage was done peace had returned and the king was dead.

Cross the drawbridge and enter the castle grounds. The most famous sight here, well worth the journey in itself, is the monumental **Apocalypse Tapestry**, housed in a specially built structure. This incomparable 14th-century series of wall hangings present a shattering representation of the text of Saint John in the Book of Revelations. Be sure to allow enough time to carefully study the seventy pieces which survived out of the original ninety. An explanation in English will be loaned to you at the door, or you can purchase an illustrated booklet.

More outstanding medieval tapestries are displayed in the **Logis Royal** which, together with the superb **Chapel**, can be seen on guided tours included in the castle admission. The Logis du Gouverneur, beyond the gardens, also exhibits some of this art. A climb to the top of the highest tower, facing the river, reveals a magnificent panorama of the city. From here it is easy to understand why the fortress was so impregnable. A walk around the ramparts and through the gardens will complete your visit. The castle is open every day except for a few major holidays. Its hours are from 9:30 a.m. to noon and 2–6 p.m. between Palm Sunday and the end of June; from 9:30 a.m. to 6:30 p.m. from July through September; and from 9:30 a.m. to noon and 2–5:30

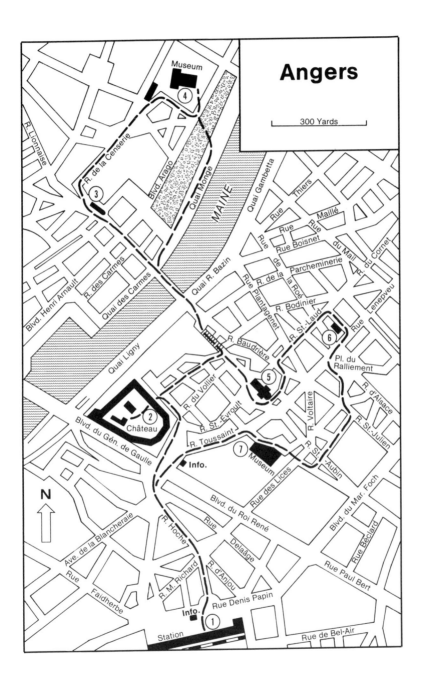

Angers

300 Yards

Museum

④

R. Lionnaise

R. de la Censerie

R. Arago

Quai Monge

MAINE

Quai Gambetta

③

Thiers

Maillé

Rue

Rue

du Mail

du Cornet

Rue

Rue Boisnet

Rue de la

R. des Carmes

Blvd. Henri Arnault

Quai des Carmes

Quai R. Bazin

Rue Plantagenet

Parcheminerie

R. de la Roe

R. Bodinier

Lenepveu

Rue

Quai Ligny

R. Baudrière

R. St.-Laud

⑥

Pl. du
Ralliement

R. d'Alsace

R. du Vollier

⑤

R. St.-Julien

Château

②

R. St.-Évroult

R. Voltaire

Blvd. du Gén. de Gaulle

R. Toussaint

R. St

⑦ Museum

R. St.-Aubin

Info.

N

Rue des Lices

Blvd. du Mar. Foch

Ave. de la Blancheraie

R. Hoche

Rue

Blvd. du Roi René

Delaâge

Rue Béclard

Rue

Faidherbe

R. M. Richard

R. d'Anjou

Rue Paul Bert

Info.

Rue Denis Papin

①

Station

Rue de Bel-Air

p.m. the rest of the year.

Now follow the map across the river and into the colorful old quarter called La Doutre, noted for its ancient half-timbered houses. Turn right at the 12th-century **Church of La Trinité** (3) and continue on to the former **Hospital of St.-Jean** (4). Take a look at the elaborate 12th-century granary, whose cellars have some old wine presses, then enter the ancient hospital. Founded in 1175 by Henry II of England as part of his penance for the murder of Thomas à Becket, it cared for the sick until 1865. The very lovely interior now houses the **Jean Lurçat Museum**, displaying a huge modern ten-piece tapestry completed by Lurçat in 1966. You can also see the old dispensary, a medieval chapel, and the delightful 12th-century cloister. The museum is open daily except on Mondays and major holidays; from 10 a.m. to noon and 2–6 p.m.

The route now leads back across the river to the **Cathedral of St-Maurice** (5). Dating from the 12th and 13th centuries, its unusual design is embellished with a peculiar central tower. Biblical figures decorate the splendid doorway, which opens into a very wide nave illuminated by stained-glass windows from the 12th century to modern times. The treasury, to the left as you enter, has some interesting artifacts including a Roman bathtub used as a baptismal font.

Continue on to the **Hôtel Pincé** (6), a Renaissance mansion now used as the **Turpin de Crissé Museum**. The collections inside are rather eclectic but focus mainly on Oriental works, especially Japanese Ukiyo-é. Visits may be made from 10 a.m. to noon and 2–6 p.m., daily except on Mondays and major holidays.

One other major attraction remains before returning to the train station. This is the **Fine Arts Museum** (*Musée des Beaux-Arts*) in the **Logis Barrault** (7), an impressive 15th-century palace. Medieval and Renaissance items are displayed along with a fine collection of paintings by such artists as Boucher, Tiepolo, Fragonard, David, Géricault, Ingres and Millet. The most outstanding exhibits, however, are the oversized plaster casts by the locally-born 19th-century sculptor David d'Angers. The museum is open daily except on Mondays and holidays; from 10 a.m. to noon and 2–6 p.m.

Amboise

Rising majestically above the banks of the Loire, the magnificent château of Amboise totally dominates its attractive little town. A castle has stood on this rocky spur, guarding the strategic bridgehead since Gallo-Roman times, when it was known as *Ambacia*. The present structure, however, is a product of the 15th century and incorporates some of the earliest examples of Renaissance architecture in France. Charles VIII, who was born and raised at Amboise, had invaded Italy in 1494. While there, he became captivated by the new Italian style and brought some of its craftsmen back with him to finish off his favorite château.

The real effect of the Renaissance came with the succession to the throne of François I in 1515. This outstanding king also spent his childhood at Amboise and continued residence there during the first years of his reign. It was he who invited Leonardo da Vinci to France, installing him in a luxurious home just blocks from the château, where the great artist and inventor spent the last years of his life.

One of the most notorious carnages in French history occurred at Amboise in 1560 when Protestant militants plotted to capture the young king, François II, to demand their religious freedom. The coup was defeated and all involved were hideously executed, with corpses decorating the château and town for weeks afterward. After that, Amboise was rarely used except as a prison until the 19th century, when Louis-Philippe, the "Citizen King," lived there on occasion.

Amboise makes a good alternative base for visits to the famous châteaux of the Loire which lie beyond daytrip range of Paris. Ask at the tourist office about bus trips to these.

GETTING THERE:

Trains leave Austerlitz station in Paris in the morning for Amboise, a trip of under two and a half hours. Be careful to get on the right car as some trains split en route. Return service operates until early evening. A change at Orléans or Blois might be necessary.

By car, take the A-10 Autoroute past Blois, then the D-31 into Amboise. The total distance from Paris is 137 miles.

WHEN TO GO:

Amboise may be visited at any time. The Clos Lucé is closed in January and the Postal Museum on Tuesdays and some holidays.

FOOD AND DRINK:

Being a popular tourist center, the town has quite a few restaurants and cafés. Some of the better choices are:

> **Le Monseigneur** (12 Quai Charles Guinot, on the river beneath the castle) $$

> **Lion d'Or** (17 Quai Charles Guinot, on the river beneath the castle) An inn. $$

> **Du Parc** (8 Rue Leonardo de Vinci, between Clos Lucé and the Postal Museum) An inn. $$

> **Auberge du Mail** (32 Quai du Gén. de Gaulle, near St.-Denis Church) $$

> **La Brèche** (25 Rue Jules Ferry, near the train station) $

TOURIST INFORMATION:

A tourist information office, phone 47-57-09-28, is located on the Quai du Général de Gaulle, near the bridge.

SUGGESTED TOUR:

Leave the **train station** (1) and follow the map across the Loire to the **Château** (2), perched dramatically above the river and town. You may prefer to have lunch before visiting any of the sights as they are closed between noon and 2 p.m. A long ramp leads up to the castle grounds. Climb this and join one of the frequent guided tours, which are given in French with a printed English translation provided. During its time of glory the château was considerably larger than it is today, much of it having been demolished in the early 19th century for lack of maintenance funds. Some of the best parts, however, remained intact and have been beautifully restored to the delight of today's visitors.

The tour begins with the exquisite **Chapel of St.-Hubert**, dedicated to the patron saint of huntsmen. Begun in 1491, shortly before Charles VIII acquired his passion for the Renaissance, it is a triumph of the Flamboyant Gothic style. What are thought to be the bones of Leonardo da Vinci are buried here, under a slab in the north transept.

Following this you will enter the **King's Apartments** (*Logis du Roi*), consisting of two wings, one Gothic and the other Renaissance. These are the only major buildings of any size left at the castle. Their interiors are splendidly decorated in a variety of period styles, ranging from the 15th through the 19th centuries. From the fascinating **Minimes Tower** with its spiral equestrian ramp there is a stunning view up and down the Loire valley.

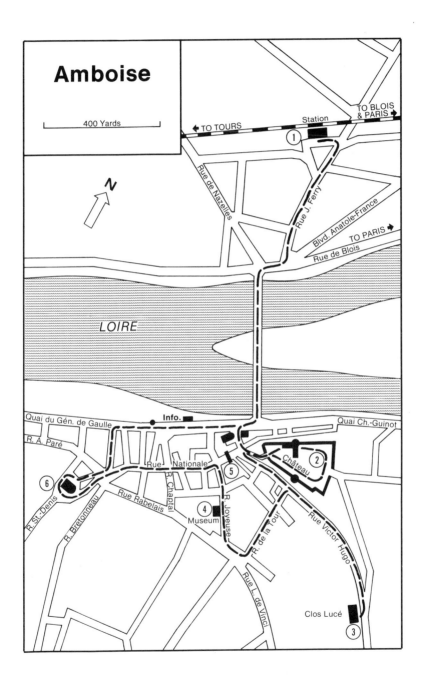

Amboise

400 Yards

N

TO TOURS → | Station | ← TO BLOIS & PARIS

1

Rue de Nazelles

Rue J. Ferry

Blvd. Anatole-France

TO PARIS →

Rue de Blois

LOIRE

Quai du Gén. de Gaulle | Info. | Quai Ch.-Guinot

R. A. Paré

Rue Nationale

Château

2

R. St.-Denis

R. Bretonneau

Rue Rabelais

R. Chaptal

5

6

4
Museum

R. Joyeuse

R. de la Tour

Rue Victor Hugo

Rue L. de Vinci

Clos Lucé

3

The Château and the Loire from the Gardens

Don't miss taking a stroll through the **gardens** behind the château after the guided tour has ended. The château is open every day, from 9 a.m. to noon and 2–6:30 p.m., closing an hour earlier in winter.

A ten-minute walk along Rue Victor Hugo leads to **Clos Lucé** (3). This was the home of Leonardo da Vinci, that visionary genius of the Renaissance, from 1516 until his death three years later. Prior to that it was a residence of Anne of Brittany, the wife of King Charles VIII. The manor house has marvelous period furnishings, worth a visit in themselves, but the main interest lies in the many models of his inventions, built by IBM from Leonardo's original plans. Frequent guided tours, with a printed English translation, are conducted daily between 9 a.m. and noon and from 2–6 p.m. During the summer the hours are from 9 a.m. to 7 p.m. The house is closed on Christmas and during the month of January.

Return along Rue Victor Hugo and follow the map to the **Postal Museum** (4). Located in an elegant 16th-century mansion, the museum features an intriguing exhibition of the history of transportation from horse-drawn coaches to modern airlines. There are also, of course, many rare stamps to be seen, along with old manuscripts and engravings. The museum is open from 9:30 a.m. to noon and 2–6:30 p.m., closing at 5 during the winter season. It is closed on Tuesdays and some holidays.

Some of Leonardo's Inventions at Clos Lucé

Continue on to the 15th-century **Clock Tower** *(Beffroi)* (5), a picturesque structure built by Charles VIII on earlier foundations. Now follow the pedestrians-only Rue Nationale to the **Church of St.-Denis** (6). This 12th-century example of the Romanesque style was built on the site of a Roman temple. Step inside for a look at some exceptional works of art including a fine *Pietà* and an astonishingly realistic sculpture of a drowned woman.

Returning via Quai du Général de Gaulle you will pass an outstanding modern fountain designed by Max Ernst, the tourist information office, the 15th-century Church of St-Florentin, and the 16th-century Town Hall.

Blois

While certainly not the loveliest château of the Loire, Blois may well prove to be the most interesting. Often called the "Versailles of the Renaissance" — and for a crucial time virtually the capital of France — it exudes a deep sense of history exceeding even that of Angers or Amboise.

Although a castle had stood there since feudal times, it was not until the end of the 15th century that Blois became a royal residence. The first king to move in was Louis XII, in 1498, who promptly added a wing in the Late Gothic style. Another large section, in the new Renaissance style, was built by his successor François I. This flamboyant king later went on to greater architectural triumphs, notably the châteaux of Fontainebleau and Chambord, but he continued to use Blois as a waystop in an endless pursuit of courtly pleasure. Royalty remained in residence there until the Valois line died out in 1589 with the assassination of the miserable Henri III.

After that, the château was used by Louis XIII as a place to get rid of troublesome members of his family. The first to go was his mother, Marie de Medici, who was banished to Blois in 1617 but later managed to escape. He then gave it to his scheming brother, Gaston d'Orléans, to keep him out of political mischief. As did the previous owners, Gaston added a wing, thus completing the château you see today.

The town of Blois has several other nice attractions of its own, including a picturesque old quarter near the river. The name, incidentally, is pronounced "Blwah." It also makes a convenient overnight base for visits to those splendid châteaux which unfortunately lie beyond reasonable daytrip range of Paris, most notably Chambord and Chenonceau. You can ask at the tourist office about bus excursions to these, or rent a car and see them on your own.

GETTING THERE:

Trains for Blois depart Austerlitz station in Paris several times in the morning. The run takes a bit under two hours, with return service until early evening. Be sure to get on the right car as some trains split en route.

By car, Blois is 112 miles from Paris via the A-10 Autoroute.

The François I Wing of the Château

WHEN TO GO:

The Château of Blois is open every day, but is less crowded during the week. Good weather will make the trip much more enjoyable.

FOOD AND DRINK:

There are quite a few restaurants and cafés along the walking route, of which some choice selections are:

> **Hostellerie de la Loire** (8 Rue Mar. de Lattre de Tassigny, near the bridge) An inn. $$

> **La Péniche** (Promenade du Mail, along the river, beyond the cathedral)   On a moored floating barge, specializes in seafood. $$

> **La Taupinère** (52 Rue de la Foulérie, in the Old Town below the cathedral) Crêperie. $

> **Le Monarque** (61 Rue Porte Chartraine, two blocks northwest from the top of the Papin steps) $

> **Viennois** (5 Quai Amédée Contant, just across the bridge) $

TOURIST INFORMATION:

The tourist information office is located at 3 Ave. Jean Laigret, between the train station and the château. You can call them at 54-74-06-49.

SUGGESTED TOUR:

Leave the **train station** (1) and follow Ave. Jean Laigret past the tourist office to **Place Victor Hugo** (2). Before climbing the ramp to the château it would be a good idea to check your watch and determine whether you have enough time — well over an hour — to enjoy it properly before lunch, or whether to see some other sights and eat first. The château is open daily from 9 a.m. to 6:30 p.m. between June 1st and August 31st. From mid-March until May 31st and during the month of September its hours are 9 a.m. to noon and 2–6:30 p.m.; and from October 1st until mid-March they are 9 a.m. to noon and 2–5 p.m. The walking route is quite short so you can always return to the château later.

The **Château of Blois** (3), overlooking the town and the Loire river, is a dramatic study in the evolution of French architecture from the Middle Ages to the Neo-Classical period. After the Valois line of kings died out in the late 16th century it ceased to be a royal residence and was used during Napoleon's time as an army barracks. What you see today is the result of a highly romanticized mid-19th-century restoration, perhaps more theatrical than accurate, but certainly fun to visit.

Pass through the doorway under the equestrian statue of Louis XII and enter the château. You are now in the **Louis XII wing**, built between 1498 and 1503. Purchase your ticket and decide whether to take a guided tour or just wander around on your own, which is entirely practical as there are printed explanations of everything in English.

Stepping into the inner courtyard you will see the famous open staircase of the **François I wing**, dating from 1515–1524. Climb this to the first floor and go in. The route through this wing is well laid out, taking you eventually to the second floor, where a notorious assassination took place in 1588. Henri III, a weak and effeminate king, was able to remain in office only as long as it suited a powerful duke, Henri de Guise, Lieutenant-General of the kingdom and leader of the extremist Catholics. Guise threatened Henri's rule by forcing a meeting of the States-General at the château. While there, the king summoned him to a private meeting, on the way to which he was brutally murdered by twenty of the king's devoted minions. He died at the foot of the royal bed while the cowering Henri looked on through a peephole. The next

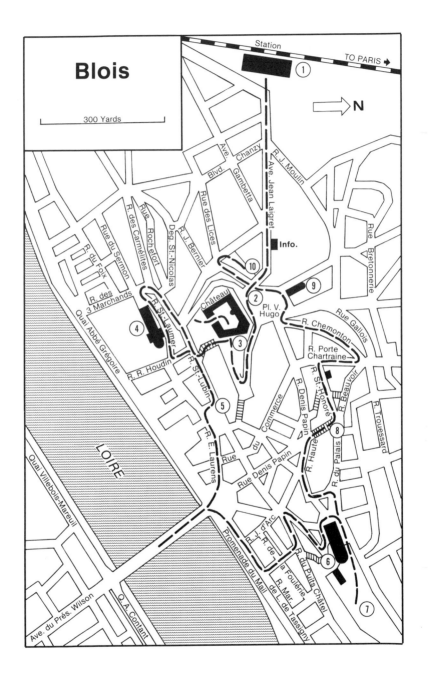

Blois

300 Yards

Station
TO PARIS →

N

1

TO PARIS →

Ave. Chanzy
Blvd. Gambetta
Rue des Lices
Ave. Jean Laigret
R. J. Moulin
Rue Bretonnerie

Rue Rochefort
Rue des Carmélites
R. du Foix
Rue du Sermon
Deg. St-Nicolas
R. J. Bernier

Info.

10

R. des 3 Marchands

R. St-Laumer

Château

2

9

Rue Gallois

4

3

Pl. V. Hugo

R. Chemonton

R. R. Houdin

R. St-Lubin

5

R. Porte Chartraine

R. St-Honoré
R. Denis Papin
R. Beauvoir
R. Trouessard

Quai Abbé Grégoire

LOIRE

R. E. Laurens

Rue du Commerce

R. Haute

8

R. du Palais

Rue Denis Papin

Quai Villebois-Mareuil

R. J.: R. de la Foulerie

R. d'Arc

R. du Puits Châtel

6

R. Mar. de L. de Tassigny

Promenade du Mail

7

Ave. du Prés. Wilson

Q. A. Contant

day the king had the duke's brother, Cardinal de Lorraine, killed as well. But justice was to come. Within days, the king's scheming mother, Catherine de Medici, was dead and Henri III himself fell to an assassin's knife eight months later. He was the last of the Valois line.

The 13th-century **Salle des États**, the oldest surviving part of the château, joins the François I and Louis XII wings together. Take a look inside, then visit the adjacent archaeological museum and the **Fine Arts Museum** in the Louis XII wing.

At the far end of the courtyard stands the 17th-century **Gaston d'Orléans wing**, a Neo-Classical structure designed by François Mansart. Other interesting buildings are the **Charles d'Orléans Gallery** and the **Chapel of St.-Calais**, both dating from the late 15th century. Amble over to the 13th-century **Tour de Foix**, part of the old feudal walls, which offers a splendid panorama of the town.

Leave the château and follow the map down to the lovely **Church of St.-Nicolas** (4), whose interior merits a visit. Built in the 12th century as part of an abbey which was destroyed during the 16th-century Wars of Religion, it is noted for its harmonious blend of Romanesque and Gothic elements.

Continue on to **Place Louis XII** (5), with its Flamboyant Gothic fountain, passing some picturesque old houses on Rue St.-Lubin along the way. Now cut down to the river and stroll out on the elegant 18th-century bridge for a gorgeous view of the town and its château.

Return to the quay and follow the map through a delightful part of old Blois. Rue du Puits-Châtel has two particularly attractive houses at numbers 7 and 5, both dating from the time of Louis XII. When you come to Place Ave-Maria look to your left down Rue Fontaine des Élus, where the noteworthy Hôtel de Jassaud stands at number 5. Now turn hard right and climb Rue des Papegaults. Passing another 16th-century house, the Hôtel de Belot at number 10, this charming street leads to the Petits-Degrés-St.-Louis, which takes you uphill to Place St.-Louis.

The **Cathedral of St.-Louis** (6), facing you, was largely rebuilt in the 17th century. Although the church itself is not particularly outstanding, its 10th-century **Crypt of St.-Solenne** certainly is. Entry to this is from the side of the altar.

Continue around to the rear of the Town Hall, reached via a gate next to the cathedral. The **park** (7) beyond this commands an excellent vantage point for views of the Loire valley.

Now thread your way through a maze of narrow streets lined

Street Scene near the Cathedral of St.-Louis

with medieval and Renaissance houses, many of which are half-timbered. Follow the map up the Denis Papin stairs to the **statue of Denis Papin** (8), a local lad of the 17th century who discovered many of the mysteries of steam power. He is shown holding his greatest invention, an early pressure cooker.

Turn left on Rue St.-Honoré past the Hôtel d'Alluye, a splendid Renaissance mansion whose double-galleried courtyard can be seen during office hours. Continue on Rue Porte Chartraine and return on Rue Chemonton, noting the fine Hôtel de Guise at number 8. This returns you to Place Victor Hugo (2).

If you have a bit more time you may be interested in visiting the 17th-century **Church of St.-Vincent-de-Paul** (9) and, especially, the beautiful **Jardin du Roi** (10), all that remains of the château gardens which once extended all the way to the train station. From here you will get a magnificent close-up view of the château and a last glimpse of Blois before returning to Paris.

Bourges

Located in the very heartland of France, Bourges is an ancient and colorful town whose winding, cobbled streets contain some of the very best medieval architecture anywhere. Although relatively unknown to foreign tourists, it makes an excellent daytrip destination for seasoned travelers looking for a delightful new experience.

Originally populated by Gauls, Bourges fell to Caesar's legions in 52 B.C. and became the Roman town of *Avaricum*. Since A.D. 250 it was ruled by archbishops. Later, as the capital of Aquitaine, it passed into the hands of a succession of counts who in 1101 sold it to Philip I, king of France. During the 14th century, Jean, duke of Berry and son of King John the Good, made Bourges the seat of his duchy. For a while the town became a flourishing center of the arts, a role which was enhanced by the immensely wealthy Jacques Coeur whose palace there is probably the best example of a medieval town mansion to be found in France.

During the Hundred Years War, Charles VII, cynically referred to by the English as the "King of Bourges," sat in that beleaguered city and slowly gathered the strength, aided by Joan of Arc, which enabled him to drive the English out. His son, Louis XI, born in Bourges, was a brilliant schemer who overcame the feudal system and began development of the modern state. He also founded a university there which became a hotbed of the Reformation, thus plunging Bourges into the Wars of Religion, a catastrophe from which it never recovered.

In the ensuing centuries, Bourges fell into obscurity, far too poor to rebuild its narrow streets and ancient façades. Not until modern times did its economy revive, with industry locating outside the town proper. This newly found prosperity in the setting of a basically unchanged medieval town makes Bourges a fascinating place to visit.

GETTING THERE:

Trains leave Austerlitz station in Paris several times in the morning for Bourges. Some of these may require a change at Vierzon. Be careful to board the right car as some trains split en route. The fastest direct route takes a bit under two and a half hours. Return trains run until early evening.

By car, take the A-10 Autoroute to Orléans, then the N-20 to Vierzon followed by the N-76 into Bourges. The distance from Paris is 147 miles.

WHEN TO GO:

Avoid going to Bourges on a Tuesday, when several of its best attractions are closed. The trip can be made in any season as the old part of town is quite small and most of your time will be spent indoors.

FOOD AND DRINK:

The cooking in this region of farmland tends to be simple and wholesome. Some good restaurant choices, in the order that you will pass or come close to them along the walking route, are:

Hostellerie du Grand Argentier (9 Rue Parerie, near the Church of Notre-Dame) $$

Au Sénat (8 Rue de la Poissonnerie, just off Place Gordaine) $

Le D'Artagnan (19 Place Séraucourt, four blocks south of the cathedral) In a hotel. $

Central et Angleterre (1 Place Quatre Piliers, one block south of the palace) In a hotel. $$

Jacques Coeur (3 Place Jacques Coeur, next to the palace) The traditional favorite. $$$

La Marée (14 Rue Prinal, two blocks west of the palace) $

Ile d'Or (39 Blvd. de Juranville, near Rue Gambon) $$$

TOURIST INFORMATION:

The tourist information office, phone 48-24-75-33, is located on Rue Moyenne, near the front of the cathedral.

SUGGESTED TOUR:

Leave the **train station** (1) and follow the map to the **Church of Notre-Dame** (2), whose brooding atmosphere encompasses a wide variety of styles. Built in the early 15th century, it was badly damaged during the great fire of 1487 which consumed much of Bourges. Reconstruction began in 1520, with considerable later additions having been made.

Take a look down Rue Pellevoysin, which has some fine old houses, many of them half-timbered. The most noted of these is the **Maison de Pellevoysin** at number 17, built of stone in the 15th century. Continue on Rue Mirebeau and take the passageway through to Rue Branly, leading to the **Hôtel des Échevins** (3). This 15th-century guildhall features a marvelous octagonal stair tower of unusual design. Return on Rue Branly to the picturesque Place Gordaine, lined with 15th- and 16th-century gabled houses.

The **Hôtel Lallemant** (4), just a few steps away on Rue Bourbonnoux, is an outstanding 15th-century mansion built for a wealthy cloth merchant. Heavily altered during the 17th century in the Renaissance style, it is now a museum of decorative art. Step inside to admire the richly ornamented rooms, antique furniture and various *objets d'art*.

Now follow the map past the Grange aux Dimes, a 13th-century tithe barn on Rue Molière, to the **Cathedral of St.-Étienne** (5). The major attraction of Bourges, this is one of the very finest Gothic structures in France. Erected at the same time as the great cathedral at Chartres, it differs greatly in both layout and concept. Construction began around 1192 as a replacement for a Romanesque basilica which occupied the site. The crypt, which was built first, is like no other. Never intended to house tombs or relics, it is basically a substructure supporting the cathedral over uneven ground. Above this the choir was erected and slowly the new church grew toward the west, surrounding the old building as work progressed. It was consecrated in 1324.

Notice, as you stand in the square facing the cathedral, the five curiously asymmetrical portals which pierce its west front. Take a few moments to examine the magnificent **carvings** depicting the Last Judgement above the central doorway — one of the great masterpieces of Gothic art. To the left, the **north tower** rises to a height of 213 feet, which can be climbed on foot for a splendid view. The south tower, never completed, is supported by a very peculiar buttress.

Inside, the **stained-glass windows** — especially those above the chancel at the east end — are among the best to be found in France and cover a period from the early Gothic to the Renaissance. Be sure to visit the **crypt**, the entrance to which is by the north doorway. Near the reclining figure of Jean, duke of Berry, is a stairway leading down to the remains of an earlier 9th-century church. The cathedral closes between noon and 2 p.m. every day.

Stroll over to the 17th-century City Hall (*Hôtel de Ville*), once the archbishop's palace. The lovely **gardens** (*Jardins de l'Archevêché*) (6) adjacent to this, attributed to Le Nôtre, offer an excellent view of the cathedral's east end as well as a welcome spot to relax.

Now follow the map past the tourist information office to the **Palace of Jacques Coeur** (7), surely one of the most splendid private buildings of the Middle Ages. It was begun in 1443 and completed, at fabulous cost, nearly ten years later for Charles

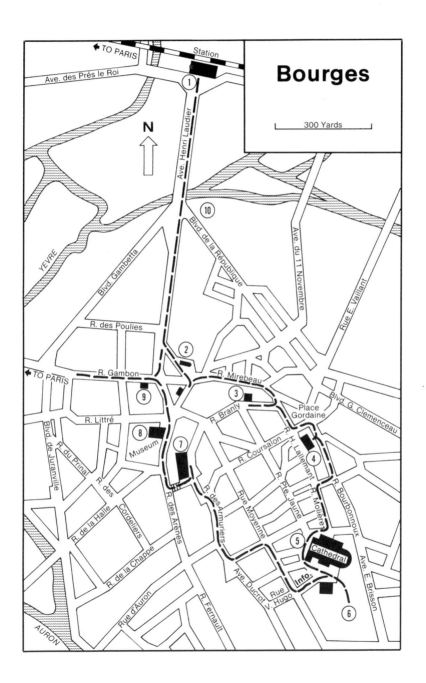

Bourges

300 Yards

TO PARIS

Station

Ave. des Prés le Roi

① c

N

Ave. Henri Laudier

YEVRE

Blvd Gambetta

⑩

Blvd. de la République

Ave. du 11 Novembre

Rue E. Vaillant

R. des Poulies

②

TO PARIS

R. Gambon

R. Mirebeau

③

Place Gordaine

Blvd. G. Clemenceau

⑨

R. Littré

⑧ Museum

⑦

R. Branly

R. Coursalon

R. H. Lallemant

④

R. Molière

R. Bourbonnoux

Blvd. de Juranville

R. du Prinal

R. des Cordeliers

R. de la Halle

R. des Arènes

R. des Armuriers

Rue Moyenne

R. Pte Jaune

Ave. E. Brisson

R. de la Chappe

⑤ Cathedral

Info.

Ave. Ducrot

Rue V. Hugo

⑥

Rue d'Auron

R. Fernault

AURON

The Palace of Jacques Coeur

VII's finance minister, a gifted merchant and banker named Jacques Coeur. Alas, poor Jacques never got to enjoy his mansion as he fell from grace in 1451 and was permanently exiled. In 1457 the palace was returned to his heirs and later used by the city as a *Palais de Justice*. Now restored to original condition, its marvelously sumptuous interior may be seen on guided tours. The palace is open from 9–11:15 a.m. and 2–5:15 p.m. between Easter and October, and from 10–11:15 a.m. and 2–4:15 p.m. the rest of the year, but closed on Tuesdays. Don't miss seeing this.

Continue on, descending the steps next to the palace and go into the gardens of Place Berry. From here you can see how the west wall of the mansion was built on top of the original Roman town walls. A short stroll down Rue des Arènes brings you to the **Hôtel Cujas** (8), an elegant mansion built around 1515 for a wealthy merchant and later the residence of Jacques Cujas, a noted jurist. It now houses the **Musée du Berry**, featuring an archaeological exhibition of artifacts dating from the Roman period back to prehistoric times. Displays of local country life from more recent centuries occupy the first floor, while the rest

A Street Scene near Place Gordaine

of the museum is given over to the fine arts. Visits may be made from 10 a.m. to noon and 2–6 p.m., daily except on Tuesdays.

Cross Place Planchat and turn left onto Rue Gambon. At number 19 stands the ornate **Maison de la Reine Blanche** (9), a 16th-century wooden house decorated with religious motifs. Farther on, at number 32, there is the Hôtel Dieu with its elaborate Renaissance doorway. Return to Place de Mirepied and continue down Avenue Jean Jaurès past the beautiful **Prés-Fichaux Gardens** (10), where you can spend some delightful moments before returning to the station.

Section VI

Daytrips in

Provence

Going to Provence is like stepping into a different world, one far removed from Paris and the north. This is a Mediterranean region with a distinctly Latin culture reflecting its ancient Roman heritage. It is also a sun-drenched land whose dazzling clarity was made famous by such painters as Van Gogh and Cézanne. Few areas of Europe — or of the world — can begin to match its broad variety of intriguing sights and delicious experiences.

The five destinations in this section are linked by frequent rail service and excellent highways. Any of them could be used as a base for exploring the others without having to change hotels. In terms of convenience, Marseille is the best situated for this purpose since it lies at the hub of major transportation routes. Those who prefer to avoid large cities will find that Arles or Avignon also make excellent bases, with Aix-en-Provence and Nîmes a little less handy, especially for rail travelers.

One-day bus excursions to other attractions in Provence, including the hauntingly beautiful Camargue, mysterious Les Baux, the Roman relics of Orange and the Pont du Gard, or the strange walled town of Aigues-Mortes are available from the base towns. Ask at the local tourist office for current information and schedules. Those with cars can easily visit several of these in one day. Descriptions are not included in this book since these places are a bit difficult to reach by regular public transportation and, being quite small, do not really lend themselves to structured walking tours.

Although it is technically a part of Provence, the Riviera is in a realm of its own, one thoroughly covered in the next section beginning on page 195.

Marseille

No one ever accused Marseille of being charming or quaint, or even lovely, but it certainly is unique — and more than a little intriguing. This brash, noisy, teeming metropolis throbs with such a vitality that to ignore it would be to miss out on a very colorful aspect of Mediterranean life.

Founded around 600 B.C. by Greek colonists from Phocea in Asia Minor, Marseille is the oldest city in France. Depending on how you count heads, it is also the second largest. Then known as *Massalia,* it developed a network of satellite towns in Nice, Antibes, Arles and other places. Threatened by native tribes, the port later turned to Rome for defense and prospered for centuries afterwards. A major setback came in 49 B.C. when it backed Pompey in his dispute with Julius Caesar. The victorious Caesar got his revenge by shifting trade to Arles, but eventually the 11th-century Crusades brought about an economic resurgence.

Although it became a part of France in 1482, Marseille has always been more a Mediterranean than a French city, caring little for Paris and its kings. It enthusiastically joined the Revolution in 1789, and in 1792 its volunteers sang a new patriotic song with such lusty fervor that the tune became known as *La Marseillaise,* the French national anthem. Commercial development during the 19th century, especially the opening of the Suez Canal in 1869, greatly expanded the city into the metropolis it is today.

With all that history, it is amazing how little of the past remains. The *Marseillais* have never been much interested in antiquity, preferring to focus their energies on trade and the future. For this reason Marseille is more a city to relish for its spicy flavor than for the few bona-fide sights it offers.

Is Marseille really as wicked as its reputation suggests? No, despite the open prostitution that thrives between the Old Port and the opera, the drunken sailors and sleazy dives off La Canebière, it is no longer the drug capital of the world — if it ever was. There are, however, a few obvious areas which are best avoided at night.

With its superb transportation facilities and many hotels, Marseille is the most convenient base for daytrips throughout

Provence. And it has a few other drawing cards as well, such as the best seafood restaurants in Europe and a truly spectacular setting on steep hills spilling down to the Old Port and the Mediterranean.

GETTING THERE:

Trains connect Marseille's St. Charles station with other towns in Provence at fairly frequent intervals. Average running times are: Aix-en-Provence—32 minutes, Arles—45 minutes, Avignon—1 hour (*TGV service also available*), and Nîmes—1 hour and 15 minutes. For more details consult the chapters for those specific towns. There are also convenient schedules to both the Riviera and Paris, the latter being served by speedy TGVs (*under five hours*) as well as conventional trains.

By car, Marseille is 19 miles from Aix-en-Provence, 57 miles from Arles, 62 miles from Avignon and 75 miles from Nîmes. Recommended routes are given in the chapters dealing with those towns.

GETTING AROUND:

You may want to make use of the magnificent new **Métro** (subway) or bus service during your exploration of Marseille. Both use the same tickets, sold singly or in a discounted *carnet* package of six. A ticket is valid for one continuous journey, which may combine both the métro and bus, for a period of 70 minutes after cancellation on first boarding the bus or entering the subway station. The tourist office can supply you with a free map of the system. Rail travelers making Marseille their base will be happy to know that both métro lines (and several bus routes) stop at St. Charles station.

WHEN TO GO:

Marseille may be visited at any time, although good weather will make the suggested tour much more enjoyable. Most of the museums are closed on Tuesdays and on Wednesday mornings.

FOOD AND DRINK:

Bouillabaisse, a fish and seafood stew flavored with saffron, garlic, cayenne and other tasty ingredients, is the classic dish of Marseille — a treat not to be missed by seafood fanciers. As befits one of the world's greatest ports, the city has a wide selection of inexpensive foreign restaurants, particularly North African, Indian and Vietnamese. Some of the more traditional restaurants, in the order that you will pass or come close to them along the suggested walking route, are:

Georges Mavro (2 La Canebière, near the Old Port) $$$

Brasserie New York Vieux Port   (7 Quai des Belges) Noted for its seafood. $$

Piment Rouge   (20 Rue Beauvau, near the opera and the Quai des Belges) $$

Miramar   (12 Quai du Port, near the Quai des Belges) Noted for seafood. $$

Chez Caruso   (158 Quai du Port, near the Town Hall) Italian cuisine. $$

Le Chaudron Provençal   (48 Rue Caisserie, near the Roman Docks Museum in the old town) $$

L'Oursinade   (Rue Neuve St.-Martin, in the Hôtel Frantel overlooking the archaeological gardens) $$$

Chez Antoine   (35 Rue Musée, two blocks south of La Canebière) Italian cuisine. $$

La Charpenterie   (22 Rue Paix, near Quai de Rive Neuve and Quai des Belges) $$

Maurice Brun   (18 Quai de Rive Neuve, well hidden near the Old Port) A traditional dining experience with no menu but a lot of seafood to sample. Reservations are needed, phone 91-33-35-38. $$$

Les Trois Forts   (In the Hôtel Sofitel, 36 Blvd. Charles Livon, near the Jardin du Pharo and Fort St.-Nicolas) $$$

Michel   (6 Rue des Catalans, near the Jardin du Pharo, facing the sea) Awarded one Michelin star, famous for its seafood. $$$

Calypso   (3 Rue des Catalans, as above)   Rates one Michelin star, noted seafood place. $$$

TOURIST INFORMATION:

The tourist information office, phone 91-54-91-11, is located at the foot of La Canebière, near the Old Port. They can arrange for hotel reservations and tours, as well as provide you with maps and transit information.

SUGGESTED TOUR:

Rail travelers using another base in Provence will begin their tour at **St. Charles station** (1), oddly located at the top of a hill. This marvelous old structure has recently been completely restored, with modern underground levels, while the exterior retains all of its considerable 19th-century charm. Walk outside for a panoramic view across the harbor, then descend the steps to Blvd. d'Athènes and walk downhill to **La Canebière**. Long known to foreign sailors as "The Can o' Beer," this once-glamorous main street of Marseille has faded somewhat in recent years, but its vitality remains as alive as ever.

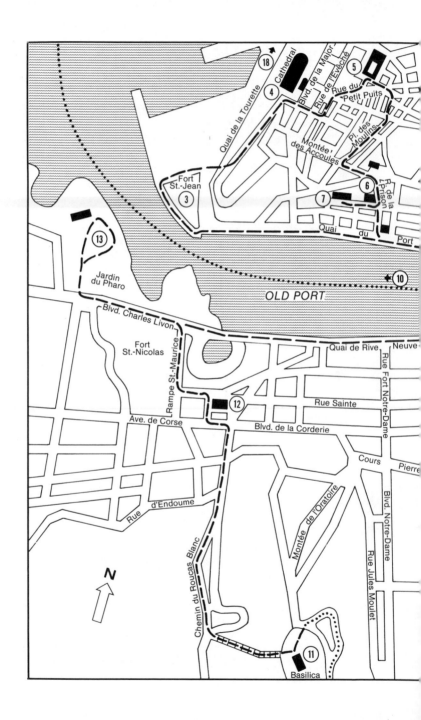

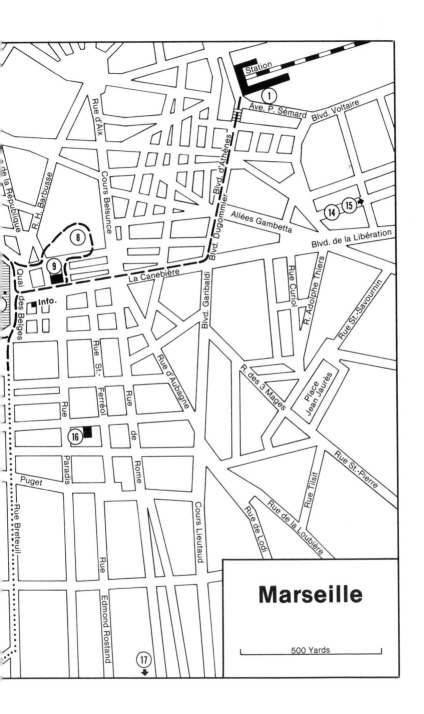

Turn right and continue downhill past the tourist information office to the Quai des Belges and the **Old Port** *(Vieux Port)* (2), the real start of this tour. Those in a hurry could also get here from the train station by métro, although doing so misses a lot of the city's character. Until 1844 this was the only harbor at Marseille, but large ships now dock beyond the breakwater and the Old Port is used for fishing and pleasure vessels. If you arrive fairly early in the morning you will be treated to the sight of fishermen hawking their fresh catch right off the boats. Excursions by boat through the harbors or to the outlying islands are available here, but it is perhaps better to wait until you return to this spot for that exciting experience.

Follow the map along the Quai du Port past the elegant 17th-century **Town Hall** *(Hôtel de Ville)*, easily singled out among the hideous modern apartment blocks lining that side of the port. This was once a fascinating warren of narrow alleyways and fetid slums, but all that ended in 1943 when the occupying Germans blew the area up in an attempt to deny the Resistance a base of operations. They only got two blocks inland, however, and the rest of the colorful old quarter still survives intact.

Continue on to the 17th-century bastion of **Fort St.-Jean** (3), which guards the narrow entrance to the harbor, and take the pedestrian promenade around it. In a few blocks you will come to a huge, remarkably ugly neo-Byzantine church, the **Cathédrale de la Major** (4). Built in the late 19th century, it replaces the much smaller **Old Major Cathedral**, which fortunately still stands directly to its side. This 12th-century Romanesque structure, erected on the site of a Roman temple and no longer used as a church, is in rather poor condition but contains some outstanding works of religious art. It may be visited any day except Tuesdays, from 9–11:30 a.m. and 2:30–5 p.m.

The walk now enters the old Panier quarter and follows an uphill route to the **Old Charity Hospice** *(La Vieille Charité)* (5), a magnificent 17th-century almshouse which has been beautifully restored and is now used for temporary art exhibitions. You can stop in for a look between 10 a.m. and noon and 2–6:30 p.m., except on Tuesdays or on Wednesday mornings.

This is the very heart of Old Marseille, a colorful but somewhat seedy area of tiny alleyways that is slowly yielding to gentrification. Follow the map through Place des Moulins and downhill past the belfry of the 12th-century Notre-Dame des Accoules Church. In a few more steps you will come to the **Museum of Old Marseille** *(Musée du Vieux Marseille)* (6) on Rue de la Prison. Housed in a 16th-century mansion with an

Selling Fish on the Quai des Belges

unusual stone façade, the fascinating displays here are devoted to local life in former times and include a model of the highly intriguing Transporter bridge which until World War II carried traffic across the harbor entrance in a most unorthodox manner. The museum is open from 10 a.m. to noon and 2–6:30 p.m., every day except on Tuesdays, holidays, and Wednesday mornings.

The **Roman Docks Museum** (7), nearby, features the *in situ* remains of Roman port installations discovered when the neighborhood was rebuilt in 1947. There are also interesting displays of ancient maritime artifacts. Visits may be made from 10 a.m. to noon and 2–6:30 p.m., except on Tuesdays, some holidays, and on Wednesday mornings.

Now return to the Old Port and follow the map to an enormous modern indoor shopping mall, the Centre Bourse. Just in front of this is a lovely **archaeological garden** where remains of the Greek port from the third century B.C. may be explored. These were discovered only recently, and digs are still going on. Adjoining this, on the lower level of the shopping mall, is the new **Museum of the History of Marseille** (8). The very well displayed artifacts include a second-century Roman merchant ship unearthed on the spot in 1974. The museum is open from noon until 7 p.m. daily, except on Sundays and Mondays.

Continue past the former stock exchange *(Bourse)*, which now houses an interesting **Marine Museum** (9) devoted to the city's long tradition of maritime trade, from the Greek era to the present. The ship models alone are worth the visit. You can see this between 10 a.m. and noon and 2:30–7 p.m., any day except Sundays.

Turn the corner onto La Canebière and return to the Quai des Belges (2). Several establishments along the quay offer very enjoyable boat excursions to the **Château d'If** (10, off the map), a 16th-century military fortress on a small island well beyond the breakwater. Long used as a prison, it was made famous by its description in *"The Count of Monte Cristo"* by Alexandre Dumas. Many of these boats also call at the nearby **Frioul Islands**, where a pleasant resort village offers numerous outdoor cafés. Allow at least an hour and a half for the round trip and be prepared for a rough ride. Anyone foolish enough to sit on the outdoor deck will probably get wet.

Back at the Quai des Belges you will find a wide selection of restaurants and cafés in all price ranges. Stroll over to the adjacent Cours d'Estienne-d'Orves and board bus number 60 — running every 30 minutes — for the very steep climb to Marseille's most spectacular landmark. The **Basilica of Notre-Dame de la Garde** (11), crowned with a huge golden statue of the Virgin, is yet another 19th-century neo-Byzantine monstrosity. It is visible from virtually anywhere in the city, even at night, and after a while you may actually get to like it. Step inside to see the literally thousands of interesting sailors' ex-votos. The real reason to come up here, however, is for the fabulous panorama it offers of the port, city, islands and seacoast.

Marseille does have at least one genuinely superb ancient church. Follow the map down a stepped path and along city streets to the **Basilica of St.-Victor** (12). The above-ground portion of this dates from the 11th to the 14th centuries and looks like a fortress, but the main interest lies in its spooky 5th-century crypt, which may be visited from 10–11:15 a.m. and 3–6 p.m. It is closed on Sunday mornings. Filled with a mysterious early-Christian atmosphere, the catacombs contain the relics of two 3rd-century martyrs. Don't miss exploring this strange, dark and wonderful place.

Continue on, following the map. When you come to a short tunnel be sure to use the sidewalk to the left; otherwise you will be caught in horrendous traffic. Just beyond this there is a Foreign Legion post, whose sidewalk recruiting office is open day and night — in case you feel so inclined. Those who would

The Archaeological Garden by the Centre Bourse

rather rest in a beautiful park with an unusually good view of the harbor will enjoy a visit to the nearby **Jardin du Pharo** (13). Luckily, it has an outdoor café overlooking the yacht basin, a perfect spot to unwind before walking or taking a bus back to the Quai des Belges. If you are heading for St. Charles station, you can take the métro from there and avoid a long uphill climb.

ADDITIONAL SIGHTS:

Travelers staying in Marseille may want to see some of these attractions on another day.

The **Fine Arts Museum** *(Musée des Beaux Arts)* (14) has an extensive collection of works by major artists, especially those of native son Honoré Daumier. Located in the splendid 19th-century Longchamp Palace, it is a fairly long walk from the top of La Canebière, or can be reached by métro line 1 to Cinq-Avenues Longchamp. The museum is open from 10 a.m. to noon and 2–6:30 p.m., but closed on Tuesdays, some holidays, and Wednesday mornings. The same building also houses the Natural History Museum.

The **Grobet-Labadié Museum** (15) displays the private collections and furniture of a wealthy musician in his own 19th-century mansion. It is very close to the front of the Longchamp Palace, above, and has similar hours.

The Old Port and the Basilica of Notre-Dame

The **Cantini Museum** (16), close to downtown and just off Rue Paradis, features contemporary art along with traditional objects. Again, the hours are about the same as those for the Fine Arts Museum. The closest métro stop is Estrangin Préfecture on line 1.

Unité d'Habitation (17). The famous architect Le Corbusier built this noted — and controversial — complex in 1952 as part of a larger project, the *Cité Radieuse,* which was never completed. Architectural mavens will find it fascinating, although its social goals failed to materialize. To get there, take bus 21 or 22 from the La Canebière area to the Le Corbusier stop.

Visits to the modern commercial **harbor installations** (18) beyond the Cathédrale de la Major may be made on Sundays and holidays only. You may want to ask at the tourist information office about this first.

Aix-en-Provence

Only nineteen miles from Marseille, Aix-en-Provence is light years removed in character. Elegant, refined, gracious, dignified, sophisticated — all of these adjectives and more can be honestly used to describe the former capital of Provence, which many consider to be nothing less than the loveliest town in France. Whether you feel the same depends, of course, on your interests, but a few hours spent sitting at an outdoor café on the Cours Mirabeau does leave most visitors with a contented perspective on life.

First settled by the Romans in 122 B.C. after their victory over a local tribe, *Aquae Sextiae,* as it was then called, was already famous as a warm spring spa. By the 6th century A.D., however, it was nearly abandoned, the ancient buildings being used as a convenient stone quarry. Good King René, that marvelous figure who keeps popping up in French history, made it his capital in the 15th century. René was the count of Provence, the duke of Anjou (see page 136), and more or less the king of Sicily, albeit in exile. He was also a true Renaissance man — one of the most civilized, diversely educated and decent men of his age.

Though united to France in 1482, Provence retained much of its independence and maintained a parliament at Aix until the Revolution. After that the town declined in importance until the recent post-war era, which has seen a nearly explosive growth in population. Much of this is due to the development of modern light industries in the outlying areas, but some of the credit goes to both its university and to its world-famous summer music festival held annually during July and August.

Those with cars will find Aix to be a good base for exploring the rest of Provence, although it is somewhat inconvenient for rail travelers.

GETTING THERE:

Trains depart St. Charles station in Marseille nearly hourly for the 30-minute run to Aix-en-Provence, with returns until mid-evening. To get anywhere else in Provence or the Riviera by rail requires a change at Marseille. There is also fairly frequent bus service to other areas of Provence, leaving from near the tourist office.

By car, Aix is 19 miles from Marseille via the A-7 and A-51 Autoroutes. Other distances are: Arles—47 miles, Avignon—50 miles, Nîmes—66 miles; all via the A-8 and A-7 Autoroutes followed by local roads.

WHEN TO GO:

Good weather will make a stroll around Aix much more pleasant. Some of the major sights are closed on Tuesdays and holidays. Hotel rooms are scarce during July and August.

FOOD AND DRINK:

The many restaurants of Aix reflect a broad range of cuisines and prices. Some of the better choices, in trip sequence, are:

Vendôme (2 bis Ave. Napoléon Bonaparte, near Place de Gaulle and the casino) $$$

Brasserie Royale (17 Cours Mirabeau) Sidewalk café with regional cooking. $$

Caves Henri IV (Banzo) (32 Rue Espariat, just north of the Cours Mirabeau) Awarded one Michelin star. Reservations recommended, phone 42-27-86-39. $$$

Les Augustins (59 Rue Espariat, just north of the Cours Mirabeau) Italian and Provençal cuisine. $$

Abbaye des Cordeliers (21 Rue Lieutaud, two blocks west of the Town Hall) Reservations are needed, phone 42-27-29-47. $$

Poivre et Sel (9 Rue Constantin, three blocks east of the Town Hall) $$

Charvet (9 Rue Lacépède, slightly northeast of the eastern end of the Cours Mirabeau) Refined, elegant, a traditional favorite. Reservations suggested, phone 42-38-43-82. $$$

TOURIST INFORMATION:

The tourist information office, phone 42-26-02-93, is conveniently located on Place du Général de Gaulle, near the foot of the Cours Mirabeau. Ask them about local bus service to Cézanne's studio, the Vasarely Foundation, and about short regional tours. They can also find you a hotel room.

SUGGESTED TOUR:

Leave the **train station** (1) and follow the map to Place du Général de Gaulle, also called La Rotonde, where the tourist information office and gambling casino are located. In a few more steps you will be on the **Cours Mirabeau** (2), one of the most utterly delightful avenues on earth. It was named for the unscrupulous Count Mirabeau, a popular 18th-century demagogue who represented the common people of Aix in the States-General of 1789 which led to the French Revolution. Although

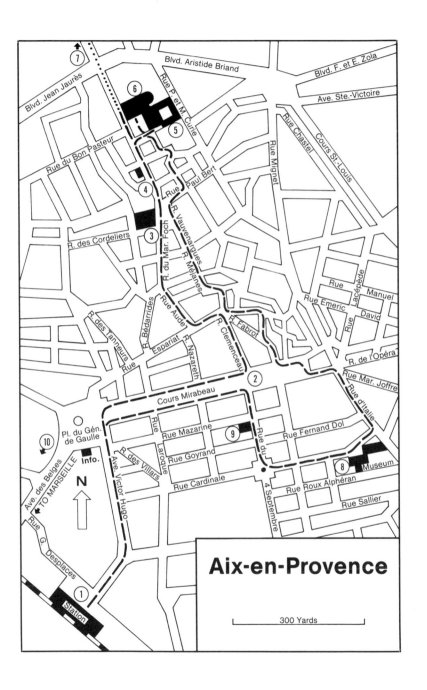

Aix-en-Provence

300 Yards

only a quarter of a mile in length, it is very wide and completely shaded by four rows of ancient plane trees forming a cool green canopy. There are several fountains along its length, the most intriguing being the curious moss-covered Fontaine Chaude at the intersection of Rue Clemenceau, which runs with the warm thermal waters that made Aix famous. The south side is lined with strikingly elegant mansions while the north is the preserve of trendy shops and a great many outdoor cafés. One of the great pleasures of a trip to France is to sit at one of these and just watch the world go by.

Stroll north on Rue Clemenceau and follow the map through a colorful old district of narrow streets to the **Town Hall** *(Hôtel de Ville)* (3), a 17th-century classical building with a lovely court-yard. Step into this, then climb the inside staircase to the first floor where there are some interesting displays in the Biblio-thèque Méjanes. The handsome 16th-century **clock tower** in the adjacent square is topped with one of those ornate wrought-iron bell cages so typical of Provence. In a niche below this is a mechanical "calendar" which rotates wooden figures repre-senting the seasons four times a year. A fountain graces the square, where an outdoor **flower market** is held on Tuesday, Thursday and Saturday mornings.

The **Museum of Old Aix** *(Musée du Vieil Aix)* (4), reached in a few minutes, has one of the best folklore collections in the south of France. Particularly noteworthy are the traditional *santons* — colored clay figures used in home Christmas displays — and larger puppets made to be drawn through the streets in the now-discontinued Corpus Christi processions. The museum is open from 10 a.m. to noon and 2–6 p.m. (5 p.m. in winter), but closed on Mondays and during the entire month of February.

Continue on to the **Tapestry Museum** (5) in the former archbishop's palace. The inner courtyard of this building is the center of the annual music festival held in July and August. You may be interested in the outstanding collection of 17th- and 18th-century Beauvais tapestries, some of which depict the life of Don Quixote. Visits may be made from 10 a.m. to noon and 2–5 p.m., daily except on Tuesdays, some holidays, and the month of January.

Next to this stands the **Cathedral of St.-Sauveur** (6), a curious architectural *mélange* incorporating elements from the 5th century onwards. Enter through an enchanting 12th-century Romanesque cloister, then step inside to enjoy the richly varied interior. The main attraction here is the famous *Triptych of the Burning Bush,* painted about 1476 by Nicolas Froment for King René, who appears on the left panel, with his wife on the right

Along the Cours Mirabeau

panel. These are usually closed, but will be opened for you by the caretaker on request. Outside again, take a look at the west front. All of the sculptures except one are replacements, the originals having been destroyed in the Revolution. The sole survivor is that of the Virgin on the central pillar of the main portal, which escaped harm when some quick-witted person crowned her with a red cap of Liberty.

Art lovers might want to make a side trip at this point to the **Atelier Paul Cézanne** (7, off the map), the small studio where the renowned painter worked until his death in 1906. Although everything there is pretty much as he left it, the effect is curiously unmoving. Still, if you are an admirer of Cézanne — a native of Aix — this is a worthwhile stop, which can be made from 10 a.m. to noon and 2:30–6 p.m. (2–5 p.m. off season), except on Tuesdays and holidays. To get there on foot continue straight ahead and follow Ave. Pasteur a short distance, then make a right uphill on Ave. Paul Cézanne to the studio on the left. The distance is about three-quarters of a mile. It is also possible to take bus number 1 from the front of the tourist information office to the Cézanne stop, which follows an entirely different route.

Return to the cathedral and follow the map through a highly picturesque old part of town to the eastern end of the Cours

Mirabeau. Continue on Rue d'Italie and turn right at the 13th-century Church of St.-Jean-de-Malte, the first Gothic structure in Provence — worth a visit for its stained-glass windows. Adjacent to this stands the **Granet Museum** (8), whose collections of fine art and pre-Roman archaeological artifacts are among the best in Provence. Some of the more outstanding paintings on display include a magnificent self-portrait by Rembrandt, several works by the locally-born early-19th-century artist François Granet, a portrait of Granet by Ingres, and a few minor works by Cézanne. The museum is open from 10 a.m. to noon and 2–6 p.m. (5 p.m. in winter), every day except Tuesdays and major holidays.

You are now in the Mazarin Quarter, laid out in the 17th century by the archbishop of Aix, a brother of the great statesman. Stroll past the charming Fountain of the Four Dolphins, which has been merrily splashing away since 1667.

A right turn leads to the **Paul Arbaud Museum** (9), featuring interesting displays of local Provençal ceramics, art and culture. Visits may be made from 2–5 p.m., any day except Sundays and certain holidays. From here it is only a few steps back to the Cours Mirabeau.

ADDITIONAL SIGHTS:

The **Vasarely Foundation** (10, off the map), in the suburbs of Aix, is devoted to the work of the contemporary Hungarian Op-artist Victor Vasarely. Housed in a stunningly modern building of hexagonal shapes, the vibrant displays appeal to some, while others find them literally painful to the eye. The foundation is open from 9:30 a.m. to 12:30 p.m. and 2–5:30 p.m., every day except Tuesdays and certain holidays. You can get there via local bus from near the front of the tourist office. Ask them about current route information. You might also inquire about their bus excursions along the "Route Cézanne," seeing places made famous by the painter.

Arles

Few towns in France are as rich in ancient monuments as Arles, yet it remains a delightfully unpretentious country place, captivating in its honest simplicity. Virtually everyone who goes there enjoys the experience.

Founded by Greeks from Marseille in the sixth century B.C., Arles became an important Roman colony in 49 B.C. after it sided with Julius Caesar in his victorious struggle against the rival general, Pompey. Having backed the wrong man, Marseille was humbled and its wealth transferred to Arles.

At that time the town was already a major port, linked to the Mediterranean by canal and set astride the main highway between Italy and Spain. The prosperity which followed brought about the construction of major public projects, several of which still stand today. Christianity came to Arles at an early date, along with political importance as the capital of Gaul. With the fall of the empire, however, the city fell to barbarians from the north and was invaded by the Arab Saracens. Although later a kingdom in its own right, it never really recovered and soon drifted into the dreamy backwater that it is today.

Arles is probably best known for its association with the artist Vincent van Gogh, who created some 200 of his greatest works while living there in 1888 and 1889, just prior to his insanity and suicide.

As an alternative to Marseille, Arles is an excellent base for daytrips throughout Provence, particularly for those with cars. Ask at the tourist office for information about bus excursions to the Camargue region, Les Baux, Aigues-Mortes and other nearby attractions. They can also make hotel reservations for you.

GETTING THERE:

Trains depart St. Charles station in Marseille several times in the morning for the 45-minute run to Arles, with returns until late evening. There is also convenient service to and from Avignon and, less frequently, with Nîmes. Aix-en-Provence is reached via Marseille.

175

By car, Arles is connected via the N-113 road and the A-7 Autoroute to Marseille, 57 miles away. Other distances are: Aix-en-Provence—47 miles, Avignon—23 miles, and Nîmes—19 miles.

WHEN TO GO:

Good weather, which fortunately is common in Provence, will make this trip much more enjoyable. All of the major sights, except the Muséon Arlaten, are open every day except January 1st, May Day and Christmas. An economical all-inclusive "global" ticket is available. With a few minor variations, each attraction is open from 8:30 a.m. to 12:30 p.m. and 2–7 p.m. during the summer, with slightly shorter hours the rest of the year.

FOOD AND DRINK:

Arles has a wide variety of restaurants and outdoor cafés, particularly near the arena, on the Boulevard des Lices, and at Place du Forum. Some outstanding choices are:

> **Lou Marquès** (In the Jules César hotel on Blvd. des Lices, near the tourist office) Awarded one Michelin star. $$$
>
> **Le Vaccarès** (9 Rue Favorin, by Place du Forum, upstairs) Original versions of regional specialties. $$$
>
> **La Paillote** (28 Rue Dr. Fanton, north of Place du Forum) $$
>
> **Le Tambourin** (65 Rue Amédée Pichot, just off Place Voltaire, between the town gate and the arena) $$
>
> **Hostellerie des Arènes** (62 Rue du Refuge, by the arena) An excellent value. $

TOURIST INFORMATION:

The tourist information office, phone 90-96-29-35, is along the Boulevard des Lices, near the center of town.

SUGGESTED TOUR:

Leave the **train station** (1) and stroll down to Place Lamartine, a good place to park if you are coming by car. Vincent van Gogh lived in a bistro here, sharing his place with the painter Gauguin for a while, and it was here that he cut off his ear. The house, alas, was destroyed by a bomb in 1944.

Continue on through the town gates and follow the map to the **Arena** (Les Arènes) (2), one of the largest, oldest and best-preserved Roman amphitheatres in existence. Probably built around A.D. 80 to seat some 25,000 spectators, it is now used for bullfights. During the Middle Ages the amphitheatre was converted into a fortress, with the top row of arches being demolished to furnish stones for the defensive towers. An entire town, with a church and some 200 houses, was built within it; and this provided some measure of safety from the marauding bands and

Inside the Roman Arena

incessant wars of those troubled times. The arena was restored to its present condition only during the 19th century. Step inside and make a circular tour through the various passageways, exploring the inner chambers, then climb to the top of the medieval tower for a splendid view.

Walk up the stepped Rue Renan to the Romanesque **Notre-Dame-de-la-Major Church** (3), now closed. Directly aside of this there is a good lookout spot above the ancient ramparts which offers a spectacular panorama of the region.

Return via the arena and amble over to the nearby **Roman Theatre** (*Théâtre Antique*) (4). It was built during the reign of the emperor Augustus toward the end of the first century B.C. and was used for elaborate theatrical productions, which often tended to be obscene. The Christians put an end to all that and tore the place down, using most of the stones to build churches and convents. Miraculously, two Corinthian columns survived *in situ* and are still there. Excavations in the 18th century revealed the long-forgotten structure which, only partially restored, is now used for festival productions. You can wander inside for a close look at the stage and seating arrangements.

Continue on to Place de la République and the Romanesque former **Cathedral of St.-Trophîme** (5), now used as a parish church. Although parts of it may date from the Carolingian era,

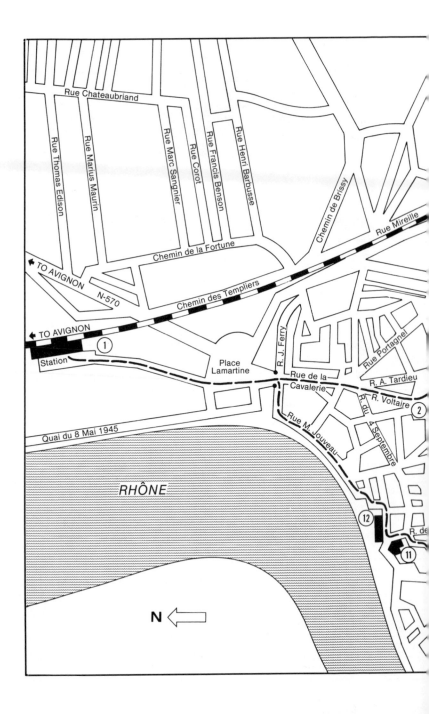

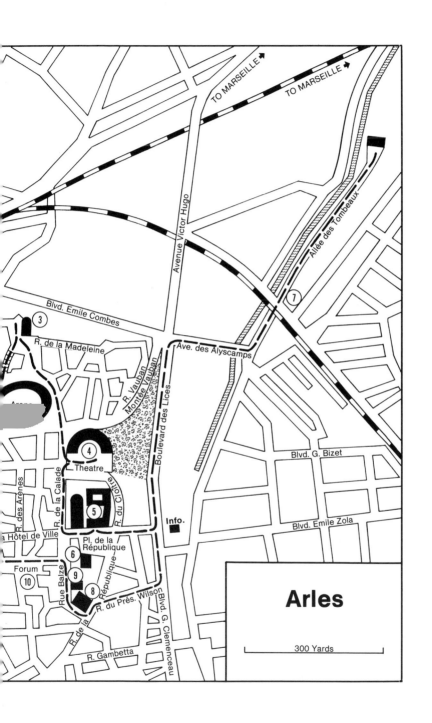

TO MARSEILLE

TO MARSEILLE

Avenue Victor Hugo

Allée des Tombeaux

Blvd. Emile Combes

③

R. de la Madeleine

Ave. des Alyscamps

⑦

R. Vauban

Montée Vauban

Boulevard des Lices

Blvd. G. Bizet

④

Theatre

R. du Cloître

R. des Arènes

R. de la Calade

⑤

Info.

Blvd. Emile Zola

Hôtel de Ville

Pl. de la République

Forum

⑥

⑩

⑨

R. de la République

⑧

R. du Prés. Wilson

Blvd. G. Clemenceau

Rue Balze

R. de la

R. Gambetta

Arles

300 Yards

it is basically an 11th-century structure, much altered in later years. The marvelous west front is richly carved with a *Last Judgement* above the portal, a procession of the redeemed on the left frieze and, on the right, figures of the damned being marched naked into hell.

Next door to the cathedral is the entrance to the incomparable **St.-Trophîme Cloister** *(Cloître)*, considered to be the best in Provence. Be sure to go upstairs to see the many small exhibits, and to carefully examine the marvelously sculpted details of Biblical stories and local legends on the pillars.

Just across the square, next to the Town Hall, is the **Museum of Pagan Art** *(Musée Lapidaire Païen)* (6), which features Greek and Roman statues and mosaics dug up nearby. The head of *Venus of Arles,* found in the Roman Theatre, is a cast — the original is in the Louvre in Paris.

Follow the map past the tourist information office to **Les Alyscamps** (7), the strangely evocative remnant of what was once a great necropolis. Begun in pagan times and later taken over by Christians, it formerly covered an immense area nearly a mile in length, with many thousands of tombs. Desecrated during the 16th century, it fell to ruin and what few sarcophagi survived were lined up along the sole remaining alley. Dante described the place in his *Divine Comedy,* while both Van Gogh and Gauguin painted its melancholy beauty. At the end of the lane stands the fittingly ruined remains of an ancient church.

Return to the animated Boulevard des Lices and take Rue du Président Wilson to the extraordinarily fascinating **Muséon Arlaten** (8), whose name is appropriately in the Provençal language. Allow yourself at least an hour to get lost in this vast storage attic of a museum, filled to the brim with just about everything imaginable that might relate to Provençal folklore. It was founded by the noted writer Frédéric Mistral using funds he received for winning the Nobel Prize in 1904, and many of the faded display cards are still in his hand. The total disregard for conventional museum values is what makes this place so intriguing, like a perverse visit to a huge junkshop. It is open from 9 a.m. to noon and 2–6 p.m. (5 p.m. in winter), every day except out-of-season Mondays and holidays. Don't miss seeing this.

Turn the corner to the **Museum of Christian Art** *(Musée Lapidaire Chrétien)* (9). By this time you may be weary of old sarcophagi, but don't let that discourage you from entering. In the midst of all those burial pieces is a staircase leading down to the **subterranean galleries** *(Cryptoportiques),* a very spooky

Les Alyscamps

place built by the Romans in the first century B.C. as a storage center for grain. The passageways were probably the substructure of the original Roman forum, near today's Place du Forum. If it is closed just ask the caretaker to turn on the lights.

Continue on through the **Place du Forum** (10), a charming square with several inviting outdoor cafés, a statue of Frédéric Mistral, and a few relics of the Roman forum. The **Baths of Constantine** *(Palais des Thermes)* (11), nearby, are all that remain of a great 4th-century bathing establishment built by the emperor Constantine. The water came via an aqueduct some forty miles long which crossed the wide Rhône river.

The last important sight to visit in Arles is right next door, the **Museum of Fine Arts** *(Musée Réattu)* (12). Located in the 15th-century former priory of the Knights of Malta, it is best known for its collection of late Picasso drawings, donated by the artist just prior to his death in 1973. There is also a fine collection of other modern works by French artists as well as local art, 17th-century tapestries, and a famous section devoted to photography. From here you can walk along the banks of the Rhône to the town gates, or return through the town.

Avignon

Lively, cosmopolitan Avignon is far more sophisticated than its size would suggest. Ever since the 14th century, when it was the capital of Christendom, it has retained a worldly atmosphere which today makes it a popular tourist and convention center as well as the setting for one of Europe's major theatrical festivals.

Although the town has existed since Gallo-Roman times, and its famous bridge has stood since the 12th century, Avignon did not really gain significance until 1309. Pope Clement V, a Frenchman, was driven from Rome by the endless wars between the Guelfs and the Ghibellines. Desiring to be closer to the French king, he moved the Papacy to a territory it owned on the banks of the Rhône, on the edge of France. Avignon, although a part of Provence, bordered on this, and was the town best suited as their new capital. The "Second Babylonian Captivity" had begun, lasting through seven French Popes, until Gregory XI moved back to Rome in 1377. This did not sit well with a faction of Cardinals who preferred to remain in Avignon. They resisted by electing their own Pope, thus creating the "Great Schism" in which the Pope in Rome and the Antipope in Avignon hurled anathemas at one another until 1403.

After that, Avignon became a peaceful but still worldly place. Having been purchased from Provence in 1348, it remained the property of the Papacy right up until the French Revolution, when it was annexed to France.

With its superb tourist facilities, Avignon makes a fine base for daytrips throughout Provence. Those staying there may want to explore the city in greater depth, or make short excursions to nearby Villeneuve-lès-Avignon, Orange, Pont du Gard, Tarascon or Les Baux. Avignon plays host to its famous drama festival during the last three weeks of July.

GETTING THERE:

Trains, including speedy TGVs, connect St. Charles station in Marseille with Avignon at fairly frequent intervals, with return service until late evening. Regular trains take about one hour, TGVs a bit less. There is also direct service to and from Arles (under 20 minutes) and with Nîmes (about 30 minutes, with faster TGV service available). To get to Aix-en-Provence requires a change at Marseille.

By car, Avignon is linked with Marseille via the N-7 road and the A-7 Autoroute, a distance of 62 miles. Other distances are: Aix-en-Provence—50 miles, Arles—23 miles, and Nîmes—27 miles.

WHEN TO GO:
The Palace of the Popes is open daily except for a few major holidays. Most of the museums close on Tuesdays and holidays. Good weather will make this trip more rewarding. The town is crowded during the international drama festival held in the last three weeks of July.

FOOD AND DRINK:
Sophisticated Avignon is endowed with an exceptional range of restaurants and cafés in all price ranges. Some excellent choices, in the order that you will pass or come close to them on the walking tour, are:

Hiély-Lucullus (5 Rue de la République, by Place de l'Horloge, upstairs) For the traditional gourmet. Awarded two Michelin stars, reservations needed, phone 90-86-17-07. $$$

Auberge de France (28 Place de l'Horloge) Rates one Michelin star for its regional dishes. $$$

Salon de la Fourchette (7 Rue Racine, almost behind the Town Hall) Popular with the locals, reservations suggested, phone 90-82-56-01. $$

La Fourchette II (17 Rue Racine, as above) Same as above. $$

Crêperie du Cloître (9 Place des Chataignes, two blocks east of Place de l'Horloge) Crêpes. $

Brunel (46 Rue de la Balance, near the Palace of the Popes) One Michelin star. $$$

La Férigoulo (30 Rue Joseph Vernet, near St.-Agricol church) Modern, with a young crowd. $$

Le Patio (2 Rue Petite-Calade, one block north of the Calvet Museum) $

Le Vernet (58 Rue Joseph Vernet, opposite the Calvet Museum) Very elegant. $$

St. Didier (41 Rue Saraillerie, by St. Didier Church, at the Rue du Roi René) $$

Les Trois Clefs (26 Rue des Trois Faucons, two blocks northeast of the tourist office) Intimate atmosphere. $$

The local wines are those from the Côtes du Rhône, especially Châteauneuf du Pape.

TOURIST INFORMATION:

The helpful tourist information office, phone   90-82-65-11, is located at 41 Cours Jean Jaurès, not far from the train station. They can make hotel reservations for you.

SUGGESTED TOUR:

Leave the **train station** (1) and follow the map through the 14th-century ramparts, which completely encircle the old part of town. They were restored in the 19th century by Viollet-le-Duc, the architect who did so much to preserve medieval France. Continue past the tourist office to **Place de l'Horloge** (2), a delightfully animated spot on the site of the ancient Roman forum, with many outdoor cafés, a 14th-century clock tower and the Town Hall.

Just beyond this is Avignon's stellar attraction, the **Palace of the Popes** (*Palais des Papes*) (3). Looking more like a mighty fortress than the residence of a religious leader, it is really two very different structures joined together. The austere **Old Palace**, to the left, was built by Benedict XII between 1335 and 1342. His successor, Clement VI, was a more flamboyant Pope, as the **New Palace** (1342-1352) on the right suggests. Both buildings were badly damaged and looted during the Revolution, then used as a prison and, later, as an army barracks until 1906. An enormous amount of restoration has been done since then, but most of the rooms are still pretty much devoid of furnishings. Still, they are extremely interesting and well worth the visit. One-hour guided tours are offered in French, English or German; but between Easter and the end of September you can just walk through on your own if you wish. A descriptive English-language brochure with detailed floor plans will be given to you at the entrance. The palace is open daily from 9 a.m. to 6 p.m. between July 1st and September 30th; from 9–11 a.m. and 2–4 p.m. from October 1st until the Easter holidays; and from 9–11:30 a.m. and 2–5:30 p.m. between then and June 30th. It is closed on New Year's Day, May Day and Christmas.

The **Cathedral of Notre-Dame-des-Doms** (4) stands next to the palace. Dating from the 12th century, it was greatly altered in later years. The gilded statue of the Virgin atop the steeple, added in 1859, is visible from all over town. Step inside to see the 12th-century white marble archbishop's throne and the fine canopied tomb of Pope John XXII.

Stroll down to the nearby **Petit Palais** (5), built in 1317 as a palace for the Archbishop of Avignon and greatly altered in later centuries. It now houses the splendid **Museum of Medieval**

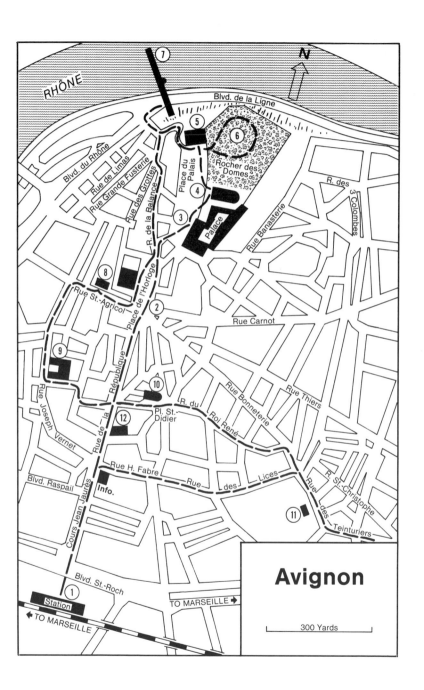

RHÔNE

Blvd. de la Ligne

N

Blvd. du Rhône

Rue de Limas

Rue Grande Fusterie

Rue des Grottes

R. de la Balance

Place du Palais

Rocher des Domes

R. des 3 Colombes

Palace

Rue Banasterie

Place de l'Horloge

Rue St.-Agricol

Rue Carnot

Rue de la République

Rue Joseph Vernet

Rue Bonneterie

Rue Thiers

R. du Roi René

Pl. St.-Didier

Blvd. Raspail

Rue H. Fabre

Rue des Lices

R. St.-Christophe

Rue des Teinturiers

Info.

Cours Jean Jaurès

Blvd. St.-Roch

Station

TO MARSEILLE →

← TO MARSEILLE

Avignon

300 Yards

Painting and Sculpture *(Musée du Petit Palais)*. Aside from the quality of the art, which is quite high, this is a beautiful example of museum organization at its very best — a situation all too rare in provincial France. Don't miss ambling through the lovely rooms. Visits may be made from 9:15–11:50 a.m. and 2–6 p.m., daily except Tuesdays and holidays.

Climb up to the **Rocher des Doms** (6), a beautiful park on the site of Avignon's prehistoric origins. The highest point in town, it overlooks a bend in the river and the famous **Pont St.-Bénézet** (7), a 12th-century bridge known to generations of French children as the *Pont d'Avignon* of the familiar nursery rhyme. Storms and floods over the centuries have reduced the original twenty-two arches which were once the only stone span across the Rhône south of Lyon to a mere four, but those certainly make a spectacular sight. According to legend, the bridge was begun after a young shepherd lad named Bénézet experienced a divine vision, then convinced the authorities by performing a miracle. It turned out to be a good investment, bringing prosperity to Avignon for centuries to come. If you wish to walk out on it you can follow the map — steeply downhill — to its foot, where the entrance is hidden in a souvenir shop. It is usually open during the tourist season, except for a break between noon and 2 p.m.

Return to Place de l'Horloge (2), using the route on the map if you went down to the bridge. A right on Rue St.-Agricol leads to the interesting **Church of St.-Agricol** (8), up a flight of stairs, rebuilt in the 14th century and much altered since. It contains several excellent works of art including a superb altarpiece.

Continue on Rue Joseph Vernet to the **Calvet Museum** (9), housed in a magnificent 18th-century mansion. The collections of art, displayed in an old-fashioned manner, are certainly an eclectic lot, with several great masterpieces by such talents as Breughel, David, Géricault, Manet, Corot, Toulouse-Lautrec, Dufy and Utrillo scattered among a mass of decidedly lesser works, some of which are just awful. There is also a fascinating collection of medieval wrought-iron objects. The museum has a certain charm about it that is difficult to describe but worth experiencing. Visits may be made from 9 a.m. to noon and 2–6 p.m., daily except Tuesdays and holidays.

Follow the map to the 14th-century **Church of St.-Didier** (10). In the first chapel on the right you will see a noted altarpiece of 1478, called *"Our Lady of the Spasm"* for its realistic

The Palace of the Popes

depiction of the Virgin in anguish. There are also some outstanding 14th-century frescoes in the first chapel on the left.

The route now wanders through a picturesque old part of town to the **Rue des Teinturiers**, an ancient cobbled street running along a stream lined with old water wheels once used in the production of dyed fabrics. Stop in at the **Chapel of the Grey Penitents** *(Pénitents Gris)* (11) to admire its splendid 17th-century golden glory. Continue on to the ramparts, then return to the tourist office, following the map. You may be interested in visiting the nearby **Lapidary Museum** (12) on Rue de la République, which features Gallo-Roman and prehistoric archaeological finds from the region. Housed in a former Jesuit chapel of the 17th century, it is open during the same times as the Calvet Museum. From here it is only a short stroll back to the station.

Nîmes

Some of the most remarkable Roman structures outside Italy are to be found in Nîmes, a handsome city on the fringe of Provence which bills itself as *"La Rome Française."* A visit here will be made even more enjoyable by the magnificent gardens, the fine museums, and by a stroll through the colorful medieval quarter.

Centered around a sacred spring, Nîmes was already a large tribal settlement when the Romans came in 121 B.C. Then known as *Nemausus,* it flourished as a colony of veterans set at the junction of several trade routes. During this time it became a showplace of the Roman Empire, with many fine buildings, some of which are still in excellent condition.

Occupation by the Visigoths in the 5th century A.D. prevented the spread of Christianity, which did not arrive until the 8th century. After that it was annexed to the Counts of Toulouse. During the 16th century Nîmes became a Protestant stronghold, with religious strife continuing until the Revolution. Since then it has prospered with the development of various light industries.

The city is noted for the manufacture of textiles, particularly a rough twill fabric long marketed abroad as being *"de Nîmes,"* from which we get the word denim.

Nîmes can be used as a base for daytrips in Provence, although it is not quite as convenient for this purpose as Marseille, Arles or Avignon. Other short excursion possibilities are to the ancient walled town of Aigues-Mortes or the famous Roman aqueduct at Pont du Gard, both served by regional buses. Ask at the tourist office for current schedules.

GETTING THERE:

Trains depart St. Charles station in Marseille in the morning for Nîmes, a trip of about one hour and 15 minutes. Return service operates until early evening. Most of these also stop at Arles en route. There are direct trains between Nîmes and Avignon, including TGVs, taking about 30 minutes. To get to Aix-en-Provence requires a change at Marseille.

By car, Nîmes is easy to reach following local maps. Distances are: from Marseille—75 miles, Aix-en-Provence—66 miles, Arles—19 miles, and Avignon—27 miles.

WHEN TO GO:

The attractions in Nîmes are open every day except for a few major holidays and Tuesdays in winter. The Roman Arena, of course, cannot be visited on bullfight days. Good weather will make this trip much more enjoyable.

FOOD AND DRINK:

Nîmes offers a fairly good selection of restaurants, several of which are in hotels. Among the best choices are:

Impérator (Place Aristide Briand, between the Maison Carrée and the Jardin de la Fontaine) In a hotel, classic cuisine, regarded as the best in town and awarded one Michelin star. $$$

Le Cheval Blanc (1 Place des Arènes) In a hotel. $$

Le Lisita (2 Blvd. des Arènes, next to the arena) $$

La Louve (1 Place de la République, next to the arena) $$

Au Chapon Fin (3 Rue Château Fadaise, between the arena and the Maison Carrée) $$

La Pergola (11 Rue de l'Enclos-Rey, near Blvd. Gambetta and the Porte Auguste) $$

Le Louvre (2 Square Couronne, between the Archaeology Museum and the arena) In a hotel. $$

Carrière (6 Rue Grizot, near the Archaeology Museum) In a hotel. $

There are quite a few inviting sidewalk cafés behind the arena and along Blvd. Victor Hugo.

TOURIST INFORMATION:

The tourist information office, phone 66-67-29-11, is located at 6 Rue Auguste, close to the Maison Carrée. They can find hotel rooms for you and provide bus schedules for nearby excursions.

SUGGESTED TOUR:

Leave the **train station** (1) and follow the map to the **Roman Arena** (Arènes) (2). Built around A.D. 50, it is a bit smaller than the similar amphitheatre in Arles, but is actually in better condition. Following the fall of the empire it became a fortress, and during the Middle Ages a slum with some 150 houses erected within the walls. As a result of a complete renovation carried out in the 19th century, the amphitheatre is now used for bullfights, concerts and other events. You may explore the interior

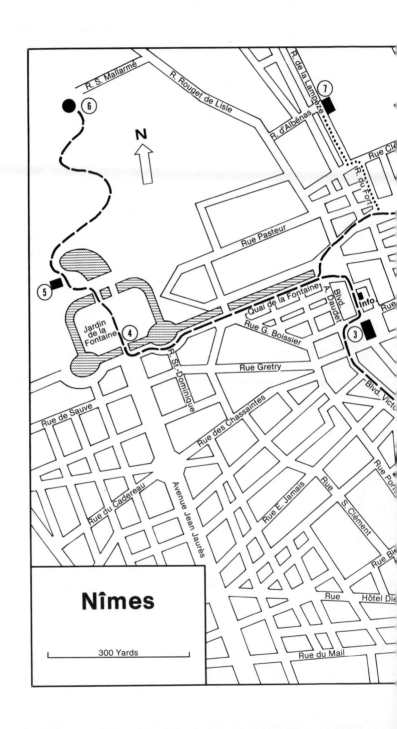

R. S. Mallarmé

R. Rouget de Lisle

R. de la Lampèze

⑦

R. d'Albénas

Rue Cl

N

⑥

R. du Fort

Rue Pasteur

⑤

Quai de la Fontaine

A. Daudet

Blvd.

Info

Rue

④

Rue G. Boissier

③

Jardin de la Fontaine

Blvd. Victo

R. St.-Dominique

Rue Gretry

Rue de Sauve

Rue des Chassaintes

Rue du Cadereau

Avenue Jean Jaurès

Rue E. Jamais

Rue

S. Clément

Rue Por

Rue Bi

Rue

Hôtel Di

Nîmes

300 Yards

Rue du Mail

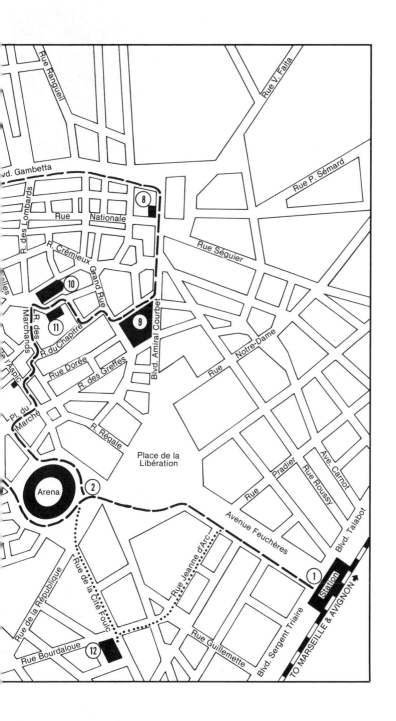

The Roman Arena

— when it is not in use — from 9 a.m. to noon and 2–5 p.m. (8:30 a.m. to 7:30 p.m. during the summer), every day except a few major holidays and Tuesdays in winter. An economical all-inclusive "global" ticket for the Roman monuments is available. If you happen to come on a bullfight day, don't despair — the running of the bulls down Boulevard Victor Hugo is an exciting event in itself.

Continue along Boulevard Victor Hugo to the **Maison Carrée** (3) which, despite its name, is rectangular in shape. This splendid Greek-style temple was built around 20 B.C. and is probably the best-preserved Roman temple anywhere. Unlike most structures from antiquity, it has been in continuous use for a variety of functions for over two thousand years, which no doubt accounts for the fine shape it is in today. In the late 18th century it even provided inspiration for Thomas Jefferson in his design of the Virginia State Capitol. The Maison Carrée now serves as a museum of local Roman artifacts and may be visited during the same hours that the Arena is open, with a few minor variations.

Now follow the map past the tourist office to the very impressive **Fountain Gardens** (*Jardins de la Fontaine*) (4), laid out in the 18th century around the sacred spring of Nemausus. Stroll over to the exquisite **Temple of Diana** (5), a highly

The Maison Carrée

romantic second-century ruin which may have been part of a long-vanished Roman bath.

The route now climbs through a park to the **Tour Magne** (6), a massive Roman defensive tower which was once part of the town walls. At the time of its construction, about 16 B.C., it was some thirty feet taller than it is today, but it is still a fairly stiff climb to the top. The magnificent panoramic view from up there, extending as far as the Pyrenees on a clear day, makes it all worth the effort. The ascent may be made during the same hours that the Arena is open, with slight variations, but not between noon and 2 p.m.

Return to the Jardins de la Fontaine (4) and follow Quai de la Fontaine to Boulevard Gambetta. Those interested in early Roman plumbing may want to make a short side trip up Rue du Fort and Rue de la Lampèze to the **Castellum** (7), an ancient distribution center for water flowing in via the Pont du Gard aqueduct.

Continue along to the **Augustus Gate** (*or Porte d'Arles*) (8), a well-preserved part of the Roman ramparts from the first century B.C. A few blocks beyond this lies a 17th-century Jesuit monastery which now houses the intriguing **Museum of Archae-**

ology (9), displaying many artifacts from prehistoric as well as Roman times. The Natural History Museum, in the same building, is also worth a visit. Both are open from 9 a.m. to noon and 2–5 p.m. daily, but closed on certain holidays and on Tuesdays in winter.

You are now on the edge of **Old Nîmes** *(Vieux Nîmes)*, the medieval core from which the modern city emerged. Follow the map to the **Cathedral of St.-Castor** (10), a small and much-altered structure with its roots in the 11th century. The partly Romanesque frieze on its west front depicts scenes from the Old Testament.

Step over to the former Bishop's Palace, a 17th-century mansion which now houses the **Museum of Old Nîmes** (11). Open during the same hours as the Museum of Archaeology, its collections include some truly magnificent furniture in beautiful surroundings. In addition, there are interesting displays devoted to textiles and bullfighting.

The route now leads through some highly picturesque streets lined with nicely-restored houses of mixed ages, several of which are medieval. Take a look into the courtyard at number 14 Rue de l'Aspic, noted for its magnificent double staircase. There are many other pleasant surprises in this charming neighborhood, best seen by just wandering around and poking your head into doorways.

Return to the station via the Arena. You may be interested in making a slight detour to the **Fine Arts Museum** *(Musée des Beaux-Arts)* (12), open during the same hours as the Museum of Archaeology. The most remarkable item there is a major Roman mosaic on the ground floor. There are also a number of paintings representing various European schools from the 16th through the 19th centuries.

Section VII

Daytrips on

The Riviera

There is something for everyone on the French Riviera. Whether your tastes run to hedonistic resorts, half-hidden hill towns, vibrant art colonies, medieval strongholds, golden beaches, mountains and forests, sophisticated urban centers or gambling casinos, you're sure to find some little corner of this enchanted, sun-drenched land that will call you back again and again. And that, precisely, is the reason why daytrips throughout the region are such a good idea. They allow you to sample many different facets of the Riviera in a relatively short time and at reasonable cost, so when you return — and you probably will return — you'll know just where to head.

There is no exact definition of what constitutes the Riviera or, as it is often called, the Côte d'Azur. For the purposes of this book, however, it includes the Mediterranean seacoast from St. Tropez to the Italian border, and extends north to the beginnings of the Alps.

For lovers of modern art, a trip to the Riviera is virtually a pilgrimage. This is where Picasso painted, as did Renoir, Chagall, Matisse and many others. Museums abound along with the homes of the artists themselves.

Although almost any of the coastal towns can be used as a base for your daytrips, there is no denying that Nice is the most convenient for those traveling by rail or bus since it is the transportation hub of the entire region, with frequent services to the other attractions. A large and very attractive city with a Mediterranean flair all its own, Nice has a broad range of hotels and restaurants in every conceivable price bracket, as well as a major airport with connections to all of Europe and beyond. Other towns which make particularly good bases are Cannes, Antibes, Monaco and Menton.

Old Nice

Nice is, well, nice. That is probably the best possible word to describe this appealing city — the fifth largest in France — beautifully situated on the edge of the Mediterranean and practically in the shadow of the Alps. Not extravagantly spectacular in any one aspect, its harmonious blend of qualities makes it quite endearing to the many visitors who return year after year. A great commercial center in its own right, Nice does not have to depend on tourists for a living and is all the more attractive for that.

Since there is an excellent chance that Nice will be the base for your Riviera daytrips, two walking tours are included which cover the most interesting parts of town. Either of these can be done in just a few hours, leaving the rest of the day free for a possible half-day excursion to a nearby uncomplicated destination such as Cagnes-sur-Mer or Menton. Or for taking the other tour, or for just relaxing.

The first walking tour explores the picturesque narrow alleyways, outdoor markets, hilltop fortress and bustling port of Old Nice, a delightful district which retains much of its ancient charm. The second tour — described in the next chapter — turns inland to the relics of Roman Nice on the Cimiez hill.

Founded as a trading post by the Phocean Greeks of Marseille around 350 B.C., the settlement was first called *Nikêa* in honor of Nike, the goddess of victory, following a defeat of the local Ligurian tribes. Two centuries later, the Romans established a town — *Cemenelum* — on the Cimiez hill, but this was later destroyed by the Barbarians and the Saracens. In the tenth century A.D. Nice came to life again and prospered, first as a part of Provence and later under the Italian house of Savoy. Although it changed hands several times, the city remained essentially an Italian one until 1860, when it was ceded to France after a popular plebiscite. Much of its Italian heritage still lingers in the twisting lanes of Old Nice, and especially on the menus of many of its best restaurants.

GETTING THERE:

Trains connect Nice with virtually all coastal towns along the Riviera, from St. Raphaël to the Italian border, at frequent intervals, with service operating until late evening. Expresses stop at major towns including St. Raphaël, Cannes, Antibes, Monaco and Menton; while locals *(omnibus)* make halts virtually everywhere. Typical running times to Nice are: from Cannes—under 30 minutes; from Antibes—15 minutes; from Monaco—20 minutes; and from Menton—under 30 minutes. The main station in Nice *(Gare Nice-Ville)* is about a 10- to 15-minute stroll from the starting point of this walking tour, Place Masséna. There is also frequent bus service, as well as taxis. You can get a free city map at the tourist office in the train station.

By car, Nice is 11 miles from Monaco, 17 miles from Menton, 8 miles from Cagnes-sur-Mer, 15 miles from Antibes and 21 miles from Cannes. Recommended routes are given in the chapters dealing with those towns.

WHEN TO GO:

Old Nice may be explored at any time, but note the schedules of the museums if these are of interest to you.

FOOD AND DRINK:

Nice is blessed with an exceptionally wide range of restaurants at every possible price level. Many of these feature seafood or Italian cuisine. The choices listed below are located in or near the old part of town covered by this walking tour.

> **La Poularde Chez Lucullus** (9 Rue Gustave Deloye, three blocks north of Place Masséna) A classic, with one Michelin star. $$$

> **Ane Rouge (Vidalot)** (7 Quai des Deux Emmanuel, on the far side of the old port) Seafood, rates one Michelin star. $$$

> **Los Caracolès** (5 Rue St. François de Paule, behind the opera in the old town) $$$

> **La Mérenda** (4 Rue de la Terrasse, two blocks north of the opera in the old town) Local cuisine. $$

> **Chez Rolando** (3 Rue Desboutins, in the old town near Place Masséna) Italian cuisine. $$

> **La Nissarda** (17 Rue Gubernatis, just north of the old town) French and Italian cuisine. $$

> **Le Rive Droite** (22 Ave. St.-Jean Baptiste, near Place Garibaldi) $$

> **Chez Les Pêcheurs** (18 Quai des Docks, on the far side of the old port) Seafood. $$

Chez Don Camillo (5 Rue des Ponchettes, near the base of the château elevator) Italian cuisine. $$

La Madrague (13 bis Cours Saleya, by the flower market) Seafood. $$

L'Estocaficada (2 Rue de l'Hôtel de Ville, by the town hall in the old town) Seafood. $

TOURIST INFORMATION:

Nice has several tourist information offices. One of these is located in the main train station and can be phoned at 93-87-07-07. Another conveniently located branch, phone 93-87-60-60, is at 5 Ave. Gustave V, at the west end of the Jardin Albert I near the old town and Place Masséna. There is also a third branch in the huge Palais des Congrès, a few blocks north of Place Garibaldi, as well as another near the airport. Ask for a free city map — essential for finding your way around the parts of town not covered by these walking tours.

SUGGESTED TOUR:

Begin your walk at the very heart of Nice, the elegant **Place Masséna** (1), located near the beach and many of the city's best hotels and shopping areas. It can easily be reached from other parts of town by bus or on foot. For those lucky enough to be in Nice during the annual Carnival, beginning two weeks before Lent and coming to a spectacular end on Shrove Tuesday, this is the best possible place for viewing the festivities.

Continue around the **Jardin Albert I**, a lovely garden filled with exotic plants and palm trees. The Quai des États-Unis is an extension of the world-renowned **Promenade des Anglais**, a seaside avenue laid out by the resident English colony in the early 1800s. The beach along here is certainly pretty to look at but not very comfortable for sunbathing since it is all pebbles.

A left turn at the handsome, late-19th-century Opera House leads to the Cours Saleya and the outdoor **Flower Market** (2), a colorful spot which comes to life with the vending of flowers and produce from early morning until mid-afternoon, every day except Sundays.

Follow the map to the base of a steep, rocky plateau over-looking the city, port and seacoast. An **elevator** (ascenseur) (3), reached through a short tunnel, will quickly lift you some 300 feet for a marvelous view from the top. It is also possible to walk up. Still known as **Le Château** (4), its summit is crowned with the ruins of a 16th-century fortress, destroyed in 1706 on orders from Louis XIV. Close by are the foundations of an 11th-century cathedral and some early Greek structures. A stroll through

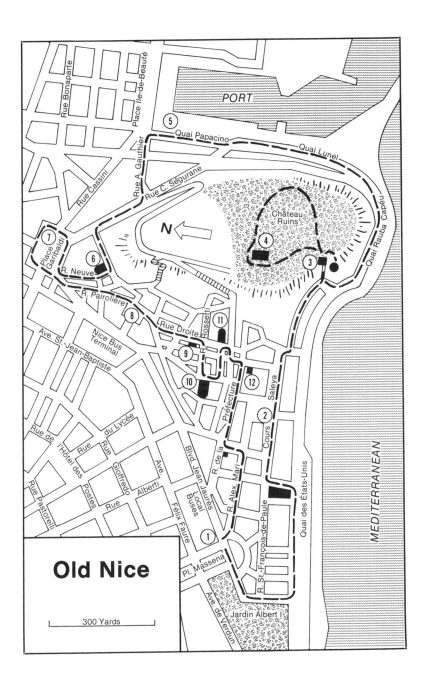

Rue Bonaparte

Place Île-de-Beauté

PORT

⑤

Quai Papacino

Quai Lunel

Rue A. Gauthier

Rue Cassini

Rue C. Ségurane

Château Ruins

Quai Rauba Capéu

N

①

Place Garibaldi

④

③

⑥

R. Neuve

R. Pairolière

⑧

Rue Droite

⑪

Rossetti

Ave. St.-Jean-Baptiste

Nice Bus Terminal

⑨

R.

⑩

⑫

Préfecture

Saleya

Rue du Lycée

②

Cours

Rue de l'Hôtel des

Rue Gioffredo

Ave. Alberti

Rue

Blvd Jean Jaurès

Local Buses

R. de la

R. Alex. Mari

Quai des États-Unis

MEDITERRANEAN

Rue Postes

Rue Pastorelli

Félix Faure

①

R. St-François-de-Paule

Pl. Massena

Ave. de Verdun

Jardin Albert I

Old Nice

300 Yards

Le Château from the Quai des États-Unis

the lush gardens leads to a viewing platform, several outdoor cafés, and an utterly delightful artificial waterfall *(cascade).*

On the way back be sure to stop at the **Bellanda Tower**, a 16th-century circular bastion near the elevator, now housing the Naval Museum. Step inside to admire the splendid ship models and nautical artifacts, which may be seen from 10 a.m. to noon and 2–5 p.m. (7 p.m. in summer), every day except Tuesdays, some holidays, and the period between mid-November and the end of December. Interestingly, the tower was once occupied by Hector Berlioz, who composed the music to *"King Lear"* in these rooms. From here you can easily walk down or rejoin the elevator — it makes a special stop at the museum, part way down the hill.

Continue around the base of the hill to **Port Lympia** (5), the lively old harbor of Nice. Begun in 1750, it provides a safe haven for the boats which, prior to that, just docked along the foot of the castle hill. Regular cruises are offered to other points along the Riviera, as well as to Corsica. The north end of the harbor, known as Place de l'Ile-de-Beauté, is very reminiscent of Italy, and it was in fact near the Customs House that Giuseppe Garibaldi, the hero of the Italian Revolution, was born in 1807.

Now follow the map to the **Church of St.-Martin and St.-Augustin** (6), a richly-decorated 17th-century baroque structure which contains a wonderful Pietà by Louis Bréa. It was here that

Port Lympia from Le Château

Garibaldi was baptized. Continue down the narrow alleyways to **Place Garibaldi** (7), a magnificent arcaded square in the 18th-century Italian style with an equestrian statue of Garibaldi.

Rue Pairolière leads to **Place St.-François** (8), where an animated outdoor fish market is held in the mornings. Nearby, on Boulevard Jean Jaurès, is the modern bus terminal *(Gare Routière)*, which you might be using for some of the other daytrips.

A stop at the **Lascaris Palace** (9) on Rue Droite is a "must" for visitors to Old Nice. This 17th-century mansion in the Genoese style has been well restored and furnished with period pieces along with fascinating displays of folk traditions. The palace is open from 9:30 a.m. to noon and 2:30–6 p.m. (6:30 p.m. in season), daily except Mondays and some holidays. During the winter season it is also closed on Tuesdays.

Wander around to the **Cathedral of Ste.-Réparate** (10), a mid-17th-century classical building with a fine dome of glazed tiles and an 18th-century tower. Step inside to view the marvelous baroque carvings, then continue on to the **Church of St.-Jacques** (11), also known as the Gesù Church. Again, there is a truly magnificent baroque interior well worth inspecting. One other church you may be interested in is the **Chapel of St.-Giaume** (12), another splendid example of baroque decoration. From here follow the map back to Place Masséna.

Nice-Cimiez

When the Romans came to Nice around 150 B.C., they immediately moved inland to the heights of Cimiez, commanding a view of the surrounding countryside. Previously, this had been the site of a Ligurian fort. Known as *Cemenelum,* the Roman town rapidly grew to an estimated population of 20,000, and soon acquired the usual features including an arena, baths and so on. This gradually fell to ruin during the Barbarian invasions and was abandoned by the sixth century A.D.

Cimiez is now an attractive residential area with many splendid homes. During the 19th century it was especially favored by the British. Queen Victoria was a frequent winter guest, staying at the old Hôtel Règina at the top of the main boulevard, from which her statue still surveys the scene.

Scattered among the elegant homes and gardens on the Cimiez hill are two outstanding art museums, some fascinating Roman ruins and an interesting monastery. This trip can easily be done in half a day, leaving the remaining hours to explore Old Nice.

GETTING THERE:

City buses *(Route #15)* leave from Place Masséna in downtown Nice *(see map on page 199)* very frequently for the starting point of this tour, the Marc Chagall Museum (1). Get off at the "Docteur Moriez" stop. The same bus continues on to the Roman Arena (2), whose stop is marked "Arènes."

Those starting at the **main train station** in Nice can easily walk to the Chagall museum, using the free city map offered by the tourist office as a guide. This should take about ten minutes but does involve a short, steep climb. Taxis are also available.

By car, start at the wide promenade between Place Garibaldi and the Palais des Congrès, then follow Boulevard Carabacel and Boulevard de Cimiez to the Chagall museum. Ample parking is available everywhere.

WHEN TO GO:

The Chagall Museum is closed on Tuesdays, while the Matisse and Archaeological museums close on Mondays, some holidays and Sunday mornings. The Franciscan Museum is closed on Sundays and holidays. Good weather will make this trip much more enjoyable.

In the Marc Chagall Museum

FOOD AND DRINK:

There are virtually no restaurants in the Cimiez area, so plan on eating in Nice proper *(see page 197).* Snacks and drinks are available outdoors at or near each of the attractions.

TOURIST INFORMATION:

See page 198 for the location of tourist information offices in Nice.

SUGGESTED TOUR:

The **Marc Chagall Museum** (1) was opened in 1973 as the only national museum dedicated to a then-living artist. It is devoted primarily to a series of large canvases created during the 1960s in which Chagall depicted his own unique vision of stories from the Bible. These were donated to the State on the condition that the government would erect a suitable museum. Chagall's strange and colorful fantasies are enormously popular, attracting a great many visitors to this rather out-of-the-way spot. The museum itself is a delightful place — modern, well lit and beautifully arranged. In addition to the Biblical series, don't miss the sculptures, tapestry, stained-glass windows, graphic works and, especially, the outdoor mosaic of the prophet Elijah rising to Heaven. Chagall, who died nearby in 1985 at the age of 97, was himself a sometime visitor to the museum. It is open every day except Tuesdays, from 10 a.m. to 7 p.m. between July 1st and

September 30th; and from 10 a.m. to 12:30 p.m. and 2–5:30 p.m. between October 1st and June 30th.

From here it is a pleasant but slightly uphill walk of a bit less than a mile to the **Roman Arena** (2), located in a public park. You can also get there by taking bus number 15 from the stop on the far side of Boulevard de Cimiez. One of the smallest amphitheatres in the Roman world, it probably dates from the first century A.D. and could seat some 5,000 spectators after its enlargement in the third century. Although in poor condition, the arena is still used for occasional performances.

Stroll over to the charming 17th-century **Villa des Arènes** (3), which houses two fine museums. The more interesting of these is the **Matisse Museum** on the upper floor, whose collections span the entire career of the famous artist Henri Matisse. Born in 1869, Matisse spent much of his life around Nice and died in Cimiez in 1954. It is absolutely fascinating to see such a broad scope of artistic talent covering such a long period of time displayed in just a few rooms. Don't miss his sketches and models for the Chapel of the Rosary in Vence *(see page 248)*. The ground floor of the villa contains the **Archaeological Museum** with its exhibits of local artifacts from the seventh century B.C. through the Roman era. Both museums are open from 10 a.m. to noon and 2:30–6:30 p.m. between May 2nd and September 30th, and from 10 a.m. to noon and 2–5 p.m. between October 1st and April 30th. They are closed on Mondays, some holidays, and Sunday mornings.

Step outside and visit the adjacent **Archaeological Site** (4), where you can wander around a large area of Roman ruins. The 3rd-century baths, one of which is incorrectly called the "Temple of Apollo," are possibly the best to be found in Gaul. Just south of the villa are the remains of a 5th-century Paleo-Christian basilica. A guide booklet in English is available at the museum entrance to help you understand the ongoing digs.

A short stroll through the park leads to the **Cimiez Monastery** (5), heavily rebuilt in the 19th century. This originally dates from the 16th century, when it replaced a 9th-century Benedictine monastery erected on the site of a temple of Diana. The church interior contains some remarkable works of art including both a 15th-century Pietà and a Crucifixion by Louis Bréa. Guided tours of the complex are conducted at 10 and 11 a.m. and 3, 4 and 5 p.m. daily, except Saturday afternoons, Sundays, and holidays.

The **Franciscan Museum** (6), next to this, tells the story of the order's life and works in several intriguing displays, with

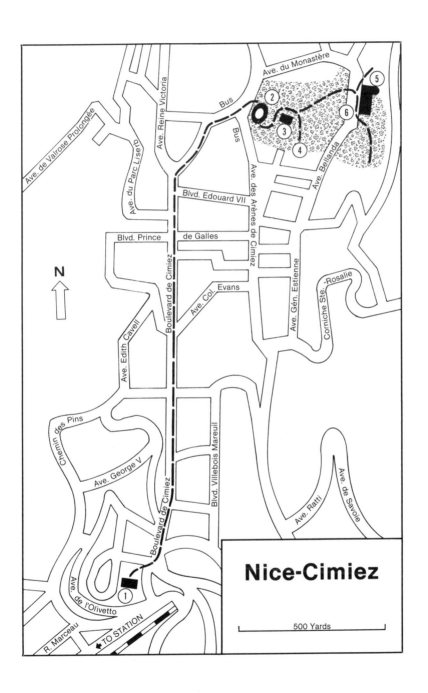

N

Ave. de Valrose Prolongée

Ave. du Parc Liserb

Ave. Reine Victoria

Ave. du Monastère

Bus

Bus

Bus

Ave. des Arènes de Cimiez

Ave. Bellanda

Blvd. Edouard VII

Blvd. Prince   de Galles

Ave. Col.   Evans

Ave. Gén. Estienne

Corniche Ste.-Rosalie

Boulevard de Cimiez

Ave. Edith Cavell

Chemin   des   Pins

Ave. George V

Blvd. Villebois Mareuil

Ave. Ratti

Ave. de Savoie

Boulevard de Cimiez

Ave. de l'Olivetto

R. Marceau

← TO STATION

Nice-Cimiez

500 Yards

2

3

4

5

6

1

The "Temple of Apollo"

a re-created 17th-century monk's cell and an 18th-century chapel as highlights. A descriptive brochure in English is available. The museum is open from 10 a.m. to noon and 3–6 p.m., daily except on Sundays and holidays.

Be sure to stroll out into the magnificent terraced **gardens** which overlook the city and the Mediterranean. The view from here is just fabulous. Before leaving, you may want to stop at the little **cemetery** just north of the church. Both Matisse and his fellow artist Raoul Dufy are buried there. Return to the arena and take bus number 15 back to Nice proper. You can also take bus number 17 from the opposite corner, whichever comes first.

Monaco

Somewhat less than a square mile in size, the Principality of Monaco is an independent country which thrives on tourism. Its casino is world famous, and the palace adds a touch of theatricality that only a mini-state could muster. The panoramic view from its heights is simply stupendous. Not surprisingly, the two towns of Monaco-Ville and Monte-Carlo, separated by a small harbor, offer more than their share of attractions.

The Grimaldi family has more or less ruled Monaco since 1308, when they bought it from the Genoese. They also once controlled other choice pieces of real estate along the coast, including Antibes and Cagnes. The last of their holdings, Menton, was sold to France in 1860 at the same time that Nice was ceded and the French-Italian border moved eastward. The family did, however, manage to hang on to Monaco, which was then practically bankrupt. Financial salvation came with the opening of the Principality's first successful casino in 1865 and the arrival of the railroad in 1868. Growth since then has been spectacular, with much of the land now covered by concrete high-rises. Gambling is no longer the major industry, having been replaced by tourism, conventions, and more traditional businesses.

Although it is not a part of France, French money is used in Monaco along with its own coinage. There are no customs to go through between the two countries; in fact the border is virtually invisible. As you probably know, the lucky Monégasques pay no taxes.

GETTING THERE:

Trains connect Monaco/Monte-Carlo with virtually all coastal towns along the Riviera at frequent intervals. Service operates until late evening. From Nice the ride takes about 20 minutes.

By car, Monaco is best reached via the N-7 road, the famous "Moyenne Corniche." It is 11 miles from Nice. There are many underground parking lots — just follow the "P" signs.

GETTING AROUND:

Two-dimensional maps make Monaco seem like a walker's paradise. It isn't. Most of the Principality is extremely hilly, so much so that public elevators have been installed. You will probably wind up using buses for part of the walking tour. These run quite frequently, with route maps at the bus stops. Fares may be paid directly to the driver.

WHEN TO GO:

Monaco is always open for business, but some sights may be closed in winter or on major holidays. Visits to the Prince's Palace can be made from July through September.

FOOD AND DRINK:

Sumptuous dining in Monaco can be a very expensive proposition. Those with thinner wallets will find adequate meals in the many bistro-type places, particularly along the Rue de la Turbie near the station, and in the alleyways behind the Prince's Palace. Some outstanding choices, in trip sequence, are:

Terminus   (9 Ave. Prince Pierre, by the station)   In a hotel. $$

Castelroc   (Place du Palais, in front of the Palace)   Lunch only. $$

Saint Nicolas   (6 Rue de l'Eglise, on the west side of the cathedral) $$

L'Aurore   (8 Rue Princesse Marie de Lorraine, one block north of the Oceanographic museum) $$

Restaurant du Port   (Quai Albert I, at the north end of the port) Italian cuisine. $$$

Le Grill de l'Hôtel de Paris   (Place du Casino, by the casino)   On the rooftop of the Hôtel de Paris, an experience to remember. Reservations: 93-50-80-80. $$$

La Belle Époque   (Square Beaumarchais, one block southwest of the casino)   In the Hôtel Hermitage. Haute cuisine. $$$

Dominique le Stanc   (18 Blvd. des Moulins, between the tourist office and the National Museum)   Awarded one Michelin star. $$$

La Calanque   (33 Ave. St.-Charles, near the tourist office)   Seafood. $$$

Polpetta   (6 Ave. de Roqueville, Monte Carlo)   Italian. $$

TOURIST INFORMATION:

The tourist information office, phone 93-30-87-01, is at 2 Boulevard des Moulins in Monte-Carlo, near the casino. They can make hotel reservations for you.

The Prince's Palace

SUGGESTED TOUR:

Leave the **train station** (1) and walk straight ahead to Place d'Armes. From here you can climb up the Rampe Major to the **Old Town** *(Monaco-Ville)*, perched high above the port on a promontory rock *(Le Rocher)*. Alternatively, you can take a bus which drops you off a few level blocks from the first attraction. However you get there, you will have the first of many spectacular views.

The **Prince's Palace** (2), surveying the entire domain, is open to tourists from July through September, when the reigning prince is not in residence. Guided tours are then conducted daily between 9:30 a.m. and 12:30 p.m., and 2–6:30 p.m. Even if you miss this, however, you can still enjoy the slightly ludicrous operetta-like changing-of-the-guard ceremony held daily at 11:55 a.m. in front of the palace. Several outdoor cafés are grouped around here so you can watch in comfort. The palace itself was begun in 1215 and greatly altered during the ensuing centuries. Besides being home to Prince Rainier III, whose wife, Grace Kelly, was tragically killed in a car accident in 1982, it also houses the small but interesting **Napoleonic Museum**. Step inside to see the many personal effects of the great French leader along with items relating to the history of Monaco. It is

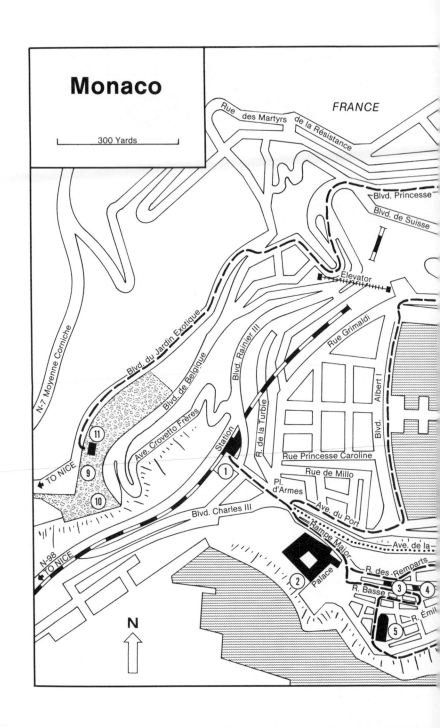

Monaco

300 Yards

FRANCE

Rue des Martyrs de la Résistance

Blvd. Princesse

Blvd. de Suisse

Elevator

Blvd. du Jardin Exotique

Blvd. Rainier III

Rue Grimaldi

N-7 Moyenne Corniche

Blvd. de Belgique

Ave. Crovetto Frères

Station

R. de la Turbie

Blvd. Albert I

Rue Princesse Caroline

Rue de Millo

TO NICE

Pl. d'Armes

Ave. du Port

Blvd. Charles III

Rampe Major

Ave. de la

N-98

TO NICE

R. des Remparts

Palace

R. Basse

R. Émil

N

The View from the Old Town

open daily from 9:30 a.m. to noon and 2–6 p.m., with somewhat shorter hours in the off season, but closed on Mondays and during the period of January 1st through February 10th.

Several of the narrow lanes in Monaco-Ville are now reserved for pedestrians. Stroll down Rue Basse to the **Historial des Princes de Monaco** (3), a beautifully arranged wax museum which depicts the history of the Grimaldi family in 24 life-size scenes. The costumes are authentic and were donated by the family. Visits may be made from 9:30 a.m. to 6 p.m., every day except between December 1st and January 31st.

Continuing down the street, you will pass the **Misericord Chapel** (4), a 17th-century structure whose interior features a fine high altar in polychrome marble and a splendid statue of Christ which is carried through the Old Town on Good Fridays.

The **Cathedral of Monaco** (5), built at the end of the 19th century in a somewhat ostentatious Neo-Romanesque style, reflects the sudden prosperity brought about by the opening of the casino. It inherited several excellent works of art from the 13th-century church which stood on the same site, including a superb 16th-century altarpiece by Louis Bréa in the right transept. The tomb of Princess Grace is among those of the princes of Monaco.

A stroll through the lovely St.-Martin Gardens leads to the renowned **Oceanographic Museum** (6), considered to be the best of its kind in the world. Now directed by the noted underwater explorer Jacques Cousteau, it was founded in 1910 by Prince Albert I, who had a passion for the sea. The large aquarium in its basement is a fascinating treat for all visitors, while the upper floors are devoted to the many aspects of oceanography. The museum is open daily from 9 or 9:30 a.m. to 7 p.m., and until 9 p.m. during July and August.

Now follow the map back to Place d'Armes and continue on past the bustling harbor. This is a good place to stop for a rest as there are many outdoor cafés along the waterfront. From here the route leads uphill along Avenue d'Ostende to the town of Monte-Carlo. You may prefer to take a bus and avoid the rather steep climb.

The **Casino of Monte-Carlo** (7) is undoubtedly the most famous gambling establishment in the world. The older section of this highly elaborate structure was designed in 1878 by Charles Garnier, the architect of the Paris Opéra — which it somewhat resembles. To your left as you enter are the gambling rooms, whose extravagant décor is worth seeing even if you're not a gambler. Admission to the first section requires only a passport to prove that you are over 21 and not a local citizen. An entrance fee is charged for the more exclusive — and much more intriguing — *salons* beyond that. Don't miss the bar with its fantastic ceiling depicting naked ladies puffing on cigars. The casino also contains a magnificent opera house, which can only be seen by attending a performance.

A short walk through the gardens brings you to the tourist information office on Boulevard des Moulins. From here you may want to make a little side trip to the **National Museum** (8), housed in a charming mansion also designed by Charles Garnier. Appropriately enough for a toy nation, the enchanting displays here feature hundreds of dolls and mechanical toys *(automata)* in exquisite settings. To reach the museum just follow the map and take the elevator down the hill. It is open from 10 a.m. to 12:15 p.m. and 2:30–6:30 p.m., but closed on some holidays.

From the corner near the tourist office you can take a bus to the next attraction, the **Exotic Gardens** *(Jardin Exotique)* (9). It is also possible to get there on foot, but the walk is long and boring. Clinging to the side of a cliff overlooking the entire Principality, the gardens contain literally thousands of varieties of weird and wonderful plants, especially a broad range of cacti

In the Exotic Gardens

from Africa and Latin America. Near the bottom of this are the **Observatory Caves** *(Grottes de l'Observatoire)* (10), where prehistoric man once lived. Guided tours are conducted through this magic world of stalactites and stalagmites at frequent intervals, a great treat for the energetic who don't mind all the hoofing involved.

Back at the entrance to the gardens is the **Museum of Prehistoric Anthropology** (11) with its collection of ancient relics. One combined ticket covers the gardens, caves and museum. They are open from 9 a.m. to 7 p.m. in season, closing at sunset out of season. The museum closes at 5:30 p.m. in the off season. The entire trio is open every day except May 1st and November 19th.

The easiest way to get back to the station is by taking a bus to Place d'Armes. You could also walk part of the way, then take the escalator and elevator down to the port.

Menton

The last town before the Italian border, Menton is a pleasantly picturesque resort blessed with the mildest climate on the Riviera. Long favored by British vacationers, it has become somewhat of a cultural center in recent years. The old quarter, remarkably well preserved, exudes a quiet charm. Menton is famous for its citrus fruits, particularly lemons. It makes a good half-day trip since all of the sights can be seen in a few hours; unless you would rather linger and enjoy yourself — not a bad idea.

GETTING THERE:

Trains link Menton with other coastal towns on the Riviera at frequent intervals, with returns until mid-evening. From Nice, the trip takes about 30 minutes.

By car, Menton is on the N-7 road, 17 miles from Nice.

WHEN TO GO:

Sunny Menton may be savored at any time, but note that the museums are closed on Mondays, Tuesdays and holidays.

FOOD AND DRINK:

This old resort offers a good selection of restaurants and cafés, especially along the Promenade du Soleil and near the port. Some choices are:

Francine (1 Quai Bonaparte, at the port) Seafood. $$$

Chez Mireille-l'Ermitage (on the Promenade du Soleil, near the casino) $$

Rocamadour (1 Square Victoria, just north of the port) Nice terrace. $$

La Calanque (13 Square Victoria, just north of the port) $$

Chez Diana (31 Quai Bonaparte, at the port) An experience. $

Bec Fin (11 Ave. Félix Faure, near the casino) $

TOURIST INFORMATION:

The tourist information office, phone 93-57-57-00, is at 8 Avenue Boyer, near the casino.

View of the Old Town from the Jetty

SUGGESTED TOUR:

Leave the **train station** (1) and follow the map through the lovely Biovès Garden along Avenue Boyer. Turn around for a splendid view of the nearby mountains framed by exotic trees. Along the way you will pass the impressive **Palais d'Europe** (2), a cultural center in the *Belle Époque* style which houses the tourist information office. Inquire here about the opening times of the Tropical Garden (*Jardin Botanique*) (5) in nearby Garavan and the Palais Carnolès Museum (10) if you intend to make those side trips.

Continue on past the casino to the **Promenade du Soleil**, an elegant avenue running alongside the beach. Follow this to the Municipal Market, brimming with morning activity in an old Victorian structure. The **Jean Cocteau Museum** (3) lies just beyond this, housed in a small fortification erected during the 17th century by the rulers of Monaco, which once owned Menton. Cocteau, who died in 1963, was primarily known as a talented poet, writer, film maker and general leader in French avant-garde circles. His reputation as a graphic artist is less secure, but the works displayed here are nonetheless fascinating. There

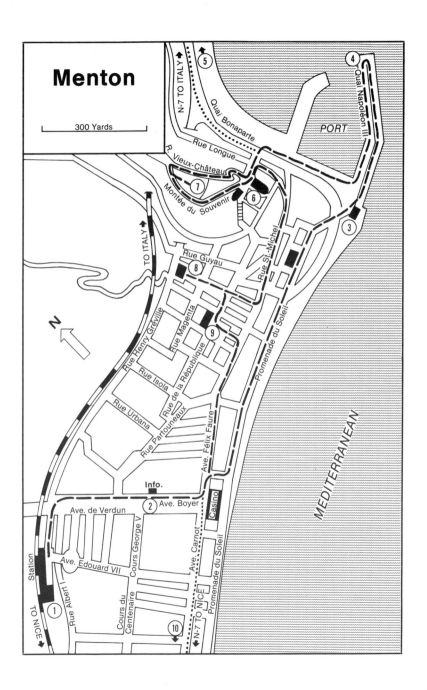

Menton

300 Yards

N

TO NICE

N-7 TO ITALY

Quai Bonaparte

Rue Longue

R. Vieux-Château

Montée du Souvenir

Quai Napoléon III

PORT

TO ITALY

Rue Guyau

Rue St.-Michel

Rue Henry Gréville

Rue Magenta

Rue Isola

Rue de la République

Rue Urbana

Rue Partouneaux

Promenade du Soleil

MEDITERRANEAN

Ave. Félix Faure

Info.

Ave. Boyer

Casino

Ave. de Verdun

Cours George V

Ave. Carnot

Station

Ave. Edouard VII

Rue Albert I

Cours du Centenaire

N-7 TO NICE

Promenade du Soleil

TO NICE

is also an outstanding drawing of him by Picasso. The museum is open from 10 a.m. to noon and 3–6 p.m. in summer; and 10 a.m. to noon and 2–5:30 p.m. the rest of the year. It is closed on Mondays, Tuesdays and holidays.

Stroll out on the **Quai Napoléon III jetty** (4), climbing the steps next to the museum for a marvelous view of the Old Town. When you get to the lighthouse at the end descend to the lower level and return.

Continue along the port and climb the steps to Quai Bonaparte, a broad street supported by arches. From here you can make a short side trip to the **Tropical Garden** (*Jardin Botanique*) (5, off the map) in the suburb of Garavan. Turn left on Chemin St.-Jacques to enter the magnificent gardens, located about one-half mile from the Italian border.

Back at the port, climb the massive staircase to the **Church of St.-Michel** (6) in the Old Town. Facing a charming little Italianate square where outdoor concerts are given in August, the 17th-century baroque church has a richly decorated interior that should be seen. At the end of the square stands another interesting church, the Chapel of the Pénitents-Blancs.

Now follow Rue du Vieux Château to the **Old Cemetery** (7), built on the site of a former castle, which offers splendid views from its grounds. Return via Montée du Souvenir and descend the steps as far as Rue Longue. A right leads through a picturesque neighborhood to the new town.

Stroll down Rue St.-Michel and turn right to the **Municipal Museum** (8). The displays here are concerned with local history, folk art and archaeology; and may be seen from 10 a.m. to noon and 3–6 p.m., daily except on Mondays, Tuesdays and holidays. The hours are shorter in winter.

Continue on to the **Town Hall** (*Hôtel de Ville*) (9), which features a fantastic Marriage Room wildly decorated by Jean Cocteau in 1957. Step inside and ask to see it. The doors are open from 9 a.m. to noon and 3–6 p.m. (2–6 p.m. in winter), daily except Saturdays, Sundays and holidays.

While in Menton you may be interested in visiting the **Palais Carnolès Museum** (10, off the map), a walk of nearly a mile from the casino. Devoted to the fine arts and located in a gorgeous old mansion, the museum may also be reached by bus. Ask at the tourist office for details.

Cagnes-sur-Mer

Primarily a modern seaside resort, Cagnes-sur-Mer offers two magnificent attractions which make a daytrip there highly worthwhile. First, there is Haut-de-Cagnes, an ancient walled village perched high atop a hill overlooking the Riviera. The other lure is Les Collettes, the enchanting country villa of the famous Impressionist painter Pierre-Auguste Renoir. Both can be seen in a few hours, making this an ideal half-day trip. You may, however, want to linger there and have dinner at one of the attractive restaurants in the upper town. This trip could be combined with one to Antibes or Cannes.

GETTING THERE:

Trains connect Cagnes-sur-Mer with other coastal Riviera towns at frequent intervals, with returns until late evening. Not all expresses stop at Cagnes.

By car, take the coastal road or the A-8. Cagnes is 8 miles from Nice.

WHEN TO GO:

The two major attractions are closed on Tuesdays, major holidays, and from mid-October through mid-November. Note that the Renoir villa is open only in the afternoons.

FOOD AND DRINK:

The walled hilltop village of Haut-de-Cagnes offers a number of charming restaurants and outdoor cafés. Among the better choices are:

Le Cagnard (Rue du Pontis Long, in the alleyways near the castle) A famous old inn with classic cuisine. $$$

Les Peintres (71 Montée de la Bourgade, just outside the walls) Regional cuisine. $$

Entre Cour et Jardin (102 Montée de la Bourgade, just outside the walls) Open evenings only. $$

Le Grimaldi (6 Place du Château) Outdoor tables by the castle. $$

Josy Jo (8 Rue Planastel, near the Chapel of Notre-Dame, just outside the walls. $$

Le Jimmy's (Place du Château) Charming outdoor tables, a good place for snacks or drinks. $

TOURIST INFORMATION:

The tourist information office, phone 93-20-61-64, is at 26 Avenue Auguste Renoir in the lower town.

SUGGESTED TOUR:

Stepping out of the **train station** (1) may leave you with that awful "what-ever-brought-me-*here*" feeling. Don't despair. A few minutes' walk past the highway intersection and tacky modern developments will bring you to the foot of one of the nicest hilltowns on the Riviera. You could also take a taxi, which would eliminate the interesting but somewhat strenuous climb.

Follow the map up the steep Montée de la Bourgade to **Haut-de-Cagnes**, the well-preserved medieval village whose history as a fortress dates from pre-Roman times. Overlooking the mouth of the Var river, which until 1860 was the Italian border, this has long been a strategically important stronghold.

The present **Castle** (*Château*) (2), around which the village developed, was originally begun in 1302 by Rainier I Grimaldi, ruler of Monaco and other Riviera towns. Transformed into an elegant residence in 1620, it remained in the Grimaldi family until 1789. The château now contains two museums, one of which is devoted to everything you could possibly want to know about olive cultivation. Stroll through the delightful inner courtyard and visit the 17th-century banqueting hall on the main floor, noted for its *trompe l'oeil* fresco of the *Fall of Phaeton,* a triumph of contrived perspective.

The rest of the castle is an **art museum**, focussing on modern works of Mediterranean inspiration. One room contains an unusual display of 40 portraits of Susy Solidor, a popular French singer, each by a different well-known 20th-century painter. Be sure to climb to the top of the tower for a spectacular view. An exhibition of contemporary art from all over the world is held in the château during the summer months. It is open from 10 a.m. to noon and 2–6 p.m., with seasonal variations, every day except Tuesdays, some holidays, and mid-October through mid-November. If the main entrance is closed, walk around to the rear.

An amble up and down the stepped passageways within the walls — too small to be shown on the map — leads to serendipitous discoveries. Find your way to **Place du Château** (3), a delightful spot with outdoor cafés. Nearby is the **Chapel of Notre-Dame-de-Protection** (4), a 14th-century structure whose charming setting inspired Renoir. Step inside to see the primitive 16th-century frescoes.

Return to the château and visit the **Church of St.-Pierre**

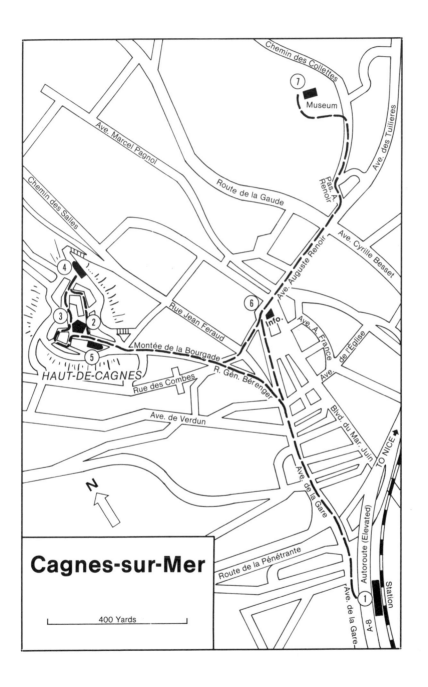

Chemin des Collettes

⑦
■
Museum

Ave. Marcel Pagnol

Ave. des Tuilieres

Route de la Gaude

Pas. A. Renoir

Chemin des Salles

Ave. Auguste Renoir

Ave. Cyrille Besset

④
■

⑥
■
Info.

Ave. A. France

Ave. de l'Église

③ ②

Rue Jean Feraud

⑤
■

Montée de la Bourgade

HAUT-DE-CAGNES

Rue des Combes

R. Gén. Bérenger

Ave.

Ave. de Verdun

Blvd. du Mar. Juin

N

TO NICE

Ave. de la Gare

Autoroute (Elevated)

Route de la Pénétrante

Ave. de la Gare

A-8

①
■
Station

Cagnes-sur-Mer

400 Yards

Renoir's Studio at Les Collettes

(5), whose double-nave interior contains some interesting works of art.

Follow the map downhill to the lower town, passing the **tourist information office** (6). From here it is a relatively short walk to Renoir's country villa, **Les Collettes** (7), where the great painter spent the last twelve years of his life. Now housing the **Renoir Museum**, it has been faithfully restored to the condition it was in when he died there in 1919. Although Renoir was very ill during his last years, he continued to paint from a wheelchair with brushes tied to his fingers. This touching scene is lovingly evoked in the studio, and throughout the property. The few works on display are, of course, minor pieces, but that in no way distracts from the wonderful experience of a visit here. The museum is open in the afternoons, from 2–6 p.m., closing at 5 p.m. in winter. It is closed on Tuesdays, holidays, and between mid-October and mid-November.

Antibes

Dating from the 4th century B.C., the ancient Greek trading post of *Antipolis* grew up to become the delightfully unpretentious Antibes of today. The narrow streets of its picturesque Old Town are an open invitation for pleasant wanderings, particularly to the seaside promenade and its castle, which today houses the fabulous Picasso Museum. Ambitious walkers, or those with cars, can also explore the lovely Cap d'Antibes, a place of great natural beauty.

A trip to Antibes can easily be combined in the same day with one to Cannes or Cagnes-sur-Mer.

GETTING THERE:

Trains link Antibes with other Riviera coastal towns quite frequently, with returns until late evening. The ride from Nice takes about 15 minutes.

By car, use the N-7 or N-98 road. It is 15 miles to Nice.

WHEN TO GO:

The Picasso Museum, which should not be missed, is closed on Tuesdays, some major holidays, and during November. Good weather is essential for a pleasant side trip to Cap d'Antibes.

FOOD AND DRINK:

Antibes has a broad range of restaurants in all price brackets. Some excellent choices, in the order that you will pass or come close to them along the walking tour, are:

> **La Marguerite** (11 Rue Sadi Carnot, near the station) Elegant. $$
>
> **L'Oursin** (16 Rue de la République, near Place des Martyrs) Seafood. $$
>
> **Le Caméo** (Place Nationale) Local specialties. $$
>
> **Auberge Provençale** (Place Nationale) $$
>
> **Les Vieux Murs** (Ave. de l'Amiral de Grasse, near the Picasso Museum) $$$
>
> **Bacon** (Blvd. de Bacon, at Pointe Bacon) Seafood, awarded one Michelin star. $$$

TOURIST INFORMATION:

The tourist information office, phone 93-33-95-64, is at 11 Place du Général de Gaulle.

SUGGESTED TOUR:

Leave the **train station** (1) and follow the town map, passing the tourist office on Place du Général de Gaulle. Rue de la République leads to Place Nationale. You are now entering the **Old Town** with its picturesque maze of narrow streets.

Thread your way through past the colorful market place on Cours Masséna to the **Grimaldi Castle** (2), home of the marvelous **Picasso Museum**. Built between the 13th and 16th centuries, this medieval stronghold overlooking the sea was for centuries home to a branch of the ruling Grimaldi family of Monaco. After seeing service as a governor's residence and later as an army barracks, the castle was bought by the town after World War I for use as a museum.

In 1946, Pablo Picasso was invited to use part of it as a studio. During the months which followed he produced some of his greatest works, many of which the artist later donated to the museum in memory of the happy times he had there. Although primarily devoted to Picasso, the museum also displays works by other contemporary artists along with some archaeological pieces. To wander through its well-arranged rooms and passageways is a sheer joy. Don't miss the sculpture-filled terrace overlooking the sea. The museum is open daily from 10 a.m. to noon and 3–6 p.m. (7 p.m. in summer), but closed on Tuesdays, some holidays, and during November.

The **Church of the Immaculate Conception** (3), next door, is still referred to as a cathedral although it lost that status as far back as 1244. Much of the present structure is from the 17th century, but the 12th-century belfry is original. Step inside to see the noted altarpiece in the south transept, attributed to Louis Bréa.

Now meander through the oldest parts of Antibes and follow the 16th-century ramparts to the **Archaeological Museum** (4) in the 17th-century Bastion of St.-André. The collections here, covering some 4,000 years of local history, include jewelry, coins and pottery; among other finds. They may be seen from 9 a.m. to noon and 2–6 p.m. (7 p.m. in summer), daily except on Tuesdays, some holidays, and during November.

Ambitious walkers have a real treat ahead of them. Turn to the area map and follow the coastal road past the public beach to **Pointe Bacon** on Cap d'Antibes (5), a distance of slightly over one mile. The views from here are marvelous, encompassing the Bay of Angels as far as Nice. Those with cars can, of course, drive there and continue completely around the wooded peninsula, long a haunt of the very rich.

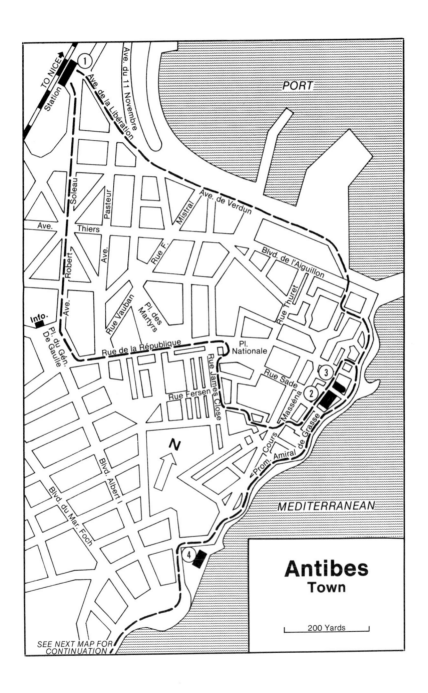

PORT

TO NICE

Station

Ave. de la Libération

Ave. du 11 Novembre

Ave. de Verdun

Soleau

Pasteur

Ave. Thiers

Rue F. Mistral

Robert

Ave.

Blvd. de l'Aiguillon

Rue Thuret

Info.

Pl. du Gén. De Gaulle

Rue Vauban

Pl. des Martyrs

Rue de la République

Pl. Nationale

Rue Sade

Rue James Close

Rue Fersen

Masséna

Cours

Rue de Grasse

Prom. Amiral

N

MEDITERRANEAN

Blvd. Albert 1

Blvd. du Mar. Foch

SEE NEXT MAP FOR CONTINUATION

Antibes
Town

200 Yards

A Game of Boules at the Bastion St.-André

Retrace your steps and turn into a stepped path called Chemin du Calvaire. This leads uphill past some Stations of the Cross to the **La Garoupe Plateau**, which offers a sweeping panorama of the seacoast, extending from Cannes to Nice, with part of the Alps in the background. The delightful **Chapel of Notre-Dame-de-la-Garoupe** (6), dating in part from the Middle Ages, has a strange and wonderful interior. Its walls are covered with touchingly naïve ex-votos offered by sailors and others in thanks for deliverance from some awful fate. You could literally spend hours examining the tales they so graphically depict. The chapel is open from 9:30 a.m. to noon and 2:30–7 p.m., with shorter hours in the winter. Nearby is a **lighthouse** *(phare)* (7), which may also be visited. The plateau can also be reached by car.

The route shown on the map takes you past the interesting **Thuret Gardens** (8), a research center for exotic trees and plants. These may be seen from 8 a.m. to noon and 1–5 p.m., daily except on Saturdays, Sundays and some holidays.

Return to Antibes via Boulevard du Cap. The route indicated on the town map follows the seacoast all the way to the train station, although it is shorter to go by way of Boulevard Albert I.

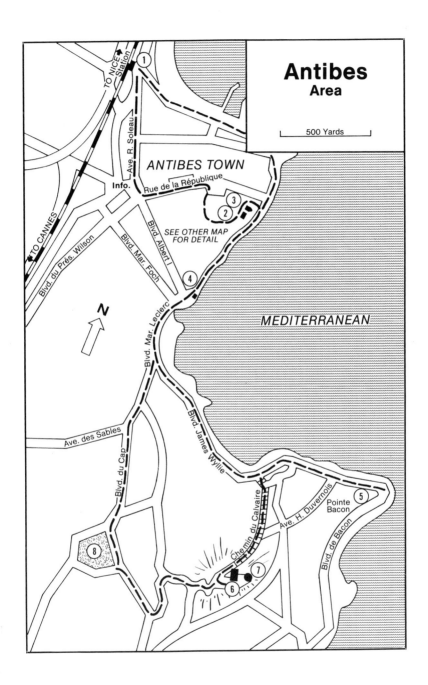

Antibes
Area

500 Yards

TO NICE
Station

1

ANTIBES TOWN

Ave. R. Soleau

Info.

Rue de la République

3

2

TO CANNES

Blvd. du Prés. Wilson

Blvd. Mar. Foch

Blvd. Albert I

SEE OTHER MAP
FOR DETAIL

4

N

Blvd. Mar. Leclerc

MEDITERRANEAN

Ave. des Sables

Blvd. du Cap

Blvd. James Wyllie

Chemin du Calvaire

Ave. H. Duvernois

Pointe
Bacon

5

Blvd. de Bacon

8

7

6

Cannes

Cannes was just a sleepy fishing village until that fateful day in 1834 when Lord Brougham, an English ex-chancellor en route to Italy, was turned back at the then-nearby border on account of an outbreak of cholera. Determined to have his vacation in the sun anyway, he built a villa near Cannes and spent the next thirty-four winters there, encouraging other aristocrats to follow suit. By the time the railway arrived in 1863, the town's destiny was sealed and the rush to build hotels began.

What was once class has now become commercial chic, existing for sensual pleasure. Cannes' main thoroughfare — La Croisette — is lined with luxury hotels, its harbor a flotilla of sumptuous yachts. This is truly the playground of the rich and famous. Fortunately, there are other diversions as well — the nearby Lérins Islands, the Old Port and the tiny medieval quarter each offer their own special charms.

A daytrip to Cannes could be combined with one to Antibes or Cagnes-sur-Mer; or by really rushing, with one to Grasse.

GETTING THERE:

Trains connect Cannes with other Riviera coastal towns, with frequent service operating until late evening. The ride from Nice takes about 30 minutes.

By car, Cannes is best reached via the A-8 Autoroute or the N-7 road. Nice is 21 miles away.

WHEN TO GO:

You can enjoy yourself in Cannes at any time. It may be crowded during festivals, but that's part of the fun. Boat service to the Lérins Islands is excellent from June through September, but greatly reduced the rest of the year.

FOOD AND DRINK:

Cannes has an enormous selection of restaurants and cafés. Some of the better choices include:

Royal Gray (in the Hôtel Gray d'Albion at 39 Rue des Serbes) Very elegant, rating two Michelin stars. $$$

La Mére Besson (13 Rue des Frères-Pradignac, two blocks north of La Croisette. $$$

View of Le Suquet from the Harbor

Le Festival (52 Blvd. de la Croisette, near the tourist office) Very swank. $$$

Le Croquant (18 Blvd. Jean Hibert, in the Old Town) $$$

La Voile au Vent (17 Quai St.-Pierre, by the Old Port) $$$

Gaston-Gastounette (7 Quai St.-Pierre, by the Old Port) $$$

Le Monaco (15 Rue du 24 Août, near the station) $$

Au Bec Fin (12 Rue du 24 Août, near the station) $$

Au Mal Assis (15 Quai St.-Pierre, by the Old Port) $$

La Pizza (3 Quai St.-Pierre, by the Old Port) Italian cuisine. $

Aux Bons Enfants (80 Rue Meynadier, in the shopping area near the port) $

TOURIST INFORMATION:

The tourist information office, phone 93-99-19-77, is in the train station. There is another office, phone 93-39-24-53, in the Convention Center by the port.

SUGGESTED TOUR:

The **train station** (1) has a tourist office on its second floor, reached by an outdoor staircase. Stop there for a free map which lists the schedule of boats to the Lérins Islands along with other useful information. Now follow Rue des Serbes to **La Croisette**, an elegant seaside promenade of world renown.

From here you may want to take a delightful walk along the bay to the **Palm Beach Casino** (2, off the map), a distance of less than a mile and a half. Along the way you will pass beaches, gardens and several opulent marinas.

Returning along the sandy beach will bring you to the new **Convention Center** (Palais des Festivals) (3), home to the famous International Film Festival held each year in May, as well as other events. Stroll through the lovely gardens behind it and over to the **Boat Terminal** (Gare Maritime) (4), where you can take an enjoyable cruise to the nearby **Lérins Islands** (5). For many, this is the best part of a visit to Cannes.

There are two islands in the group, and it is quite possible to visit both. Most tourists, however, are content to explore just the first, **Sainte-Marguerite**, reached in 15 minutes. About two miles long by a half-mile in width, it is mostly covered with a dense forest cut through with charming pathways. A massive 17th-century **fortress** lies near the dock. Within its forbidding walls you can visit the prison cell of the enigmatic "Man in the Iron Mask," confined there for sixteen years by Louis XIV, along with those of several Protestants locked up after the revocation of the Edict of Nantes. There is also a small museum of marine archaeology. Returning to the docks, you can either take a boat back to Cannes or continue on for another 15-minute cruise to the second island, **Saint-Honorat**. Considerably smaller but more enchanting, it contains an ancient 11th-century fortified monastery which may be explored. The newer Abbaye de Lérins, still in use, opens its church and museum to visitors. Boat service to both islands operates quite frequently from June through September, with greatly reduced schedules the rest of the year.

Back in Cannes, step over to the **Allées de la Liberté** (6), alive with a flower market in the mornings and games of *boules* in the afternoons. From here it is a short climb up to the old part of town known as **Le Suquet**. Follow the map to the **La Castre Museum** (7), a former citadel containing an interesting — and highly eclectic — assemblage of art, antiquities and items of ethnographic interest from around the world. It is open from 10 a.m. to noon and 2–5 p.m. (3–7 p.m. in summer), daily except on Mondays and between November 1st and December 15th. The medieval tower next to it may be climbed by asking at the museum entrance.

Continue around to the 16th- and 17th-century **Church of Notre-Dame-de-l'Espérance** (8), a late-Gothic structure featur-

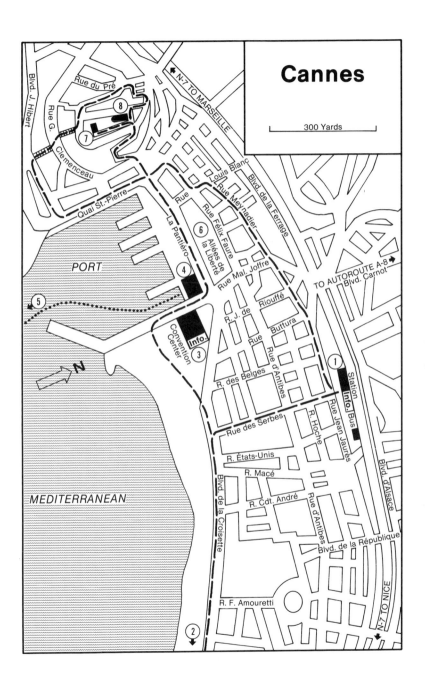

Disembarking at Ste.-Marguerite

ing some fine polychrome statues. The route now leads downhill through the old town to the port. Quai St.-Pierre is a particularly colorful spot with its popular restaurants and outdoor cafés. Wander around the lively old market area and follow Rue Meynadier — the former Main Street when Cannes was still a village — back in the direction of the train station.

Grasse

The medieval hill town of Grasse is widely known as the undisputed world center of perfume essences. A visit to one of its scent factories is a must, of course, but don't miss out on exploring the enchanting town itself. A veritable maze of ancient alleyways and half-hidden passages wind their way along the hillside, opening here and there for magnificent views. With its interesting cathedral and three small but highly intriguing museums, Grasse offers enough attractions to entertain you for an entire day, although it is possible to combine this daytrip with one to Cannes.

GETTING THERE:

Buses to Grasse depart fairly frequently from the east side of the train station in Cannes, easily reached from other Riviera towns (see page 228). The bus ride takes about 45 minutes, with return service running until early evening. There is also direct bus service with Nice.

By car, take the N-85 north from Cannes, a distance of 10 miles. Grasse is 26 miles from Nice. Park by the bus station.

WHEN TO GO:

Most of the attractions are closed on Mondays, some Sundays, and during November.

FOOD AND DRINK:

Grasse has an adequate number of rather modest restaurants, the best choices being:

Chez Pierre (3 Ave. Thiers, near the tourist office) $$

Amphitryon (16 Blvd. Victor Hugo, near the Fragonard Museum) $$

Maître Boscq (13 Rue de Fontette, near Place aux Aires) $

Crêperie Bretonne (3 Rue des Fabreries, near Place aux Aires) Crêpes. $

TOURIST INFORMATION:

The tourist information office, phone 93-36-03-56, is on Place de la Foux, near the bus station.

SUGGESTED TOUR:

Leave the **bus station** (*Gare Routière*) (1) and follow the map past the tourist office to **Place aux Aires** (2). This thoroughly delightful open area has some fine arcaded 18th-century houses and several sidewalk cafés arranged around a bubbling fountain. A lively outdoor market is held there in the mornings.

Follow the map down Rue des 4 Coins and descend the steep Rue Fontette to Place Jean Jaurès. Continue on, trying not to get lost in the tiny alleyways, to the 12th-century **Cathedral of Notre-Dame-du-Puy** (3), heavily restored in the 17th century. Step inside to view three paintings by Rubens in the south aisle, an altarpiece attributed to Louis Bréa and, above the sacristy door, one of Fragonard's rare religious works — the *Washing of the Feet*.

The square in front of the cathedral has an impressive square tower from the 12th century. Stroll around to **Place du 24 Août** (4), which offers a sweeping panorama of the countryside.

A series of steps leads to Rue Mirabeau and the **Museum of Provençal Art and History** (5). Housed in an 18th-century mansion, its splendid collections are mostly concerned with the folk arts and traditions of the region, although there are also some fine paintings and archaeological displays. These may be seen from 10 a.m. to noon and 2–6 p.m. (5 p.m. in winter), daily except on Mondays, some Sundays, and during November. The ticket is also valid for the Fragonard Villa-Museum.

Grasse produces most of the world's supply of the essences used in perfume manufacturing. This industry had its origins in the 16th-century fashion for scented gloves, which were made locally. It grew with the nearby cultivation of roses, jasmin and other plants; with more exotic ingredients now being imported from all over the world. Several of the larger factories offer free guided tours explaining their operations. One of the most interesting of these is the **Parfumerie Fragonard** (6), conveniently located a few steps away, whose tours in English are given daily at frequent intervals.

Now wander past a lovely park to the **Fragonard Villa-Museum** (7). If that name seems common around here, it is because the famous painter Jean-Honoré Fragonard was born in Grasse in 1732. Although he lived most of his life in Paris, he returned to his hometown during the Revolution and spent a year in this villa. Most of the paintings on display are copies, albeit very good ones; the originals being in the Frick Museum in New York. Still, a visit to this charming small museum is very worth-

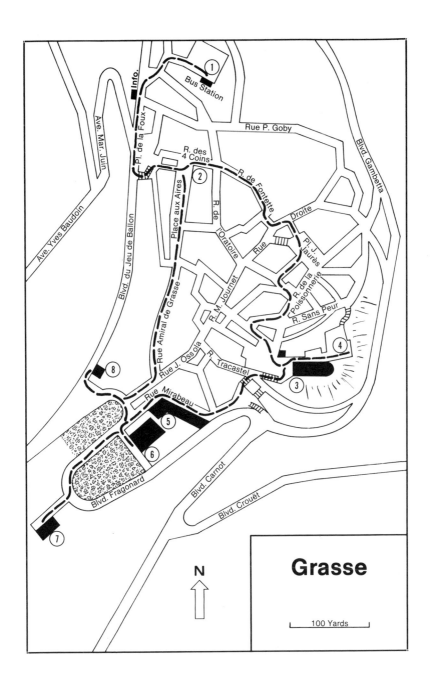

Bus Station

①

Info.

Rue P. Goby

R. des 4 Coins

②

R. de Fontette

Droite

Pl. de la Foux

Place aux Aires

R. de l'Oratoire

Rue

Pl. J. Jaurès

Ave. Mar. Juin

Ave. Yves Baudoin

Blvd. du Jeu de Ballon

Rue Amiral de Grasse

R. M. Journet

R. de la Poissonnerie

R. Sans Peur

Blvd. Gambetta

④

Rue J. Ossola

R. Tracastel

⑧

Rue Mirabeau

③

⑤

⑥

Blvd. Fragonard

Blvd. Carnot

Blvd. Crouët

⑦

N

Grasse

100 Yards

Place aux Aires

while and can be made during the same times as the Museum of Provençal Art and History described above.

American tourists will be particularly interested in the **Maritime Museum** (8), devoted primarily to the life of Amiral de Grasse. Born in nearby Bar-sur-Loup, this 18th-century French naval hero is remembered for his role in the American War of Independence, when he blockaded the British at Yorktown, Virginia. Souvenirs of the battle are on display along with ship models and related items. The museum is open from 10 a.m. to noon and 3–6 p.m. (2:30–5:30 in winter), daily except on Sundays, Mondays, holidays, and during November. From here follow the map back to Place aux Aires and the bus station.

St. Tropez

Fame and notoriety have not managed to spoil St. Tropez, which preserves all of its considerable charm. Isolated by geography from the main stream of the Riviera and far off the highways and rail line, this deliciously hedonistic place is well worth the effort of reaching.

There are many faces to St. Tropez. It is at one and the same time an art colony, a haunt of the intelligentsia, a bohemian resort, a center of fashion, and — yes — even a sleepy old fishing port. These and other facets of its paradoxical existence may or may not appeal to you, but the easiest way to at least sample its heady lifestyle is to go there for a day and try the place on for size. Who knows? You may decide to return for a real vacation. If you do, you'll be happy to know that there are sandy beaches for every taste, all within a short distance of the town.

GETTING THERE:

Trains in the morning connect coastal towns along the Riviera with St. Raphaël, a one-hour ride from Nice. From the St. Raphaël station you can get a **bus** for the 80-minute ride to St. Tropez. Return service operates until early evening.

By car, take the A-8 Autoroute to the Fréjus exit, then the N-98 to St. Tropez. It is 68 miles from Nice.

WHEN TO GO:

Good weather is essential for a visit to St. Tropez. The art museum is closed on Tuesdays, major holidays, and in November; while the maritime museum closes on Thursdays, major holidays, and from November 15th through December 15th. Unlike the rest of the Riviera, St. Tropez faces north and suffers from cold winters.

FOOD AND DRINK:

As you might expect, St. Tropez abounds in restaurants and outdoor cafés. Some of the better choices are:

Byblos (Ave. Paul Signac, below the Citadel) Nouvelle cuisine, very well known, in a luxury hotel) $$$

Leî Mouscardins (at the foot of the breakwater) Provençal cuisine. $$$

L'Escale (Quai Jean Jaurès, at the port) $$$

Auberge des Maures (4 Rue Dr. Boutin, three blocks south of the art museum) Seafood. $$$

Le Girelier (Quai Jean Jaurès, at the port) Seafood. $$

Bistrot des Lices (3 Place des Lices, also called Place Carnot) $$

Crêperie Bretonne (Quai Mistral, near the foot of the breakwater) Crêpes. $

TOURIST INFORMATION:

The tourist information office, phone 94-97-41-21, is on the quay by the port, with a branch on the road into town.

SUGGESTED TOUR:

Leave the **bus station** (1) and follow the map to the **port**. Filled with all kinds of boats, from humble fishing vessels to luxury yachts, this is the very heart of St. Tropez. Don't be surprised to see ocean-going sailboats with American registrations docked here. The quays are often the scene of uninhibited exhibitionism or joyous revelry, which can be best savored by sitting down at one of the seemingly-endless sidewalk cafés.

Be sure to stroll out to the end of the **Môle Jean Réveille** (2), a massive breakwater which encloses the harbor. The panoramic vistas from its upper level are fantastic.

Return to the quay and turn left on Rue de la Mairie, passing the Suffren Castle and the **Town Hall** (3). You are now in the picturesque Old Town, where several narrow passageways lead to lovely views. Continue on Rue de la Ponche to its end, poke around the alleyways there, then follow the map uphill to a path which goes to the nearby Graniers beach. Stroll a short way down this to a **point** (4) where you will be treated to a magnificent perspective of the town and the sea.

Walk uphill to the **Citadel** (5), a 16th-century fortress which now houses the fascinating Maritime Museum. Step inside to see the marvelous reconstruction of a Greek galley, displays on the manufacture of torpedoes (a local industry), and a section devoted to the Allied landing of 1944 — when this bastion was the last stronghold of German resistance. A climb to the roof reveals yet another fabulous panorama. The museum is open from 10 a.m. to 6 p.m. (5 p.m. in winter), daily except on Thursdays, some holidays, and between November 15th and December 15th.

Returning to town, you may want to make a little side trip to witness a more traditional aspect of life in St. Tropez. Known to residents as **Place des Lices** (6) but called Place Carnot on maps, the town's main square is a delightfully shady spot where men play *boules* all day and a market is held on some mornings.

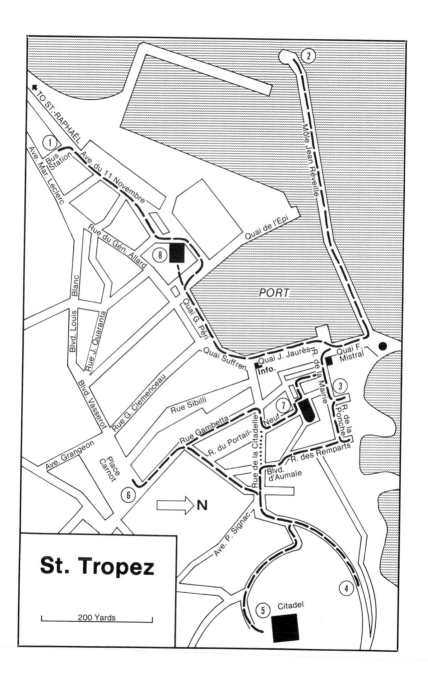

TO ST.-RAPHAËL

① Bus Station

Ave. du 11 Novembre

Ave. Mar. Leclerc

Rue du Gén. Allard

⑧

Blvd. Louis Blanc

Rue J. Quaranta

Blvd. Vasserot

Rue G. Clemenceau

Quai G. Péri

Quai de l'Épi

PORT

Môle Jean Réveille

②

Quai Suffren

Quai J. Jaurès

Info.

Quai F. Mistral

●

R. de la Marie

③

R. de la Ponche

Rue Sibilli

⑦

Neuf

Ave. Grangeon

Place Carnot

Rue Gambetta

R. du Portail-

Rue de la Citadelle

R. des Remparts

Blvd. d'Aumale

⑥

→ N

Ave. P. Signac

St. Tropez

200 Yards

④

⑤ Citadel

Along the Breakwater

Stop in for a drink at the Café des Arts, then stroll over to the 18th-century **Parish Church** (7) to see its remarkable bust of Saint Tropez himself.

No visit to St. Tropez is complete without a stop at the **Annonciade Museum** (8), housed in a 16th-century chapel right by the port. Surprisingly, this is one of the best small museums of modern art in all France. Most of the artists represented in its permanent collection have had some connection with the town, and include Signac, Matisse, Van Dongen, Derain, Bonnard, Dufy, Vuillard, Roussel and others. It is open from 10 a.m. to noon and 3–7 p.m. (2–6 p.m. in winter), daily except on Tuesdays, some holidays, and all of November.

St. Paul

Totally enclosed by its ancient ramparts, the tiny fortified hill town of St. Paul is today both an art colony and a magnet for discerning tourists. Often referred to as St.-Paul-de-Vence after its larger neighbor, this charming village is home to one of the world's greatest museums of contemporary art.

Once occupied by Ligurians, and then Romans, St. Paul was converted into a military stronghold in the 16th century by François I, who needed to defend his frontier against the dukes of Savoy. Its importance declined after the Revolution, only to be rediscovered by artists in the 1920s.

This classic daytrip is customarily combined with one to nearby Vence, described on page 245.

GETTING THERE:

Buses depart the bus station *(Gare Routière)* on Blvd. Jean Jaurès in Nice about every hour for the 45-minute ride to St. Paul. They then continue on to Vence. Return buses run until early evening. A special round-trip ticket allowing stops at both towns is available.

By car, take the A-8 Autoroute or other coastal roads to Cagnes-sur-Mer, then the D-6 and D-7 north to St. Paul. From there the D-2 continues on to Vence, three miles to the north. St. Paul is 12 miles from Nice.

WHEN TO GO:

This trip can be made at any time. Good weather will make it much more enjoyable.

FOOD AND DRINK:

The village of St. Paul has several restaurants, most of which are quite simple. A few of the better choices are:

La Colombe d'Or (at the entrance to the town) World-famous for its magnificent collection of modern art, given to the owner by the painters in payment for meals. The terrace restaurant of this inn is enchanting. $$$

Morateur (98 Rue Grande) $$

Bar Le Tilleul (by the North Gate). A simple café with outdoor tables. $

Rue Grande near the North Gate

Les Oliviers   (one mile outside the village, on the D-7
   Route de la Colle)   Regional cuisine in an attractive
   setting. $$$
Snacks and drinks are also available at the Maeght Foundation.

TOURIST INFORMATION:
   The tourist information office, phone 93-32-86-95, is at 2
Rue Grande, just inside the town gate.

SUGGESTED TOUR:
   Leave the **bus stop** (1) and stroll past the famous Colombe
d'Or inn to the North Gate of the village. Just inside this is the
tourist office (2).
   The narrow pedestrians-only Rue Grande, lined with antique
shops, art galleries, boutiques and restaurants, is the main street
of the village. Follow it to the utterly delightful urn-shaped
fountain (3) which splashes away merrily in a tiny square.
   Turn left and climb the steps to the 13th-century **Church**
(4), heavily rebuilt during the 17th century. Its attractive interior
contains some remarkable works of art, including a painting of
St. Catherine attributed to Tintoretto at the far end of the north

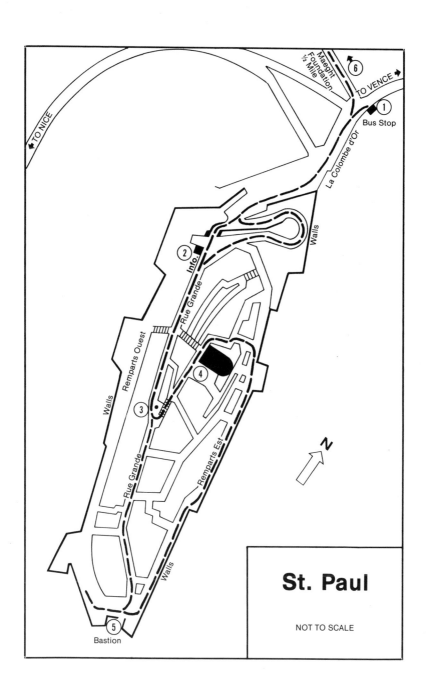

To Nice

Maeght
Foundation
½ Mile

To Vence

⑥

① Bus Stop

La Colombe d'Or

Walls

② Info.

Rue Grande

Remparts Ouest

Walls

④

③

Rue Grande

Remparts Est

Walls

N

⑤ Bastion

St. Paul

NOT TO SCALE

aisle. Step into the Treasury for a look at a few unusually fine items dating from the 12th to the 15th centuries.

Amble over to the east ramparts. It is possible, if you're feeling sure-footed, to walk along the top of these for some good views. Continue on to the **South Gate Bastion** (5), from which you may ⸺ in clear weather — have a sweeping panorama from the Alps to the Mediterranean.

Now meander back to the North Gate, exploring the hidden stepped alleys along the way. Return to the bus stop and follow the secondary road to the left. This leads, in half a mile (800 meters), to St. Paul's major attraction. Those with cars should follow the road signs instead.

A visit to the **Maeght Foundation** (6, off the map) is an experience no lover of modern art should miss. Established in 1964 by a Paris gallery owner and publisher to promote an understanding of contemporary art, it is housed in a stunning cluster of buildings set atop a hill surrounded by pine forests. More than just a museum, the foundation embraces a wide range of artistic endeavors, with theatres, libraries, studios and other facilities on the premises. Its permanent collections cover works by many of the leading artists of this century. More important than this, however, are the renowned temporary exhibitions, usually devoted to the work of one particular artist. The Maeght Foundation is open daily, with hours of operation displayed on signs near the village entrance and elsewhere. You can call them at 93-32-81-63 for current information.

Return to the bus stop, from which you can continue on to Vence or head back to Nice.

Vence

Once a Ligurian tribal capital of some importance, Vence, then known by its Roman name of *Vintium,* became the seat of a bishop as early as A.D. 374 — a distinction it retained until 1790. Its ancient town walls and medieval quarter are still virtually intact, complete with a maze of quaint little passageways and picturesque squares.

Sheltered from the north winds by a mountain range, Vence is noted for its mild climate and luminous air. This, together with its charming Old Town, has long attracted artists and writers as well as numerous tourists. A daytrip here can easily be combined with one to St. Paul, described on page 241.

GETTING THERE:

Buses connect Vence with Nice by way of St. Paul at nearly hourly intervals. The trip takes a bit less than one hour. See page 241 for details.

By car, follow the directions to St. Paul on page 241 and continue on for three more miles to Vence. A faster route, bypassing St. Paul, is to take the A-8 Autoroute or coastal roads to Cagnes-sur-Mer, then the D-36 north to Vence. It is 14 miles from Nice. The most convenient place to park is at Place du Grand Jardin.

WHEN TO GO:

Vence may be visited at any time. The nearby Chapel of the Rosary is usually open on Tuesdays and Thursdays only, but possibly more frequently during the summer or by special arrangement. Ask at the tourist office about this.

FOOD AND DRINK:

Vence has several restaurants and outdoor cafés in and around the Old Town. Some of the better selections include:

Auberge des Seigneurs (Place du Frêne) A traditional Provençal inn with regional cuisine. $$

Les Portiques (6 Rue St.-Véran, behind the cathedral) A local favorite. $$

La Farigoule (15 Rue Henri Isnard, north of the tourist office) A Provençal inn with regional cooking. $

Closerie des Genets (4 Impasse Maurel, on the south side, just outside the walls) $

Rue Ste.-Luce in the Old Town

TOURIST INFORMATION:

The tourist information office, phone 93-58-06-38, is located at Place du Grand Jardin, near the bus stop.

SUGGESTED TOUR:

Leave the **bus stop** (1) and stroll over to the **tourist office** (2), where you can ask about seeing the famous Chapel of the Rosary (7), designed and decorated by the artist Henri Matisse.

Place du Peyra (3), on the site of the ancient Roman forum, is reached via a medieval gateway standing next to a 15th-century tower. This delightful little square in the Old Town is enlivened by a gurgling urn-shaped fountain and several outdoor cafés.

Turn right and follow the map to the 11th-century former **Cathedral** (4), which still retains parts of its 5th-century predecessor, erected on the site of a Roman temple. The present structure was greatly altered during the 17th century. To the left of the main door there is an ancient inscription in honor of the 3rd-century Roman emperor Gordianus. Step inside to see the wonderfully satirical carvings on the 15th-century choir stalls. These are in a gallery which is sometimes open — just ask if it isn't.

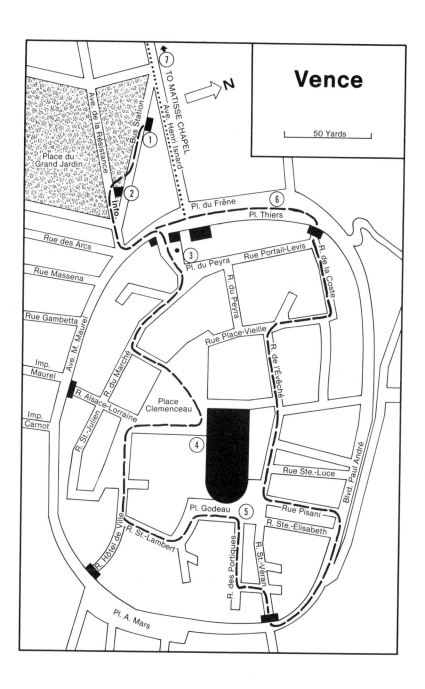

Now follow the map around to **Place Godeau** (5), at the center of which stands a Roman column dedicated to the god Mars. Continue on and pass through the Porte d'Orient gate, then turn left and follow the line of the walls, re-entering the medieval quarter by way of Rue Pisani.

Meander along through the ancient narrow streets and exit the Old Town at the 13th-century Levis Portal. **Place du Frêne** (6), also known as Place Thiers, is noted for its enormously thick, centuries-old ash tree. Legend has it that this was planted in 1538 to commemorate a visit by François I. From the north end of the square you can get a good view of the nearby mountains and, if you can pick it out, the Chapel of the Rosary. The 15th-century Château des Villeneuve, near the Peyra Gate, is now restored and used for exhibitions.

You may want to walk — or drive — to the nearby **Chapel of the Rosary** (7, off the map), a bit less than one mile away. Although this is the best-known attraction in Vence, it is generally open only on Tuesdays and Thursdays, from 10–11:30 a.m. and 2:30–5:30 p.m. Visits on other days may be possible, especially during the summer, but be sure to check with the tourist office before making the trek. Designed and decorated by the noted artist Henri Matisse around 1950, the simple chapel is considered to be a great masterpiece of modern art and architecture. To get there just follow Avenue Henri Isnard and Avenue des Poilus, then turn right on Avenue Henri Matisse across a bridge and uphill to the Chapelle du Rosaire.

Var Valley

Little known to foreign visitors, the narrow-gauge rail line through the Var Valley offers a magnificent visual treat coupled with an exciting ride. The private railway, properly known as the *Chemins de Fer de la Provence*, operates along a spectacular mountain route in the lower Alps between Nice and Digne. This same trip can also be made by car.

GETTING THERE:

Trains of the private railway depart from the Provence station (*Gare du Sud*) in Nice, just a few blocks north of the main station. It is necessary to get to the station well before 9 a.m. Both the Eurailpass and the special voucher in the France Vacances Pass are accepted (see page 16). Be sure to pick up a current schedule to determine which stops can be made — and for how long. Schedules are also available at the main Nice station.

By car, you can cover most of the same route by following the N-202 north from the Nice airport. There are difficult mountain roads between Scaffarels and St.-André-les-Alpes, but these can be bypassed by sticking to the N-202.

WHEN TO GO:

Trains operate all year round, although on a reduced schedule in winter. The castle at Entrevaux is closed on Mondays.

FOOD AND DRINK:

There are simple restaurants and cafés at each of the stops. Some of the better choices are:

> **Le Grand Hôtel** (by the station in St.-André-les-Alpes) $
> **Hôtel du Parc** (Place de l'Eglise in St.-André-les-Alpes) $
> **Grand Hôtel Grac** (in the village of Annot) An old country inn with good food) $$
> **De l'Avenue** (in the village of Annot) $
> **Le Vauban** (by the main road in Entrevaux) $

TOURIST INFORMATION:

The tourist office in Entrevaux, phone 93-05-40-04, is inside the town gate. The telephone number in Nice for the Provence Railway is 93-88-28-56.

SUGGESTED TOUR:

Board the train in **Nice** (1) and ride it all the way to **St.-André-les-Alpes** (2), a trip of about two and a half hours, or

The Entrance to Entrevaux

74 miles. Along the way you will climb through narrow gorges to an elevation of 3,353 feet, then begin a short descent to the pleasant little mountain resort. This is a fine place for a delightful country lunch, or you may decide to take the next train back to Annot or Entrevaux and eat there, depending on the schedule.

The wonderfully picturesque old town of **Annot** (3), founded in the 12th century, is another excellent place to have lunch. If you do stop here, be sure to check the schedule so you don't miss out on seeing Entrevaux.

The most visually exciting town along this route is **Entrevaux** (4), an ancient walled fortress approached via a drawbridge over the Var stream. Once a frontier between France and the kingdom of Savoy, its present ramparts were built in 1695 by Vauban, Louis XIV's great military engineer. Wander through the unspoiled passageways to the former **Cathedral**, known for its richly-decorated interior. Perched high above the village is the mighty **Citadelle** — a castle which may be visited.

If time permits, you may also want to make a stop at **Puget-Théniers** (5) before returning to Nice. This lovely old town, dominated by the ruins of an ancient castle, has a fine 13th-century church and an attractive square.

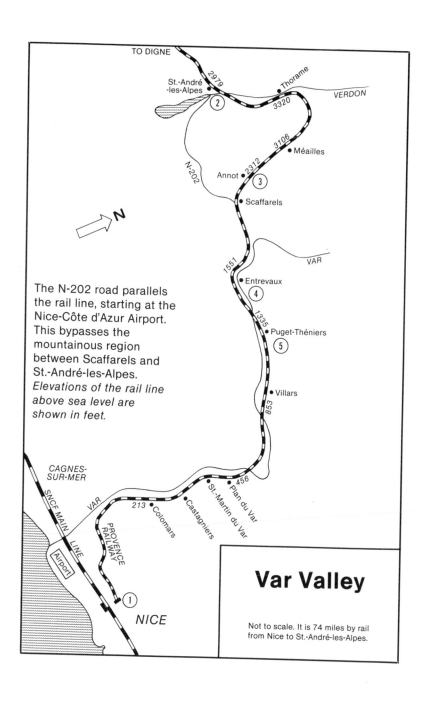

TO DIGNE

St.-André
-les-Alpes

2979

Thorame

VERDON

② 3320

3106

Méailles

2312

Annot ③

N-202

Scaffarels

1551

VAR

Entrevaux

④

1335

Puget-Théniers

⑤

Villars

853

The N-202 road parallels
the rail line, starting at the
Nice-Côte d'Azur Airport.
This bypasses the
mountainous region
between Scaffarels and
St.-André-les-Alpes.
*Elevations of the rail line
above sea level are
shown in feet.*

CAGNES-
SUR-MER

456

Plan du Var

VAR

St.-Martin du Var

213 Colomars

Castagniers

SNCF MAIN LINE

Airport

PROVENCE RAILWAY

①

NICE

Var Valley

Not to scale. It is 74 miles by rail
from Nice to St.-André-les-Alpes.

Index

Cathedrals, Châteaux, Museums, and Roman Relics are listed individually under those category headings. *Names of persons are in italics.*